About the Author

Carl Zigrosser was born in Indianapolis, Indiana, in 1891, and graduated from Columbia College with Phi Beta Kappa honors. He entered the employ of Frederick Keppel and Co., dealers in etchings and engravings, as research librarian in 1912. During the war he was with the United Engineering Societies Library. In 1919 he entered the employ of the bookseller, Erhard Weyhe, to found and direct the Weyhe Art Gallery. In 1939–40 he was awarded a Guggenheim Fellowship for research in American prints. In 1941 he was appointed Curator of Prints and Drawings at the Philadelphia Museum of Art, and later served as Vice Director also. He was elected, in 1952, a Trustee of the Guggenheim Museum in New York. In 1959 he was awarded the Achievement Medal of the Philadelphia Art Alliance. He was also active in the foundation of the Print Council of America. In 1964 he retired from the Museum to devote himself to writing and research. He has written over a dozen books on art, including *The Book of Fine Prints, The Artist in America, The Expressionists,* and a first volume of an autobiography, *My Own Shall Come to Me,* of which this present work is the sequel and conclusion.

Philadelphia: The Art Alliance Press
London: Associated University Presses

A
World of Art
and Museums

Also by Carl Zigrosser:

A
World of Art
and
Museums

Carl Zigrosser

Philadelphia
The Art Alliance Press

London
Associated University Presses

Associated University Presses, Inc.
Cranbury, New Jersey 08512

Associated University Presses
108 New Bond Street
London W1Y OQX, England

Library of Congress Cataloging in Publication Data

Zigrosser, Carl, 1891-
  A world of art and museums.

  Continuation and companion volume to My own shall come to me.
  Includes index.
  1. Zigrosser, Carl, 1891-   2. Philadelphia Museum of Art. I. Title.
N685.Z53   708'0092'4 [B]   74-75989
ISBN 0-87982-014-4

The Profile of Flannagan is reprinted from *The Sculpture of John B. Flannagan,* edited by Dorothy C. Miller, introduction by Carl Zigrosser. Copyright 1942, renewed 1969, the Museum of Modern Art, New York. All rights reserved. Reprinted by permission of the publisher.

To
Rockwell and Roderick,
friends for over half a century

Contents

Preface

This book, A World of Art and Museums, is a continuation and
companion volume to my autobiographical study published
in 1971 under the title *My Own Shall Come to Me.* The previous work treated largely of family affairs, of personal beliefs
and of holiday pursuits. It was a self-portrait that revealed
various aspects of my personality, but not my professional activities. It was more or less a projection of *homo ludens,* the
man at play, whereas this new work is a representation of
homo laborens, the man at work. The theme of the present
memoir could thus be designated as my relation to the world
of art and museums. Appropriately included, therefore, are
the summaries of my apprenticeship at the Keppel Gallery,
of my twenty-one years as founder and director of the
Weyhe Gallery, and my slightly longer service as Curator of
Prints and Drawings at the Philadelphia Museum of Art, as
well as a few portrait sketches of people whom I have known
or worked with. The essays in portraiture—the profiles and
vignettes—are based upon actual acquaintance with the subjects, whether for long or short duration. Because they are
limited to my direct experiences and impressions, they will, I
trust, have some value as primary source material, in spite of

being restricted to a personal point of view. Other chapters, such as the travel sketches or my review of *The Masses* magazine, are more truly period pieces, illuminating some aspects of a bygone era. In short, this is a narrative of my professional life, together with a selection of Profiles and Period Pieces in which I turn the searchlight, in varying degrees of duration and magnification, upon people and events.

I have had help from many sources in the writing of this work. Although they are not usually recorded in the text, I am nonetheless grateful for such aid and many kindnesses, including permission to quote from letters and publications. I would be remiss indeed if I did not acknowledge a special obligation to my wife, Laura, for her typing and wise counsel. Two of the chapters have been published previously: that on John B. Flannagan served as the introduction to the Memorial Exhibition catalogue at the Museum of Modern Art in 1942, and the pages on the Armory Show appeared in a slightly different form in "Art in America" in 1963. The Commencement Address, of course, was delivered orally, at the Pennsylvania Academy of the Fine Arts in June 1964.

Villarasio, Montagnola   Carl Zigrosser
Switzerland

A
World of Art
and Museums

PART I

Work and Travel

1

The Keppel Gallery

At the beginning of November 1912, I started to work for Keppel and Co., a well-established firm of print dealers founded by Frederick Paul Keppel, senior. He was descended from the Irish branch of an old English family, and he had prospered in America. The business still retained a faintly English tone—solid, reliable, conservative. He had two sons, Frederick Paul, Jr., the college dean who inherited his father's enterprise and executive ability; and David, who inherited his father's business, along with an inheritor's psychology. David was very much the English squire. His manners were always charming and courteous, his responses leisurely and unhurried. He had the outlook and bearing of a gentleman. Every summer he went abroad, chiefly to England, to buy prints for stock. In the spring he knocked off for a few weeks' fishing, and in the fall for a few weeks' duck shooting at a preserve in which he had a share in the Carolinas. The business ran more or less on the pattern and momentum established by his father. The American firm had been incorporated as a selling agent of art works supplied by the family firm located in London. The junior partners in the American company were the two chief salesmen, Fitzroy Carrington and H. V. Allison, and the office manager, Edward Nicholas.

Fitzroy Carrington was also of English birth. He was a romantic character, enterprising, passionate, extravagant. He was devoted to poetry and he loved the Renaissance. Sir Philip Sidney was his great hero (he named the little country place at Niantic, where he died, *Penshurst*). He loved primitive and Italian Renaissance engravings, without, however, appreciating them actually for their aesthetic significance. His approach was primarily literary. He was a creative salesman, that is to say he created an interest in a subject and a passion for collecting it. He succeeded so well with a group of collectors and patrons centered around the Museum of Fine Arts in Boston that he was asked to fill the post of Curator of Prints there, left vacant by the retirement of Dr. Emil Richter. He had just resigned from Keppel's when I arrived. There had been a conflict of personality between Carrington and Allison; and no doubt the call to Boston was also an opportune chance to withdraw gracefully from the scene. Carrington had big and often extravagant ideas. Just a year previously he had launched the *Print Collector's Quarterly* as a house organ for Keppel and Co. Allison considered the undertaking a huge and unwarranted expense. Carrington took the Quarterly to the Museum of Fine Arts with him, and remained its editor until Campbell Dodgson of the British Museum took over. Allison henceforth was the dominating influence in the firm. He was the prime exemplar of the substantial citizen. Dignified and soft spoken, he inspired confidence and stability. He spoke with authority, for he knew the price—if not the true value—of everything. His unshakable conservatism was not, in the long run, a sound influence. During the transition period in the visual arts soon to be inaugurated, imagination and flexibility were called for. Time and time again the firm missed the boat, and after various vicissitudes ceased to exist.

In the days when I first knew it, Keppel and Co. was a flourishing institution, and one of the leading print dealers in New York. It was by far the best firm in which to serve an apprenticeship. It was—and here I see the influence of David Keppel—more than just a place of business. As a commercial establishment it maintained a sense of dignity and decency, and some respect for art and scholarship; money was not everything. The catalogues and booklets issued by Keppel's were printed by one of the best printers in New York, The De Vinne Press. It is significant that three men associated with the house of Keppel eventually became museum curators, Fitzroy Carrington at the Museum of Fine Arts, David Keppel (Associate on a voluntary basis) at the National Gallery of Art in Washington, and myself at the Philadelphia Museum of Art.

I began as a kind of research librarian. None of the staff except David Keppel had any scholarly background or knowledge of languages essential in studying French and German reference books on prints. Carrington had previously taken care of the research, and I replaced him for that specialized branch of service. I enjoyed working with David. Although not the bookworm that I was, he had a broad and urbane culture and a wide experience with prints. His comments were often illuminating, and I began to train my eye for printing quality, and learn all the things one should know about prints. Since Keppel's had a fairly large stock of fine prints of all schools, it gave me a sound start for an all-around knowledge of prints. I began a systematic study of print history in books, often working in the Print Room of the New York Public Library, just around the corner. As I gained experience, I catalogued all the prints when they came in, supplying notes on their "states," provenance, rarity, and condition, and often finding pertinent quotations from the literature for sale's interest. Eventually I arranged and hung the special exhibitions. If there were catalogues to accompany them, I compiled them and saw to the printing. I was even allowed to write short forewords to the catalogues—miniature *causeries* on the subject—when David Keppel did not feel inclined to do so. I wrote on Rembrandt, Millet, Early Engravings, Whistler, Lithographs, Dutch Etching from Rembrandt to Bauer, and on such contemporaries as Ernest Roth, Childe Hassam, Earl Horter, and James McBey. The rather high-flown style of the forewords may be somewhat dated now, but the catalogues were well received at the time. A year or two before he died, James G. Huneker wrote me a note in which he said, among other things, "I remember with pleasure your artistic catalogues and well-written forewords." I generally took care of the critics when they came to review exhibitions and became acquainted with Royal Cortissoz of the *Tribune,* Elizabeth Luther Cary of the *Times,* and Henry McBride of the *Sun.* James Huneker, though covering music at the time, occasionally visited the gallery on his own. I remember a conversation with him in which he was discussing a man who had plagiarized his work: "I don't care if he appropriates my facts. Facts are common property. He who steals my purse, steals trash. But I am concerned when he copies my style, for my style is my trademark." I remember McBride's telling me à propos the number of exhibitions he had to cover, a burden even at that time, "I don't pretend to be a critic. Real criticism takes time, time to digest facts and verify conclusions."

I became acquainted with the artists who were connected with the gallery. Ernest Roth was one of the first. His studio—the first etcher's workshop I ever visited—was arranged with typical German order and neatness. Joseph Pennell came from London to etch New York skyscrapers, and I watched him print his plates at Peter Platt's printing shop downtown. Platt was a competent printer, but I remember him most vividly as continuously smoking a short clay pipe filled with dry Connecticut leaf tobacco. I marveled that his lips were not seared and his mouth not completely parched. He would ink the plate and remove the surplus, and then Pennell would take over to manipulate the rags and the palm of his hand, and achieve the effect he desired. He generally left a film of ink on the plate and employed retroussage. Once he turned to me and said "Do you think that you can print a plate?" I said I would try. "It is a lot better than I thought you would do", he said as he inscribed the proof to me. Pennell was a picturesque looking figure: he was easy to caricature, with his stoop, his scraggly whiskers and his squeaky voice. He was called "Scolding Joe," but his bark was

worse than his bite. His intemperate speech was a mannerism
that he adopted from his master, Whistler. He would dress a
person down with devastating vituperation, and then next
morning resume normal converse as if nothing had happened. While I was at Keppel's, I compiled a list of Pennell
etchings based upon exhibition catalogues and other available
records. It ran to over a thousand numbers, and was the
basis of Louis Wuerth's subsequently published catalogue
raisonné. Pennell was a facile draughtsman, left-handed, and
he seldom took longer than a day to complete a plate. Since
he sketched the scene directly on the plate, the image was re-
versed. He was primarily an illustrator, but documentation
also has its place in the hierarchy of art. His London, New
York, and Panama series did suggest the spirit of the place.

My association with Childe Hassam was more active.
Hassam had become interested in prints one summer at Cos
Cob. He etched and printed a sizable group. Late in the
summer Kerr Eby brought the artist and his etchings to
Keppel's. David Keppel and Allison were away, and Nicholas
was not equal to the occasion. His reaction was lukewarm if
not entirely negative. He mumbled something about the
etched lines being queer. Hassam was about to withdraw,
feeling rebuffed, when I intervened with a more enthusiastic
response. Not only did I like them, but I also was quite aware
of his standing as a painter. Would Hassam be willing, I suggested, to leave the prints there until David returned; I was
sure that his reaction would be as favorable as mine. Thus it
happened that Hassam's prints were first published by
Keppel's. I saw a great deal of Hassam for a while, both at
his New York studio on 57th Street and at Cos Cob where he
was staying with Elmer Livingston MacCrae. I remember
once that David and I spent a morning and an afternoon in
the New York studio selecting prints for a show. We had a
pleasant time looking over paintings and drawings as well as
the new etchings. We smoked cigars and exchanged jokes
and stories. Hassam told of the remark Remington made the
first time he ever saw one of Hassam's paintings: "O Hell, I
have an aunt up state who could knit a better picture than
that." Hassam told about his old friend, Col. C. E. S. Wood.
He had been a famous Indian fighter in his early days. He

was a man of wide cultural interests, a poet, an art collector, a kind of aristocratic radical who was a thorn in the flesh of conservative California. Hassam introduced me to his book *The Poet in the Desert.* The work supplemented his irreverent but very amusing *Heavenly Discourses,* which I was reading in *The Masses* at the time. Hassam was the first affluent artist I had met. His duplex studio was large and impressive and spotlessly clean. He had his press set up there. Though I never saw him print, I know that he printed all his etchings himself. He was fastidious about printing papers, too, always searching for old handmade sheets. I liked his etchings of city scenes and interiors with figures. He was adept at suggesting atmosphere and the play of light. I did not like his nudes *en plein air;* I considered them stiff and wooden. He, however, set great store by them, and was always asking me if I did not believe that they were better and solider than Zorn's photographic nudes. He could not see why Zorn should be so popular. Hassam, nonetheless, was a dedicated printmaker, and much more concerned with composition and design than one would expect from a successful colorist and impressionist painter. He once was discoursing on the mystery of art and I jotted down a few phrases which, in a sense, suggest his striving: "something baffling and elusive, that sets it apart from the easy, obvious expression—something that one labors over lovingly, glowingly."

I came to recognize the great collectors who came to the gallery, such as Harris B. Dick, the gift of whose collection precipitated the founding of the Print Room at the Metropolitan Museum; William M. Ivins, Jr., a lawyer, who was soon to become the first curator of prints at the Metropolitan; General Brayton Ives, imperious as befitted a rich man and a general; Howard Mansfield with a cold steely eye who collected Whistler and Japanese prints; Felix Warburg seeking fine impressions by Rembrandt; Paul J. Sachs, then a banker not quite sure of his taste, but soon to become director at the Fogg Art Gallery in Cambridge. Paul J. Sachs was asked by the weekly *The Nation* to suggest someone who would write articles on art and especially prints, and he referred the editor to me. I wrote an article on Ivins's first major exhibition at the Metropolitan, *Italian Renaissance Woodcuts*, that pleased him; and one on a big sale of Americana that aroused the ire of the dealer Harry Bland because I intimated that much Americana might have historic importance but little aesthetic value.

In due course I came to know some of the other print dealers operating in New York. One of the most picturesque was Ferdinand Meder. He was related to Joseph Meder, who was head of the Albertina in Vienna and author of the monumental work on drawings and on Dürer. He had a magnificent beard and looked very much like the bearded character in Zorn's etching *The Toast*. He seemed to me a relic of a past era. He was a great expert in the reproductive line engravings and portraits that were in vogue at high prices before the turn of the century. He was betrayed by his expert knowledge. He was constantly buying "bargains," rare early states that he knew had once commanded enormous prices. He did not realize that the fashions had changed; the original etchings of the British School were now in vogue, and nobody bought reproductive prints, no matter how rare or exceptional. He became discouraged and spent more and more time in a *Weinstube* on Union Square, until he died penniless. His example was my first lesson in the mutability of fashionable taste. Among the more active dealers I recollect were E. G. Kennedy, tall in stature and sharp in features—Old Hatchet Face, they called him—friend of Whistler and cataloguer of his etchings; Herman Wunderlich, his partner, a German-born dealer-expert who seldom paraded his great knowledge; Albert Roullier, of French birth, stocky and cheerful, who had left Keppel's to become the leading print dealer of Chicago and the West; William MacDonald, also a graduate of Keppel and Co., endowed with integrity and an equable temperament, and a marvelous eye for printing quality, who helped form the George W. Davison collection now at Wesleyan College in Middletown, Conn. and the A. H. Wiggin collection now at the Boston Public Library. George Sidney Hellman and Arthur Harlow were united in a partnership called the New York Cooperative Society—I never could figure out to what the cooperation referred, unless it was that the partners cooperated to sell pictures to the public. The cooperation did not last long. Arthur Harlow, who had a wide acquaintance among bankers and brokers in Wall Street, shortly thereafter entered into another partnership as Harlow, MacDonald and Co., and subsequently still another as Harlow, Keppel and Co., while MacDonald and Allison of the two respective firms branched out for themselves. E. Gottschalk had a shop at 150 Lexington Avenue. His stock, to a great extent, was junk and he sold cheaply without warranty, for he professed to know nothing. For a while, his shop served as an outlet for Keppel's old, outmoded, and unsalable stock. He had been a prize-fighter in his youth but had grown deaf and corpulent. His deafness was a business asset, for, when someone asked him an embarrassing question, he just could not hear. After his death the shop was bought by Henry Shaw Newman, who cleaned out the junk and built up a business in Americana and decorative prints under the name of The Old Print Shop. A strange and rather mysterious character, Richard Ederheimer, appeared now and then. He specialized in Dürer, Van Leyden, and early engravings. At first he had a shop, then he operated by carrying a portfolio, finally he gave up print selling and devoted all his time to painting in oils. He must have done some favors for Lord Duveen, because the latter gave him the use of a room at the Duveen Galleries on Fifth Avenue where he could bring sitters and paint portraits. He asked me to pose for him, and it was fun to have one's portrait painted at the Duveen Gallery, a legendary place even then. His pictures were in the primitive or Sunday-painter style. I do not know what became of my portrait. He called me and the painting "The Young Siegfried." Among dealers I should also mention Hugh Dunbar. When I was at Keppel's, he was in charge of the stock downstairs. He knew more about prints than the salesmen upstairs, but he was never allowed to function on the sales floor. I learned a great deal from him. Later he went to Chicago and joined Roullier. After Albert's death, his daughter Alice and Dunbar carried on the business for many years.

In the second decade of the twentieth century, the taste of

the public, as directed by the leading print dealers, was slanted chiefly toward the British School of etching. The great masters were Haden and Whistler. The arbiter of taste was Hamerton through his book *Etchers and Etching;* the touchstone was "the charm of the etched line." Cameron and Bone were eagerly collected. Among continental etchers, Zorn was fashionable. Of the French School, the only familiar printmakers were Legros, who lived in England, and Forain, who became known through the championship of Campbell Dodgson, of the British Museum. To be sure, Keppel's had introduced Lepère, Bejot, and Leheutre, but such etchers were not too different in style from the British printmakers. There was a gap in time between Corot and Millet (whose plates Keppel's owned and published) and the etchers mentioned above. It actually was one of the most exciting periods in print history and was totally unknown in this country. I became aware of this in various ways. I saw for the first time prints by Redon, Gauguin, and Munch at the Armory Show in 1913. They were a revelation, and I read Meier-Graefe's *Modern Art* and whatever else was available at the time. I also saw some unusual prints around the corner from Keppel's on Madison Avenue at the Berlin Photographic Co., dealers in fine art reproductions. The manager, Martin Birnbaum, started arranging special exhibitions of original works of art, such as drawings by Aubrey Beardsley, paintings by Maurice Sterne, and modern German prints. I saw my first prints by Käthe Kollwitz and bought one. Birnbaum later devoted all of his time to selling works of art and developed into an art advisor of wide experience and excellent taste. The Grenville Winthrop Collection, now at the Fogg Art Museum at Harvard, was formed largely by his guidance.

I had long talks with the German Alfred Strölin, one of the most astute print dealers of our time. He had had a gallery in Paris. When the war broke out in 1914, he became a war refugee in this country, and his stock of prints in Paris was sequestered. He occupied himself here by picking up bargains, rarities of which the American dealers were unaware, for he had an extensive knowledge of the European market, and he also knew what had happened in France during the last quarter of the nineteenth century. He had sponsored and published a set of Cameron etchings but he also had issued an edition of Manet's etchings. It was he who revealed to me the existence of prints by the Impressionists, Manet, Pissarro, Renoir, and Degas, Cassatt, Rodin, Toulouse-Lautrec, as well as those by such earlier masters as Delacroix (only his big *Lion* and *Tiger* were known here), Chasseriau, Gericault, and Daumier. Strölin, in his quiet way, did influence my life, not only by what he taught me about modern French prints, but also, later, by suggesting my name to E. Weyhe, when he was looking for someone to run a print gallery in connection with his book store.

What I had seen and heard of these new and modern prints, I found engaging and exhilarating. It seemed a pity that they were unknown in this country. I suggested to David Keppel and Allison that the firm introduce them here. I was careful to advocate not the young *Fauve* artists but such established painters and printmakers as Manet, Degas, Pissarro, or Toulouse-Lautrec. They were not convinced that there would be any demand for their prints in America. If there had been, collectors would have gone to Durand-Ruels, who handled their paintings. But, I argued, Durand-Ruels were not interested in selling prints; the only prints they ever displayed were a few color prints by Mary Cassatt. Besides, the two contended, they had no desire to compromise the good name of Keppel in view of the notoriety of the Armory Show. But, I countered, if they could not wholeheartedly sponsor such works, would they allow me to establish a tiny experimental gallery within the gallery on my own responsibility. There was a small alcove, adjacent to the exhibition gallery, which could be adapted for the purpose. No, they could not allow any association with experimental work, however remote, to affect the established reputation of the House of Keppel. It is ironic that many years later I happened to meet Allison, who said to me "You must come and see some wonderful new prints we have just acquired." They were wood engravings by Gauguin.

In 1917 the United States entered the war. The House

of Keppel, following the example of many other business firms, decided not to have any men of draft age in their employ for the duration of the war. Louis Wuerth and I, therefore, gave up our positions. In August of 1918 I had a letter from David, himself away in Washington on war work: "I was delighted to hear that you had landed your position [with the United Engineering Societies' Library] and am sure you will do splendidly with it. Our separation in business is, I sincerely hope, only temporary. I do not need to tell you that I never had a man who approached you for the scholarly research of our work." After the war was over, Louis Wuerth returned to the fold, but I did not. I felt that at Keppel's I would never be able to carry out some of my more advanced ideas about prints. When, therefore, Erhard Weyhe asked me to found and direct a print gallery as an adjunct to his art-book shop, I decided that it would give my initiative wider scope, and I accepted his offer. Thus, the first phase of my training as a print expert came to an end. When Dean Keppel first told me about the opening with the House of Keppel, he said that it "might possibly lay the foundation for a useful and profitable career." He went on to say that it was a highly specialized profession, but that its very specialization might well prove to be an asset, because of the relatively small number active in the field. His predictions have come true. I have never regretted my lifelong association with prints, whether as a dealer or museum curator. I never made a great deal of money, but my work has always been pleasant and never routine. I have many pleasant memories of my five years' apprenticeship at Keppel's. The Dean, Frederick P. Keppel, too, has been a kind of godfather to me. At various critical moments in my life, he has intervened with sound advice and helpful action. And it was his recollection of a casual remark I made as a freshman in college that determined my profession and career. As I have written elsewhere, I once went to the Dean's home for tea and because I had read a book on prints, I ventured some comment on the etchings he had on his walls. Later, after I had left college to work on a farm, he remembered me when his brother David asked him to recommend a young man of scholarly pursuits to work as librarian in the gallery. By that time I was fed up with working sixteen hours a day on the farm, and so I accepted. That is how I started at Keppel's.

2

Extracurricular Activities

I might mention some of the activities that occupied my spare time while working at the gallery, such as my editing of the Modern School Magazine, which I discussed in *My Own Shall Come to Me*. Another exciting event was the impact of the Armory Show. When I think of the Armory Show of 1913 it is with a certain glow of nostalgia and, still, with a tingle of excitement, for it marked a milestone in my youth. Now, so many years after the event, I shall try to revive my memories of it in the hope that I can communicate my feelings about it, reconstruct its setting, and suggest the impact of its innovations. Around 1912, New York City was a fairly comfortable place to live in. The First World War had not yet erupted to shatter the idea of unlimited progress. There was intellectual ferment of a mild sort. Wells and Galsworthy were writing controversial novels, George Bernard Shaw controversial plays, Richard Strauss controversial music. But in the visual arts, the keyword definitely was "genteel." The National Academy of Design was the dominating force in painting; its

27

galleries were practically the only public exhibition space available. The works of its members were, in the main, innocuous and noncontroversial. There were faint rumbles of revolt by a young group of Independents. Little if anything, however, was known about what had happened in art since 1900 in Europe.

Even before leaving college, I had been aware of conflicting art movements in New York. I remember going to an exhibition at the National Academy on West 57th Street. It was a cold winter afternoon. I was the only visitor, and I was struck by the loneliness of the exhibition, its complete remoteness from life, the sameness of its contrived figure pieces, the empty prettiness of its landscapes. By contrast, the first show arranged by the Independents in 1910 and held at an improvised gallery at 29-31 West 35th Street, had sparkle, variety, and vitality. Some of the pictures were not pretty, but they were alive. I was in sympathy with the new movement; I was for the underdog against the entrenched academicians.

I began to meet artists in the flesh. The first was Rockwell Kent, who came to talk to a student group at Columbia. It was a case of friendship at first sight. Kent invited me to visit him at his home at 4 Perry Street in Greenwich Village. I still remember the thrill of that first visit. Greenwich Village seemed so romantic on that cold snowy night. And the warmth of hospitality inside, music with Kathleen at the grand piano, good talk—Marsden Hartley was there between sojourns in Maine—talk of poetry, art, and nature. It was a glimpse of life at its fullest, most glamorous—the artist's life, the creative way. Kent and Hartley were among the "Independents."

I also met Walter Pach outside of Keppel's, and he opened up other vistas for me, glimpses of foreign shores. Although American-born, Pach had a slightly foreign aura about him. He and his walrus mustache appeared somewhat Spanish, and indeed he taught Spanish at night school. He smoked French cigarettes, the *paquet blue* of Maryland tobacco, or strong Italian cigars, *toscani.* He had exotic tastes in food; he introduced me to Chinese restaurants. They were cheap and neither of us had much money. We also talked about art and literature. From Pach would come intimations of exciting experiences in Paris, or casual references to Matisse, Redon, Jacques Villon, or Elie Faure, whose world history of art he was later to translate into English. During the period of the Armory Show I naturally turned to Walter Pach for enlightenment. But the artist seemed unable to explain or justify all the startling innovations, since he, in spite of more experience and an artist's training, took for granted many things that puzzled the neophyte.

I felt at the time that my lack of understanding vis-à-vis Walter was due to my own inadequacy. But I have since come to feel that the deficiency might not have been all on one side. Even if it is true that experience can not be transmitted, he might have shown a little more imagination in recapitulating the steps that led to understanding, and giving the clues to another seeker. A long time afterwards he confided to me that his own acceptance of the extreme forms of distortion in post-impressionist art had not been accomplished without considerable doubt and effort on his part. It would have helped if he had told me so at the time. He had diligently acquired a body of knowledge and experience, but he could not transmit its spirit or essence to another, because, as it turned out, he had not actually made it part of himself. He learned everything about art from without. He learned the rules, he knew the techniques. He was basically an academic painter and therefore his aesthetic reactions originated more from outside authority than from inner sensibility. His lectures and even his writings on art were dull and uninspiring. There were words—plenty of them, for he had great verbal facility—but they never came to life, never were convincing. He was not intelligent in his approach, which may be an added reason why his lectures were not too successful. They tended to be amorphous and lack any structure that the mind could grasp. He was very emotional, but his feelings never led him toward dramatic presentation: they were turned in on himself to render him constricted and ponderous. He was dreadfully serious about art—always with a capital A. He had a sense of humor but not about his chosen profession. Nonetheless, he was a warm and generous friend, and I learned many things from him. He played a major role in the constitution of the Armory Show; in fact he spent a whole year abroad assembling the foreign material. He will always be remembered for his share in introducing modern art to this country in a tangible way.

After this digression let me return to 1913 and my first visit to the Sixty-ninth Regiment Armory at Lexington Avenue and 25th Street in February of 1913. In a sense, I was better prepared than most Americans. Although I had not been to Paris and seen twentieth-century art, I had some familiarity with modern European literature and music. I had some experience in literary criticism, enough to treat the function of criticism with respect—not just to make snap judgments, but to strive to discover the artist's intention and then evaluate it. How good a critic I was is open to question; and it is with some diffidence that I contemplate revealing my notes and comments jotted down in my catalogue of the Armory Show. My justification is that my experience may be typical of many others, and since there are so few records, I submit mine for what it is.

The Armory Show was really two exhibitions in one. The first was a show of American paintings and sculpture by the young Independents and by a few sympathetic Academicians. This was both exciting and gratifying, for it meant that some of the American artists outside the pale of the Academy were getting recognition, or at least having the opportunity to show their work publicly. The second part of the show consisted of works by the French impressionists and Postimpressionists and, curiously enough, a few German expressionists, most of whom had never been shown in America. Some of these provided the shock element in the exhibition, and the press really had a field day. Among those who caused the most furor were Duchamp, Matisse, and Brancusi. My catalogue notes must have reflected some of the popular clichés. Opposite Duchamp's name I had written "shingle artist." Next to Matisse's *La Femme Blue* was written, "The one that caused the hysteria." Next to Brancusi's *Mlle. Pogany* was written, "The Duck Egg Muse." Later I came to know all three artists personally and to view their work with more sympathy and understanding.

But let me first speak of the Americans. There were so many unknown to me that I tried to arrange them in groups with some cohesive similarity. I would work from the familiar to the unfamiliar. This sometimes led to amusing results. For instance, the note: "Allied with A. B. Davies: Albert P. Ryder, Howard Coluzzi, Agnes Pelton, Van Deering Perrine." I was familiar with Davies's work, but had not seen many Ryders, thus putting the cart before the horse. I attempted to grade the artists. Those who received three stars (the highest) were Whistler, Ryder, Robert Henri, Jo Davidson, Jerome Myers (drawings), and the following, whose names have somewhat faded away: David Milne, Van Deering Perrine, and Patrick Henry Bruce. Among those with two stars were Karl Anderson, George Bellows, Robert Chandler, Arthur B. Davies, Lawson, Jonas Lie, Marin, Maurer, MacRae, Sloan, Mahonri Young. I was also interested in the cartoonists who exhibited: Art Young, Denys Wortman, O. E. Cesare (misspelled in catalogue) and Boardman Robinson, the latter two being rated with two stars.

The foreign moderns of course stole the show. I had some slight familiarity with the impressionists, Manet, Degas, Renoir (none of the late paintings were shown, as I remember), Pissarro, Monet. I welcomed them as old friends and rated them highly. But the Postimpressionists were a challenge, and I visited Galleries O, P, Q, and particularly H, I, and R many times to make myself familiar with the strange new productions. It must be remembered that at that time there was practically no interpretive literature on modern art. We Americans were confronted with odd and bizarre works without having any clue as to how to look or what to see.

I accepted Cézanne, for example, without realizing the nature of his most important contribution. I liked his *Femme au Chapelet,* and judged it to be one of the best paintings in the show, and one of those most likely to endure. What impressed me most about it was its human overtones—my note about it was a single word, "Character." I was not aware of his formal contribution, his searching analysis and realization of form.

Van Gogh presented no difficulties: I responded to him at once. One of my favorites was the *Bal à Arles* with its rich pattern of color. The picture is still vividly in my memory, although it is long since I have seen it. Gauguin likewise became one of my favorites. Perhaps his South Seas adventure aroused my romantic interest, for at the exhibition a little pamphlet was sold, giving extracts from his *Noa Noa*. But even though my response might have been partially literary, I had no difficulty in accepting his distortions and his color, so unlike that of nature. I also liked several lithographs, shown but not listed in the catalogue: *Pastorales Martinique* and *Les Drames de la Mer, Bretagne*. I was fascinated by the ethereal color of Redon's pastels; and his prints and drawings have always retained a compelling power over me. Another of my discoveries was Edvard Munch, who was represented at the show by four woodcuts and four lithographs in color. I was so taken with the lithographs that I made tiny sketches of three of them in my catalogue. I have never lost my enthusiasm for Munch's graphic work.

The hardest nut to crack was cubism. I am sure that I did not understand what it was all about at the time. I was unaware of the part that Braque and Picasso played in its genesis. Braque, it seems to me, was not well represented by the three paintings shown; at any rate I was not much impressed by him—another instance where I missed the boat. Nor did Picasso, certainly not the cubist element, impress me then. Evidently I did not respond to the austerities of analytical cubism, but preferred the later developments, for I wrote down "Villon and Picabia, best of the cubists." Likewise, I thought Gleizes was wonderful but did not understand Duchamp. About Jacques Villon I said, "I like him among the best of the cubists, he has prismatic color." If I did not comprehend the significance of cubism in all its phases, at least I did not reject it arbitrarily.

Toward a *fauve*, such as Matisse, my feelings were mixed. Some of his paintings were in my opinion "crude," but others I liked very much; and one, *Les Capucines*, I rated among the best paintings in the show. Rouault's compassionate irony did not get across to me at the exhibition. I called him "a tipsy muse" and commented on his *Nu* as "woman through fumes of absinthe." Nor did I do justice to Douanier Rousseau. I believed that his naiveté was a pose, and labeled him "consciously primitive." I missed Kandinsky, but perhaps this was not all my fault; there was only one painting, *Improvisation.* Beside my errors of omission, I committed errors of overestimation in the case of such artists as Chabaud and J. D. Innes. I made a list of thirteen works that I considered to be outstanding in the show and which I thought might have some lasting qualities. I print this list for what it is worth; the works were put down without any deliberate order of precedence:

Albert Gleizes, *L'Homme au Balcon* (sturdy crusader); Henri Matisse, *Les Capucines* (dance, motion); Wilhelm Lehmbruck, *Jeune Femme,* sculpture; Auguste Chabaud, *Le Troupeau sort après la Pluie;* Jacqueline Marval, *Odalisques au Miroir;* J. D. Innes, *Evening near Arenig, Wales* (advanced coloring); Patrick Henry Bruce, *Nature Morte* (interior effect, hard white light of whitewashed cottage); David Milne, *Distorted Tree* (most excellent design); Paul Gauguin, *Faa Ihe Ihe* (glowing warmth); Paul Cézanne, *Femme au Chapelet* (character); André Dunoyer de Segonzac, *Une Bucolique;* Augustus E. John, *Way down to the Sea;* Albert P. Ryder, *Moonlight on the Beach.* (My tiny sketch in my catalogue enabled the organizers of the Memorial Show fifty years later to identify the Ryder and to locate its whereabouts in the Duncan Phillips Collection.)

Beside the survey of the cubists, the pointillistes (Signac, Cross, Seurat), of whom Signac then seemed to me most important, and others of the School of Paris, such as Vuillard *(Les Journaux:* a fleeting glimpse—colors harmonize —beautiful) and Toulouse-Lautrec *(La Tresse:* beauty like Degas), the Armory Show assembled examples of the English School, largely from the collection of John Quinn, by Conder, Innes, Augustus John, Gwen John, Derwent Lees, A. E. Russell, Sickert, Wilson Steer, and Jack Yeats. And, surprisingly enough, a group of Germans and expressionists, such as Hodler, F. M. Jansen (I was much taken by his prints), Kandinsky, Kirchner, Lehmbruck (the two great statues), Munch, Pascin (I admired him as a draughtsman), and Slevogt. As I think back upon my reactions I am inclined to believe that I understood more readily (and was therefore more sympathetic to) the expressionist approach as exemplified by Van Gogh, Gauguin, and the like, and that I had more difficulty in accepting the formal approach of Cézanne and the cubists.

A little over 1,100 works of art were listed as shown. As one can well imagine, things were a bit helter-skelter, but the show was surprisingly well and logically organized. The original catalogue was jumbled and contained a number of misprints; during the exhibition a supplement was published, correcting some of the mistakes and listing about 65 additional paintings, which had arrived too late for insertion in the first catalogue. But there were numerous works shown that never appeared in either catalogue; about 1,600 works were actually shown.

The great hall of the Armory was divided into eighteen rooms designated from A to R. Roughly the front half of the area, or Rooms A, B, C, D, E, F, L, M, N, was devoted to American art, and the balance to foreign art. The entrance room, A, was huge, and contained American sculpture and Bob Chandler's big screens. Rooms B,C,D,E,F to the right contained American paintings. Room G, in the corner, contained mostly English and German art. Room H, somewhat larger and matching A in the rear, contained French painting and big sculpture, Lehmbruck, Bernard, Brancusi, Maillol, and the like. Corner room I contained cubist paintings and smaller sculpture by Picasso and Duchamp-Villon. Rooms J,K,L showed prints, drawings, and watercolors; J, foreign; K, foreign and American; L, exclusively American. Rooms M and N, devoted to American painting, led back into A, from the left. Between A and H,—that is to say the center of the whole area—four galleries, O,P, Q, and R were arranged, containing the impressionists and old masters, as well as Cézanne, Van Gogh, Gauguin, and Matisse. Rooms H and I were perhaps the most exciting sections, for there were found the crowds that came to laugh and scoff. It was exciting to watch people's reactions, and occasionally to argue with strangers about the pictures. The air was electric with the clash between old and new. New vistas were being opened, new discoveries made: primitive folk art, long-neglected arts of the past. The vested interests fought viciously to protect their position; accusations of charlatanism, insanity, or mildest of all, technical incompetence were directed against the innovators. The battle for freedom of expression took on aspects of a crusade that appealed to youth and all free spirits. The battle was not won in a day—it was to endure for many years. But this was the beginning of the fray, when there was hope that many young Davids would appear to slay the Goliaths of convention and reaction.

One of the shining yound Davids was Alfred Stieglitz, and I first became acquainted with him and "291" about the time of the Armory Show. His exhibitions of foreign and American works were stimulating and exciting. Indeed, he had introduced certain features of modern art even before the Armory Show. I soon became a constant visitor to the gallery and a regular reader of his publication, *Camera Work*.

This then is the story of my introduction to modern art. The beginnings may have been groping and tentative and full of mistakes, but they were stirring and exciting. I can say with assurance that, with my exposure to the Armory Show and to "291,' my education in modern art was well and happily under way. In the special number of *Camera Work* for 1912, there was an essay on Picasso by Gertrude Stein. The following quotation somehow expresses the spirit of the creative artist in those early and exciting days: "Something had been coming out of him, certainly it had been coming out of him, certainly it was something, certainly it had been coming out of him, and it had meaning, a charming meaning, a solid meaning, a struggling meaning, a clear meaning."

3

The Weyhe Gallery

To return to my narrative, my association with Erhard Weyhe began in the late summer of 1919. He had been an antiquarian bookseller with a shop on Charing Cross Road in London. When war was declared in 1914, he foresaw that as a German national he would sooner or later be interned in England, and he made a quick decision. He came to New York with his wife and a suitcase full of books. Alert, intelligent, and hard working, he knew his trade and was a good salesman. He began by peddling books, buying a choice item (which he recognized) in one shop and selling it in another. Gradually he built up a clientele and took a tiny bit of office space in a plumber's shop at 708 Lexington Avenue. He decided to specialize in art books; he sensed the growing demand, and saw that there were no American dealers knowledgeable in the field. Artists and scholars began to frequent his shop; Pach and Strölin told me about him while I was still at Keppel's. By 1919 he had the whole shop—all of it stuffed with books—and the plumber had the tiny office space. The occasion called for expansion: Weyhe rented a whole store next door and asked me to run a print gallery for him. The rear half of the place was to be made into a print gallery and the front half was to be the book shop, "Weyhe's Art-book Store and Gallery."

I was at last to have a gallery of my own. To be sure, it was an adjunct to a book store—books and prints fitted well together—but the direction and operation were to be my responsibility, for Weyhe knew little about prints. I now had a chance to try out the theories about "modern" prints that had not been acceptable at Keppel's. The first major exhibition that I held was of lithographs by Daumier and Gavarni on the first of November 1919. This was followed by lithographs by Odilon Redon. They were pioneering exhibitions. It is hard to realize nowadays the paucity of such material in this country at the time. I remember that years before I had searched everywhere in New York for lithographs by Daumier. A few of the artists, who had been to Paris, had some that they had picked up from the *bouquinistes* by the Seine. But no dealer here had any. I finally found two (taken from *La Caricature*) in an odd lot at an auction sale. Redon lithographs were just as scarce. The only other Redon prints I had seen were at the Armory Exhibition of 1913.

My appeal was not to the rich collector, but rather to the artist or collector of moderate means but good taste. The rich collector generally buys at the peak of the graph. The innovator is of course at a certain disadvantage: he has the major burden of educating the public. Afterwards the operators move in for the big financial kill. Our educational efforts at the gallery were aided by the sympathetic attitude of the press. Although the reactions of the leading critics were not always predictable or favorable, they were, in the aggregate, benevolent. Occasionally we received a heartwarming tribute, such as the following in *Arts and Decoration* for February 1921, which recognized what we were trying to do.

> At the Weyhe Gallery, in a perfectly natural manner, an atmosphere of mental activity has been created. There is nothing imposing or showy in the place, no palatial front, just some interesting books, and small interesting exhibitions which are meet-

ing with response of those who care. The gallery has life in it; and, in comparison, some of our palaces of art-dealing are mere tawdry pretense. It is a very hopeful sign that a little gallery of this kind, which appeals to the mind and love of art, and does not attempt to impress the profiteer with velvet hangings, should be thriving in its own unpretentious manner.

The decade of the 1920s was an opportune time to launch a print gallery. Prints were plentiful in Europe owing to postwar conditions, and foreign exchange was very favorable to the American dollar. And there was a potential market in this country if one could discover and cultivate it. Early in 1922 I launched a major exhibition of graphic work by Manet and the French Impressionists, including Cézanne, Degas, Cassatt, Morisot, Pissarro, Guillaumin, Renoir, Sisley, and Signac. By a coincidence Keppel's staged an exhibition of modern prints at the same time. They had by this time become more aware of "modern" graphic art, and had no doubt found encouragement, as had I, in the prestige of the Postimpressionist exhibition of paintings and prints at the Metropolitan Museum of Art of 1921. Henry McBride wrote a long review of the Keppel and Weyhe exhibitions in the *New York Sun* of February 11, 1922.

It would be tedious to mention all the exhibitions of contemporary foreign printmakers held in the decade; I might, however, cite the show of Matisse drawings in 1925 (in collaboration with Pierre Matisse, his first appearance in New York before he established his own gallery here), prints and drawings by Picasso in conjunction with bronzes by his friend Manolo, and later, shows by Pascin, Rivera, and Grosz. Of course, beside the formal exhibitions, there was active commerce in prints by the leading practitioners of the nineteenth and twentieth centuries.

The introduction of graphic art from abroad, however, was only one part of the gallery's program; the other aim was to become a center for American prints, and to encourage the native artist by creating a market for his work. As an assignment in propaganda, the launching and buildup of American printmakers proved to be an even more difficult task than that of the Europeans. The French artists had at least some prestige in their own country, and the American public, ever

since the Armory Show, began to have a slight curiosity
about them. But the American artists who needed encouragement were not known as printmakers in their own country, even though some of them were successful or potentially
successful painters. In general, the public is indifferent to
things that are unfamiliar, and the public in this instance
consisted of the customers of print dealers, each of whom
had educated his clientele to like and buy the works of artists
in his own "stable." Since the taste of the established dealers
was very much the same, the customer trained by any one of
them would not feel too uncomfortable in the gallery of any
other. But it was otherwise when the customer was confronted with works not conceived in the style of Haden,
Cameron, and their many followers. To one nurtured to appreciate only the charm of the etched line, works slanted toward realism or experimentation in design seemed, if not
ugly, at least strange and repellent. Therefore the task con-
fronting the Gallery was to educate an entirely new public to
respond to the work of the young creative artist rather than
of the technically competent craftsman. A leaflet that I wrote
in 1921, which drew favorable comment from *The Dial*, sums
up the basis of the Gallery's intention. It was entitled *The Living Artist* and was printed with decoration and typography by
Rudolph Ruzicka.

Do you realize that works of art, as vital and powerful as any
in times past, are being created today? So often people consider
art merely as the heritage of former generations, and forget that
the masterpieces, now so rare and precious, once had all the
commonplaceness of contemporary things. If you read in history
with what indifference or even hostility great works of art were
received, you would realize how little the world has changed
from yesterday to today. If we all but had the wit to see them,
we could discover for ourselves those rare living things which assume with years the dignity of great art. And there is no more
satisfactory adventure than to find, acquire, and enjoy these
works of dynamic and haunting quality.

But there is a further side to the question. The artists of today
who may have such noble potentialities, must live. They must
have food and shelter and the freedom to work unhampered;
and being human, they must have recognition and sympathy. By
buying their productions which they gladly offer at far from exorbitant prices, you serve them in all their needs. But you must

aid them when they most need your support, when they are young and struggling, not when they are old and famous. If America is ever to produce an art for all the world to see, you must foster every one who is genuinely striving to create.

We make this appeal for the searchers, the young and coming artists, and those who have never grown old. The others have their own reward—the sanction of "official" renown. But the creators work with more travail of flesh and spirit. Not only do they contend with a hostile or indifferent world but they work inceasingly to perfect their expression and clarify their vision. Most often they struggle alone.

We make this appeal in the interest of no special clique of artists working either in the old or in the new tradition. We invite you to come to our shop to look at the work of a group whose productions we happen to have. But there are others whose achievement is equally or perhaps more significant. Go to other dealers with vision and intelligence; go to the artists themselves.

We appeal to you to buy the works of the creators of our own time. If you cannot afford to buy, then see them and think about them. Collect prints and reproductions if nothing else; there are masterpieces a-plenty if you have the taste and the will to see. If you own and enjoy a genuine work of art it will repay you a hundred-fold in renewed sensitiveness to creative and human values.

Before the formal opening of the Gallery in November 1919, Weyhe had agreed to finance a publication entitled *Twelve Prints by Contemporary American Artists.* I busied myself, therefore, with assembling the material, visiting studios, commissioning prints, supervising printing, and the like. The finished work, in a linen portfolio and containing my introduction printed by Bruce Rogers, was formally published in December 1919. The twelve original signed prints comprised seven etchings or drypoints by Earl Horter, W. Auerbach Levy, Kenneth Hayes Miller, Jerome Myers, Walter Pach, John Sloan, and Mahonri Young; three lithographs by Boardman Robinson, Maurice Sterne, and Albert Sterner; and two woodcuts by Rockwell Kent and Rudolph Ruzicka. The sets sold for fifty dollars and were issued in an edition of one hundred. My high hopes of an immediate sellout were somewhat dashed by the public response. Sales were fair, but it took several years before we broke even. I learned a number of things from the experience. One lesson was that the American public did not take kindly to portfolios. Time and time again I was told "I like one or two of the prints, but what shall I do with the other ten?" As I look at the publication now, I feel that I did not exercise enough editorial judgment. The choice of several artists to be included represented a compromise with the prevailing taste, an expediency that I now regret. And I wish I had been a little firmer in my selection of individual prints: I believe I might have obtained better examples from Robinson, Ruzicka, Sterne, and Young. But on the whole, I still feel that it was a fairly representative cross section of print production around 1920, albeit slightly in advance of the prevailing taste. There were a few conspicuous omissions of printmakers whom I either discovered after the portfolio was published, or whom I wanted but were not available for one reason or another, such as A. B. Davies, George Bellows, or J. Alden Weir.

During the early years of the Gallery at 710 Lexington Avenue, from 1920 to 1923, I had exhibitions of prints and drawings by Arthur B. Davies, John Marin, Joseph Stella, Adolf Dehn, and group showings by Walt Kuhn, Walter Pach, Boardman Robinson, Max Weber, Mahonri Young, George Bellows, Charles Burchfield, Pop Hart, Marsden Hartley, and John Sloan.

In 1923 Weyhe bought a building at 794 Lexington Avenue between 61st and 62nd streets, and remodeled it as a book store on the ground floor, a gallery on the second, and storage and living quarters above. Henry Churchill was the architect, and he designed the facace with its characteristic pattern of checkerboard tiles. We commissioned Henry Varnum Poor to make a group of four decorative tiles, which were incorporated in the building. The new quarters with their cloth-covered exhibition walls and low shelf cases for print boxes, have remained the background of the Weyhe Gallery ever since. The interior and exterior aspects of the Gallery were depicted in Christmas cards by Mabel Dwight, Howard Cook, Emil Ganso, and Allan Lewis. These Christmas cards or keepsakes were a special—and possibly pioneer—feature of the Gallery's enterprise. Each year we would commission an artist to make an original lithograph or woodcut as a memento to send to our customers. In addition to those already mentioned, we sent out prints by Arthur B.

Davies, Rockwell Kent, Victoria Hutson, Pamela Bianco, Wanda Gág, and Adolf Dehn. Likewise, many of the invitation cards for one-man shows consisted of original prints made by the exhibiting artists, We tried to add distinction and typographic beauty to the announcements, title pages of catalogues, and various other publications of the gallery and bookstore. In this I sometimes had the friendly advice of such famous typographic designers as D. B. Updike, Bruce Rogers, Walter Dorwin Teague, and Rudolph Ruzicka. As might be expected from the close association with a bookstore, the gallery dealt in rare illustrated books (embellished with original prints) and other examples of fine printing. This bookish bent was also reflected in some exhibitions of specific typographic interest, such as the engraved illustrations of Stephen Gooden and the productions of the Curwen Press of London. Another activity not generally pursued in many art galleries was the commerce in decorative prints: we made a specialty of flower prints, Audubon Birds, decorative maps, views, costume, and ornament prints, and illuminated manuscript pages. In fact, these specialties helped somewhat to keep the gallery going while the sales of American art were lagging.

The gallery dealt in some paintings in addition to graphic art. There were several one-man shows by Alfred Maurer, Emil Ganso, Vincent Canadè, and Diego Rivera. Maurer and Ganso had been brought into the gallery circle by Weyhe himself. There were likewise paintings in stock for sale. I recall canvases by Redon, Picasso, Per Krohg, Masereel, Castellanos, and Siqueiros; also watercolors by Klee, Tamayo, Demuth, Marin, Burchfield, and Pascin.

Next to prints and drawings, however, sculpture was the most active branch of the gallery's business. Again, it was pioneer work, since few other galleries dealt in sculpture. The low book cases or print cabinets made appropriate bases for the display of plastic objects in bronze, wood, or stone. Sculpture was often on view even during formal shows of pictures. Besides special exhibitions of Manolo and Chana Orloff, there were in stock bronzes by Picasso, Maillol, Renoir, Daumier, Degas, and Despiau, and from the German

School, works by Lehmbruck, Barlach, Kolbe, Mataré, Marcks, and Sintenis. Whole editions of bronzes by Maillol (eight subjects) and Lachaise (six subjects) were commissioned, and became, as it were, publications of the gallery. Likewise large groups of sculpture by Flannagan were purchased outright. The gallery was his sole agent until a few years before his death. Among other American sculptors who had solo shows at the gallery may be cited: Alexander Calder (two shows, 1928 and 1929, his first exhibition anywhere), Arnold Ronnebeck, Heinz Warneke, Wharton Esherick, Dorothea Greenbaum, and Doris Caesar.

Mention should be made of our active commerce in pre-Columbian stone sculpture and African wood carvings. It seemed to me that those classes of objects represented about the only areas where it was still possible to obtain works of high aesthetic merit for a modest price. An Egyptian stone head, for example, comparable in aesthetic quality to a *Guerrero* stone mask, would cost twenty to fifty times the price of the latter. The problem was to be sure of getting genuine pieces when the market was being more and more flooded with forgeries and imitations. Fortunately we found sources where the authenticity was unassailable. Similarly we found a trained ethnologist and art historian, Dr. Hans Himmelheber, who was going to Africa in 1936. We gave him funds to collect for the Weyhe Gallery, as he had previously collected for a number of European ethnographic museums, notably that at Frankfurt. For over two years he explored the Ivory Coast, Gabun, the Grasslands of the Cameroons, and the various tribal areas of the Belgian Congo, such as *Bakuba, Bena Lulua,* and *Batshiok;* and he shipped us a large collection of art objects from each region. The "ghost masks" from the *M'Pongwe* tribes of the Gabun were particularly beautiful and also exceedingly rare, since the missionaries, some fifteen years before, had systematically destroyed all the masks and statues they could find. The Gallery held a big exhibition in 1940, and issued an illustrated catalogue of *African Negro Art,* for which I did considerable research.

As I look back on the activities of the Gallery during the

score of years that it was under my direction, I would say that it did accomplish certain things. It helped to introduce the graphic art of the Postimpressionists, the expressionists, and the Mexican School. into this country. It dealt in Old Master prints of good quality and moderate prices—Goya, Blake, Daumier, Rowlandson, Piranesi, Callot, fifteenth- and sixteenth-century woodcuts from books, the lesser but fine Durers and Rembrandts, early lithographs, and numerous other out-of-the-ordinary prints. Pre-Columbian and African sculpture were to be found there, and modern sculpture both foreign and American, with special emphasis on John B. Flannagan. It encouraged, perhaps with more enthusiasm than discrimination, a great number of American printmakers. Some of these have been described in my book *The Artist in America*. At a crucial period, the Gallery dealt in the work of Arthur B. Davies, George Bellows, John Sloan, Edward Hopper, Glenn Coleman, Pop Hart, John Marin, Yasuo Kuniyoshi, Charles Sheeler, Stuart Davis, Louis Lozowick, Andrée Ruellan, Victoria Huntley, Carolina Durieux, Peggy Bacon, Max Weber, Benton Spruance, and Reginald Marsh. But the printmakers most closely identified with the Gallery were Rockwell Kent, Adolf Dehn, Wanda Gág, Emil Ganso, Mabel Dwight, Howard Cook, Harry Sternberg, and Federico Castellon. Such is the record, for better or worse, of the Weyhe Gallery.

Some highlights stand out in my recollections of gallery events. Openings, for example: Ganso's, where we served the cake he had baked as a farewell gesture to his old profession. Openings, where customers were waiting for the gallery to open in the morning in order to get first choice. Such zeal always delights the gallery director, and it happened with Arthur B. Davies and Rockwell Kent. Davies was one of our great assets; not only was he a star performer in the gallery but he was also a big customer in the bookstore.

On February fifteenth of 1933 there was considerable commotion in the Gallery. We had been having trouble now and then with the customs officials of the Port of New York. They harassed our importing activities by their arbitrary and what we considered illegal rulings. For instance, we imported several original drawings by Odilon Redon. They were signed by the artist; the consular invoice and affidavits were in order; we had every reason to assume that they would pass through free. The tariff law states that all original works of art are free of duty, and proceeds to enumerate the categories: original paintings in oil, etchings signed by the artist, drawings in pencil and watercolor, and so on. Some smart and unscrupulous examiner noted that in the phrase "drawings in pencil and watercolor" there was no comma between *pencil* and *and*. Therefore he argued that drawings in pencil were not free (though those in pencil *and* watercolor were), and held up the shipment for duty. We argued with him in vain. He said, with a smile, that we could appeal to Washington if we liked. We reckoned the costs of an appeal to Washington whether we won or lost, and they amounted to more than the duty involved. Weyhe decided to pay the duty. The customs officials also acted as censors to screen shipments of books that they deemed obscene. It was their practice, when they found books that they considered pornographic, to send a notice to the importer that his shipment had been declared unmailable. If he signed the printed form consenting to the confiscation and destruction of the books, he would absolve himself from prosecution for illegal entry. One memorable day in February we received such a notice. The title of the culpable book was garbled—they were not very literate at the Customs House—and we were at a loss to know what piece of pornography we had wittingly or unwittingly imported. We were able to decipher one word *Michel-Ange* and then we remembered that we had ordered from Paris a book with large-scale reproductions of the frescoes in the Sistine Chapel. Fortunately we had already had a copy of the work and we looked through it to see what could possibly be considered obscene. We found nothing and we therefore did not sign and return the printed form. Instead, we sent out a release to all the papers stating that the U.S. Customs have declared the frescoes in the Pope's private chapel in the Vatican to be obscene. Thus on the fifteenth of February all hell broke loose. Reporters swarmed about for interviews, scores of news photographers came to get pictures, telephone wires were humming all day. All business at the Gallery was suspended. It was front-page stuff in all the newspapers. The head of the customs department came specially to the Customs House to face the reporters and issue a statement that it was all an unfortunate mistake, due to the officious zeal of a minor clerk. He called up on the telephone and said plaintively, "Why didn't you telephone me? I am sure that we would have corrected the mistake without all this hullabaloo in the papers." But would the arrogance and "officious zeal of the minor clerks" have been curbed without the newspaper publicity? At any rate the atmosphere at the Customs House was much more courteous for a period thereafter. Meanwhile we had had some fun (though the interviews with reporters, repeating the same thing, became a bore after the second day) and had our revenge for the numerous vexations we had suffered. Such incidents as these made life exciting in the early days of the Weyhe Gallery.

Another instance of Weyhe's enterprise in the early days was his invitation to Julius Meier-Graefe to visit the United States on the occasion of his sixtieth birthday. Weyhe paid all his expenses for the four weeks visit. Meier-Graefe and his wife arrived in New York City in February of 1928. I acted as his guide and interpreter on occasion. In addition to visiting numerous collectors such as Dr. Barnes and seeing their pictures, Meier-Graefe had contacts with American artists. They naturally wanted to do him honor. I was present at several dinners for him, notably one given by the Starrs at 88 Central Park West, to which many artists were invited. I remember seeing Stieglitz, Marin, O'Keeffe, Demuth, Wanda Gág, Emil Ganso, and Victor Frisch, among others. The occasion was also the first time I met the Baroness Hilla von Rebay.

Meier-Graefe expressed a desire to see Harlem and dancing by blacks. I therefore arranged a party to take him there. Besides Meier-Graefe and his wife, Annamarie, I invited Marya Mannes, Wanda Gág, Rockwell Kent, and Jimmy Harris, a Negro high school teacher, all of whom except Jimmy had some knowledge of German. First we had dinner at 51 West 51, then we gathered at the home of Marya's parents,

David and Clara Mannes. Finally about midnight we took taxis to the Savoy Dance Hall in Harlem, which at that time had the best jazz in town. Meier-Graefe watched the Negro couples entranced, marveling at their instinctive feeling for rhythm, and their uncanny sense of timing when they broke away from each other only to return again in perfect step. It was a delight to watch their movements, so graceful, so relaxed, yet so perfectly attuned to rhythm and gesture, so inventive in their response to the music. It was a memorable evening.

Just before Meier-Graefe left, we presented him with a portfolio that I had assembled of prints and drawings by a group of artists. From the boat he wrote in his halting English:

> I begg you to say my best thanks to the following artists, Niles Spencer, Preston Dickinson, Louis Bouché, Yasuo Kuniyoshi, Arnold Ronnebeck, Vincent Canadè, R. Lahey, Al Frueh, Eugene Fitsch, Ernest Fiene, Mahonri Young, Jo Mielziner, Edward Hopper, Walter Pach, A. Lubbers, John Marin, Wanda Gág, Emil Ganso, Max Weber, and Arthur B. Davies, These artists have greatly enjoyed me with the collectif portfolio. The gift will be a fine souvenir of my first journey to America. I hope to come back. Give to all my shaken hand.

In the mid-twenties Weyhe and I were in the habit of having our lunch in the apartment of an Italian widow nearby. Others frequented the place, and we formed a kind of Luncheon Club. Among the members were Arthur Upham Pope, Phyllis Ackerman, Rudolf M. Riefstahl, Elizabeth Titzel, and Stephan Bourgeois. Guy Eglington, writing in the *International Studio* for February 1925 has neatly described its activities:

> The food was only moderate, but the talk was good. A little peppery perhaps, but keen, and intolerant of long phrases and undigested ideas. In its small way, which in view of the fact that everyone in the art game was dragged in sooner or later, was not so very small, it played the much needed role of satirist. It laughed unmercifully and its laughter hit home. The offensive little word "artistic" was but one of its *bêtes noirs*, a symbol if you like, of the kind of thing it wouldn't stand for, the heavy earnestness of the second-rate painter, the breathless enthusiasm of

the neophyte connoisseur, the candy-coated phrases (*schleim* in the language of the Luncheon Club) of the professional critic, the pompousness of the new dealers, just fresh from Europe and all set to teach America the meaning of art. In the process, of course, we all lost our halos, but it is amazing how well we got along without them. Forbidden to speak *ex cathedra* we had to reexamine all the old words and phrases that had done such yeoman service, discover what, if any, was their exact meaning and hammer them into new shapes to approximate as closely as might be, new thoughts. It was hard work, but it did us good.

I can not recall all the thousands of people who frequented the gallery during the score of years when I was there. A few stand out in my recollection—I am not speaking of the artists: they were a host in themselves and are recalled elsewhere. For instance there were the Three Musketeers, Frederick B. Adams, Elmer Adler, and Burton Emmett (or was it Adams, Adler, and Donald Klopfer?). At any rate we labeled them such, since they arrived together every Saturday or so, making the rounds of the galleries.

W. G. Russell Allen was a cultivated *amateur* in the finest sense of the word, a *connoisseur* of the arts, a *dilettante,* again in the noble eighteenth-century tradition. He had the taste and knowledge of a professional museum man but, owing to a private income, none of the responsibilities. He was the curator of his own first-rate art collection. He had a delightful time in life, and that delight was shared by those with whom he came in contact through his collecting.

It was also a pleasure to serve Edward W. Root in the gallery. There was more direction in his collecting: he was building up a teaching collection. He had been Professor of Mathematics at Hamilton College, and it is a tribute to his character that his nickname among the students was Square Root. (This was of course long before the word *square* had acquired a pejorative meaning for a younger generation.) He retired from the mathematics faculty and while still on the campus devoted himself to teaching the appreciation of art. He had begun long ago to collect paintings—as the son of Elihu Root he had ample means—and formed close friendships with a number of distinguished artists. In his new vocation he continued to build up the collection as a teaching instrument. His manner was unassuming and retiring, partly due to his increasing deafness; but he had uncompromising integrity, an alert intelligence, and an assured aesthetic sensibility. His judgments on art, even the most advanced, were sound and stimulating. Once, at lunch at *The Passy* where he generally ate when in town, he expounded his philosophy of teaching. Most people, he said, most students never had a direct aesthetic experience. They had never been trained to look at a work of art. They went first to a book to read about it, and they never got around to look at it. He forbade his students to look at a book. He started them by looking at a statue, feeling its planes with the fingers and correlating the sensation of the inclination of the planes with the amount of light or shade reflected. Only after a thorough grounding in three-dimensional form and its conventions did he allow the student to look at two-dimensional categories, such as paintings, and go on to the exploration of design and color.

Miss Lilly Bliss, friend and confidante of Arthur B. Davies, occasionally came and bought things. She invited me to see the music room that Davies had decorated for her. She also told of an idea she had for combining three collections —John Quinn's, Arthur B. Davies's, and her own—to form a museum of modern art. Unfortunately, it was only her own that later became the nucleus of The Museum of Modern Art.

There are a few special moments that stand out in my memory. One was selling to Leonard Hanna of Cleveland, Bolton Brown's collection of Bellows's lithographs. Bolton Brown was the printer for a large part of Bellows's oeuvre, and he had the printer's privilege of keeping one proof for himself. Naturally they were very choice proofs. Another such moment was selling Judge John M. Woolsey a Redon lithograph. He was a man of dignified presence, every inch a judge, yet simple and genial in a kind of hearty British manner. He collected prints of clock towers. He already had several by Buhot and Bonington, but he was intrigued by the Redon, which was a visionary tower. He was dubious whether he should acquire a print that did not represent an actual place, but he was a good sport and bought it. This happened shortly after he had rendered his far-reaching decision on Joyce's *Ulysses*. A third moment was Dr. W. R. Valentiner's immediate response on his first view of Flannagan's sculpture. His impulsive and intuitive reactions were both an asset and a handicap to Valentiner. They alerted him to the creative aspects of some modern artists, such as Flannagan and the German expressionists, but they also led him to make snap judgments and indefensible attributions in the Old Master field. In spite of his faults he will always remain for me a warm and generous human being. One more instance was when Fritz Kreisler came in to sell a little collection of rare early books. He was quite a Latin scholar, and loved to read Vergil, Livy, Terence, and the like, in the original. After the First World War, there was suffering and starvation in his native Austria, and he felt he ought to sell his books and send the money abroad. I bought two or three of the books for myself and he inscribed them for me. I was deeply impressed by his charm and innate modesty.

Frank Crowninshield was an influential figure during the era, not so much for what he bought (though later he collected de luxe illustrated books in order to sell them at auction with great éclat) as for the publicity he was able to dispense as editor of *Vanity Fair*. He did much to make the modern art movement respectable and even chic. But his activity was on a superficial plane. He had a patter, made up largely of fashionable clichés—he could turn it off or on, and spout it by the hour—and this was used to accompany the reproductions of modern art in the magazine. He had elegant manners, and obviously was the man about town, but he could be heartless and penurious to the young artists whose work he purchased for illustrations. *Vanity Fair* was aptly named.

Musicians and actors came to the gallery to see and ocassionally to buy. Geoge Gershwin, for example, who came more to see than to buy (he was an amateur painter); the harpsichordist Ralph Kirkpatrick, ever alert to an aesthetic experience; Janos Scholtz, more cellist at the time than collector, but even then with an alert eye and always with heartwarming gusto. Alfred Lunt, occasionally with Lynn Fontaine, playing, even in real life, the role of devoted husband and romantic lover. Joseph Schildkraut used to give me tickets to his plays. We all thought his greatest role was Liliom: he *was* Liliom.

The big-name stage designers were avid customers for art books. They needed background material for their business. Jo Mielziner had more of the constitution and training of the artist than most of them. He had studied painting at the Pennsylvania Academy in the same class with Franklin Watkins, Caroline Durieux, and Paul Froelich. He had several shows in our gallery. He was friendly and likable. Lee Simonson was the consummate egotist: whatever he did was impressively important to him, and by implication to the whole world. He looked vaguely oriental, and I could easily imagine him in the guise of a *Pasha*. I saw him occasionally at social affairs and he once invited me to meet Rivera at a party he gave to introduce the Maestro to New York. The occasion was not so momentous for me, however, as he thought it was, since I was seeing Rivera every day at the time. But he did occasionally give me tickets to Theatre Guild plays for which he had designed stage settings, such as *Caesar and Cleopatra*—I remember particularly the three performances of Shaw's *Back to Methusaleh* cycle. The Guild then had the pleasant custom of offering a dress rehearsal on the Sunday before the Monday night opening, to which they invited the intelligentsia of New York. It was pleasant to see the play and one's friends also. I recall seeing Hutch Hapgood at the last play of the cycle and being impressed that he looked so much like one of the "ancients" on the stage.

Of course I had much to do with the critics who came to review the exhibitions. With most of them I was reserved, and kept the relation purely on the professional level. I never tried to influence their critical judgment. I usually stated my case in the release. (I was often amused by how easily a gallery release could be changed into critic's copy.) I answered questions when they were put to me, but in general I left the critics alone unless they demanded attention. There were one or two, however, notably Henry McBride and Lewis Mumford, with whom I could talk on matters of mutual but more general concern. I occasionally met McBride at outside parties, but only occasionally, for he had told me long ago that he had tried to avoid personal contacts with artist because they tended to impair his critical judgment. What he really meant, I believe, was that he avoided contact with all artists except those whom he accepted in a critcal sense. The judgment came first and the friendship second. He did have cordial relations with some of the best artists, such as Demuth or Lachaise, and he did go to parties given by Florine Stettheimer, Juliana Force, and the like. His conventional manners recoiled at Bohemian ways. We seemed to get along well together, and I respected his aesthetic values and his sense of style. He once said that he had modeled his style on Spenser's *Faerie Queene* but I think that Santayana also was a factor. He was an admirable crusader for the best in modern art. He adopted an easygoing bantering tone that could be devastating to the stuffy academic tribe. He knew how to make the opposition feel ridiculous. In his last years he lost much of the crusading spirit—the battles had been won—he no longer cared. He then devoted his efforts to polishing the style of his essays: they became, to a large extent, literary causeries, with little concern for the implication of his judgments in the world of art. At any rate, in the old days I welcomed my casual encounters with him. We would gossip about art or chat about literature and other topics. For instance, on October 21, 1935, I jotted down in my journal:

> McBride in and told me about Lachaise's funeral. He found it depressing: there was no release for genuine feeling, everybody present was in a false position. There was no style about the ceremony—everything hit or miss—the Catholics certainly do the thing much better. Seldes made a few remarks, but it was all impromptu. McBride confided that he had a deep feeling for Lachaise: it was not that he wanted to weep but under the circumstances he felt ridiculous, He also spoke of Stieglitz's growing touchiness, how difficult it was now to talk to him without his going into a tirade or a tailspin. And of Mabel Luhan's new book, in which she ruthlessly tore off the veils, not all of them but enough of them to make a conventional civilized man like himself squirm.

Lewis Mumford, in my opinion, and Henry McBride, also, in spite of his own disclaimer, are among the very few real art critics as opposed to art journalists we have in this country. An art critic must have the artist's sensibility, the Olympian detachment, and the wide cultural background to offer the farseeing and balanced view. Mumford has these qualifications, especially the latter two. He is a great scholar who has devoted himself to the study of man in its noblest proportions. I remember that when I read his *Technics and Civilization,* I felt it represented the reflections of a sane and normal human being. He put into words many of the attitudes and reactions that I never even bothered to speak of, but merely felt and lived. For several years he served as art critic for *The New Yorker.* When he came in to see our shows he would get around to discussing all manner of things. Once, while looking at Rockwell Kent's illustrations for Moby Dick, he recalled his own involvement with Melville, and how, when he had finished his biography of him, it had taken him many months to withdraw from the spell of Melville's thought world. Another time he discoursed on the effect of hard and soft beds on the technique of sexual intercourse. On May 3, 1935, I wrote in my journal:

> Mumford in. Told how he had become the father of a baby girl a few days before. He was proud and happy. I recounted my own experience of fatherhood and my feeling in participating in the great cycle of evolution. He told how the baby came in the night, how the Jewish doctor with a vivid sense of life had shown the newborn baby to him contrary to the rules, how its head and body were perfectly formed, how he left the Doctor's Hospital just as dawn was breaking over the East River. Spring was in the air; a few workmen were stirring about. Life seemed good indeed. . . .He is working on another book dealing with city life. I told him that the prints of Bosse and Weiditz were pertinent to the subject.

It was on October 24, 1929, that the first stock crash occurred, which was to send Wall Street reeling on its foundations. For me the events will always be graphically and appropriately symbolized by James N. Rosenberg's three lithographs, for Jimmy was both an artist and a famous lawyer specializing in bankruptcies. Although the crashes were dramatic and catastrophic, it was several years before the full impact of the depression was felt in the business of the

Weyhe Gallery. For instance, in 1930 I went to Mexico on a purchasing trip for paintings, drawings, and prints of the Mexican School; and the Gallery published prints by Rivera, Orozco, Siqueiros, and Tamayo. After all, much of the gallery's merchandise was moderate in price and did not suffer from disastrous deflation. But by 1935, even we began to feel the pinch. Sales became fewer and fewer, and many worthy people, including artists, were on the bread line.

The depression did have a far-reaching psychological effect on both Weyhe and myself. Weyhe, along with many other Americans, had speculated on the stock market. (Much discourse, both business and social, at the time, centered on "hot tips" in the market and on directives to the broker.) The crash undoubtedly caused him some monetary loss. But he was relatively fortunate because he had a thriving business and a vast stock, where others who invested on margin were wiped out. During the boom years, he had enjoyed phenomenal and unbroken financial success. The shock of disappointment had a deep and unfortunate effect upon his personality. He became, it seemed to me, a changed man: he lost his flexibility, worried unceasingly, and thought only of dollars and cents. He adopted the technique of the "hard sell"; and many an innocent customer who had come for a particular book departed with another instead, overborne by Weyhe's relentless drive. Then his interest would change, and there would be a new *livre du jour*.

Some of his actions took on a rather amusing turn—more amusing in retrospect, perhaps, than in actual occurrence. He became increasingly preoccupied with building up his own legend, or as we would say today, projecting his own favorable image. He would tell long stories to captive customers, and in general boast of his achievements as a successful business man and patron of the arts. Or in a pessimistic mood, he would tell how he was losing money every day, and enumerate how many people were dependent on him for a livelihood. He did not know how long he could keep the business going! His associates, who had heard all these stories repeated over and over, came to label them as phonograph records—"such and such a record is on today." It is a pity that he felt constrained constantly to blow his own horn and not allow others to give him credit spontaneously, for he did have a conspicuous record of achievement. His conduct during the previous decade was in strong contrast to that during the span of desperate years. He had formerly shown himself generous and understanding with artists and colleagues, and keen in his estimate of the potentialities of new undertakings. But now he was worried, excessively so.

I repeatedly urged him to relax and accept the lean years along with the fat ones. I even suggested that he retire from business and have a good time. He loved nature and the out-of-doors. Every Sunday he took a long hike, sometimes as much as ten to fifteen miles, in the neighboring counties of New York. He had terrific will power and could have found new interests for himself. As a young man he had been ill with tuberculosis and was sent to Davos Platz. He saw all the consumptive patients lying in beds, and realized that if he yielded to that treatment he would be cured only by death. He left Davos and cured himself with a strict regime elsewhere. But now he could not or would not retire, and he continued with his obsessions. I understand that when prosperous times came again, Weyhe reverted somewhat to his normal stride. But by that time I had left the Gallery.

How had the stock crash affected me? Since I never invested in stocks, I did not lose any money. But the depression did affect me in other ways. During the decade of the 1920s I had built up a flourishing gallery. It had been an exciting and satisfactory education in executive and business practice. Doubtless, if reverses had not come, I might have been constrained to continue. Basically, however, I was not a businessman. I found that selling a customer something he did not want was not challenging but, on the contrary, repugnant. The financial collapse and setback tended to bring latent ambitions to the surface, authorship and museum work. In the time of crisis, I doubtless did not keep my mind entirely on business, because the regular business techniques did not seem to work. People had no money for luxuries such as art. Even the expedient of the "hard sell" was not effective when customers would not come in to expose themselves to it. I tried to find a solution to the problem in my own way, and came up with the idea of publishing very low-priced prints by contemporary artists. It was to be a return to an earlier concept of printmaking, prints not limited in edition and not signed in pencil by the artist. The scheme was dependent upon the quantity of sales at a low price for adequate financial return, and its success was contingent on finding an efficient vehicle for mass distribution. I believed I had found it in the set-up of the greeting-card industry. Sam Golden, the president of the American Artists Group, one of the leading greeting card distributors, was sympathetic and offered full cooperation. I laid the idea before Weyhe but he rejected it emphatically. With his usual pessimistic approach toward new enterprise, he said it would not work and furthermore would ruin the print business completely.

Sam and I tried it out for two years, 1936 through 1937. It was, I would say, only moderately successful, but it certainly did not ruin the print business for the future. The fifty-four artists who made one or two prints for the enterprise received anywhere from a hundred to a thousand or more dollars as royalties, which in most cases was more than they received from their regular editions in those days of meager sales. Golden assumed all costs of production and promotion, and I approached the artists and negotiated the commissions. We tried to slant the subject matter of the prints for popular appeal—pictures for the masses. It was a difficult assignment. In the first place there is no easy formula for popularity. Even the professionals who are in the game to catch the public's eye or ear—the writers and newspapermen, the magazine and book publishers, the theater and movie producers, the song writers—can not infallibly predict success. They follow an empiric course, a hit-or-miss strategy. Furthermore, those who seek success generally have no other goal, whereas we had two aims: to furnish works of art and to be popular. Many of the artists whom we were trying to help had no conception of popular appeal. Nor, I must admit, was I always an effective counselor, for I also instinctively shied away from popularity and its compromises. Our duality of purpose involved us in a certain amount of compromise, and, as is often the case with half measures, produced neither art nor popularity. If a large number of the ninety prints we published now seem trite and commonplace, a score perhaps still have not lost their luster, and another score stood out above the average of their time. We certainly gave the public good value for their money at two dollars and seventy-five cents per print. We employed the best available printers, George Miller for the lithographs, Charles White for the etchings, and the Spiral Press for the woodcuts. We organized exhibitions and traveling shows in about 760 cities and smaller communities, many of which had never seen an exhibition before. We had many favorable comments from the press. But in spite of the slogan "good art for the price of a book," we never made the best-seller lists. Perhaps the venture was premature: the people as a whole were not interested in art then as they are now. Perhaps the austere program of prints without the collector appeal of signatures and limited editions will never be popular. At any rate the success was only moderate in spite of all our efforts. Sam Golden was a good sport to have shouldered the burden.

I was scrupulous not to do any work for the American Artists Group during gallery hours, but Weyhe resented my involvement nonetheless. He berated me on numerous occasions—I would not call them quarrels, for the tirade was all on one side. He threatened to close the gallery; he claimed he was losing money every day. He had lost interest in the gallery. It was dead. A customer told him that he had heard that I helped political prisoners, and swore that he would never come into the store again. We sold only to other dealers and drove other customers away. Why didn't I hustle around and do something. My mind was on other things, popular prints, writing books, and the like. He was just a businessman; *he* could not afford the luxury of principles.

He also went to my friends, such as Kent and Stieglitz, and told them of my shortcomings. Stieglitz replied (as he reported to me) "Why do you complain that Carl is no businessman. You know that he never was and never would be. He is honest and loyal. What more do you want?" I am sure that Weyhe did not value me for my business ability, but rather for my knowledge and judgment in matters of art, and for my idealistic attitude, my "principles" to counterbalance any excessively businesslike atmosphere. I may not have been the most wholehearted businessman, but there were very few years if any that the gallery did not gross more than expenses, nor do I believe that, by and large, Weyhe has lost much money through the purchases I advised him to make, when a reckoning is made of the prosperous years that succeeded the depression. Furthermore, I had no personal stake in the gallery: I was always a paid employee. When I first joined with Weyhe there was some talk of an eventual partnership, but as the years passed there was less and less mention of it, and I realized that it would never become a reality. I do not regret the missed opportunity. But during all the early years I acted as if I had a personal stake in the business. And so did the other members of the staff. Weyhe was very fortunate in having such loyal helpers.

The last few years at the Gallery were in many ways unpleasant and oppressive. There was a definite estrangement between Weyhe and myself. It was a pity that we both had withdrawn into our own shells and that we could not make common cause against the adversities outside us. But it was not to be. I was made to feel more and more insecure and unwelcome. When I was awarded a Guggenheim Fellowship in 1939 for research on American prints during the summer, Weyhe's response was to reduce my salary. Therefore, when I received a bid from Fiske Kimball to become a curator at the Philadelphia Museum of Art, I accepted it gladly. On my last day at the gallery, and after the great surprise party that the artists gave me the night before, I jotted down in my journal:

Was a little groggy after last night's exciting experience. So by the way was E. W. He was much impressed by it all, for he is talking about it all the time. He presented me with a book *Tides of English Taste* [his only parting gift].

And thus on Saturday, December 7, 1940, I ended my more than twenty years' service with the Weyhe Gallery.

In spite of the somewhat lame ending, my tenure at the

Weyhe Gallery was a most valuable and many-sided experience. It gave me practical business and executive training and above all a basic education in dealing with people. The management of an art gallery, especially when one also carries out most of the details, calls for many special skills and a vast store of knowledge. One learns the value of time, not only to meet deadlines but also to apportion the limited amount to the best advantage. One acquires practical psychology in meeting human beings face to face, in judging character, in drawing people out, yet not being imposed upon by them. There are many virtues inherent in the conduct of business in its finest sense: the basic habit of giving fair value in merchandise, of avoiding misrepresentation and double dealing, of fulfilling every promise or obligation promptly and honorably.

There were also specific advantages to the experience due to the close connection between the bookstore and the gallery. I became familiar with the literature of the arts in all its branches. This was my equivalent of a university education in art history, for I had never studied the subject in college. And I learned one useful lesson from the diversity of opinion expressed by the visitors to the gallery or bookstore, namely, the relativity of taste. One person would pronounce judgment on the worth of an artist or particular work of art. Half an hour later another would express precisely the opposite point of view with equal conviction. As for myself, I had ample opportunity to sharpen my critical sense, because my value judgments had to be sustained with cash. Likewise I was exposed to bad art and forgeries as well as genuine art of many varieties, an opportunity to develop connoisseurship and a sense of market values not obtainable in academic circles. Similarly I became familiar with the sources of supply—whether dealer, collector, or artist—both here and abroad, and had the chance to travel to Europe for purchase and incidentally for study in museums.

But the one thing I cherish above all others is the acquaintance I gained among artists and scholars. There were few artists of the time whom I did not know casually or intimately. Sooner or later they and the scholars, the collectors, and museum folk, all came, lured either by a book or an exhibition. We were more than a gallery and bookstore, we were a lively institution, a meeting place for the elite of the art world at a time when there was a great deal of life and ferment in that world.

4

Travels in Europe in the 1920s

I used to go to Europe to buy works of art for the gallery. My first trip was in the summer of 1923. In London I stayed at the Abbotsford, a small family hotel on Upper Montague Street in Bloomsbury, within a block or two of the British Museum. I was entranced with the place. There was a *maître d'hôtel* who looked and acted as if he had stepped out of a Dickens novel. He loved his uniform, and his cheerfulness was invincible in spite of the weather and other vexations. In the lounge I saw middle-aged respectable women smoking cigarettes, not self-consciously in a gesture of defiance, but casually as if they enjoyed it. It was there also that I was first introduced to the hearty English breakfast—huge dishes of oatmeal porridge, bacon and eggs, kippers, cold toast and marmalade, and gallons of tea. The hotel was quaint and quiet, and I read with regret that the place had been bombed out in the Second World War.

I found London delightful except for the cold rainy spells. It was easy to get around by bus or the underground, which seemed superior to the New York subway. The English had a tradition of craftsmanship and pageantry; and everywhere there were sights and buildings that recalled passages from English literature or history. Life seemed easygoing to an American. The pubs were friendly, and afternoon tea at the ubiquitous A.B.C. or Lyons tearooms was a pleasant custom. I discovered the Devonshire Dairies on Oxford Street, an outlet for Devonshire products, where one could get delicious fresh strawberries with clotted cream. But in general I did not relish English cuisine. The roast meats and chops were excellent, but other dishes were unimaginative and the soggy greens and potatoes definitely unpalatable. I often had dinner in the Soho quarter, where the French and Italians lived, partly as a sentimental pilgrimage to the scenes made familiar in Whistler's prints, but mostly as a rehearsal for experiences to come in France. When I returned to the Soho in recent years, I found it changed. Of course everything has changed, including London, and particularly myself. Perhaps I have idealized my recollections, but the quarter seemed more shoddy and the restaurants more ordinary and pseudo than they used to be.

Back in 1923, I had dinner one night with my friend Boardman Robinson, who was then serving as staff cartoonist on one of the English weeklies. He had been invited to H. G. Wells's later and he took me along. I had not brought any dinner clothes and so he went informally also. Thus I was introduced plump into a salon of English literary lights. St. John Ervine, Philip Guedella, Lady Rhonda, and H. W. Nevinson were there. Wells had a kind of easy and bantering conversational manner that put one at ease immediatley. As an unknown youngster I did not have much to say to him. And since I did not set down any notes afterwards, I have little record of the conversation. Henry W. Nevinson (I knew his son, the artist C. R. W. Nevinson) was one of my great admirations and his *Plea of Pan* one of my favorite books. My memories are mostly visual; no doubt I watched more than I talked. The company seemed a bit ridiculous in their formal evening clothes: Lady Rhonda in *décolleté* (I believe she was the only woman present) and the men in their stiff evening shirts. It is not that I am against formal clothes but that the fashions for men's wear were so ugly at the time. The starched bosom-shirt—and the equally stiff collar—was as comfortable as a breastplate of armor. It bulged out when one sat down, especially if one was inclined to be portly. I could not understand how Britons, who habitually dressed for dinner, ever stood the ordeal. The soft pleated shirt with attached collar of today seems an improvement, if not in elegance, at least in comfort. The furnishings in Wells's flat were undistinguished and almost bourgeois in taste. But the view of the Thames from the window was wonderful, since the flat was on the Embankment overlooking the river.

Another aspect of British life was revealed on my next visit to London, when I had lunch with Mukul Chandra Dey at the Anglo-Indian Club. The retired British civil servants, now relieved from carrying the white man's burden, had founded the club and took their ease there. To a young American they appeared, if not formidable, at least firmly intrenched in conservative virtues. Mukul Dey had been granted temporary membership privileges while in England to deliver to the British Museum his copies of the Ajanta Cave frescoes. I had met him years before, when he came to New York in the entourage of Rabindranath Tagore. At lunch we had a series of curry dishes, all of them delicious and some of them very hot. The club members liked their curry authentic.

Another memorable experience in 1923 was seeing Eleanor Duse act in Ibsen's *Ghosts.* She played Mrs. Alving, a relatively minor part, but she dominated the play by her presence. And it was a magical presence—no makeup, no theatrical business, wonderfully expressive hands, all so simple yet so indescribable in its living absorption of the role. In the row ahead of me was a very substantial British matron of the Victorian type. She was constantly whispering the details of the plot to her companion, since the play was in Italian. In the row just ahead was Lytton Strachey, whom I recognized from a portrait I had seen in *The Dial.* The juxtaposition of types, I felt, was amusing. He endured the whispering as long as he could, and then he turned around with his terrifying long beard and ferocious spectacles, saying in a loud tone *sh sh sh.* Later, when she started up again, he did it again, leaning on his swaying umbrella and almost spitting in her face. She subsided thereafter.

One of the things that struck me about London then was the enormous spread of American ideas. The city was full of American motion pictures and plays, music (jazz and the like), novels, manufactured goods, and even slang. Wells used a great deal of American slang in his conversation. Sinclair Lewis was very popular in London.

In the pursuit of my profession I made the rounds of the galleries and bookstores. It was fun to buy, though also a serious responsibility. I visited the big firms, Quaritch, Maggs, The Leceister Galleries, and especially Colnaghi and Co. Not only did Colnaghi's have a vast stock of prints—the redoubtable Gustave Mayer was then in charge of the print department—but it also had a tradition dating back to William Blake, who used to buy prints there for a few pence. I combed through the stock of many other dealers scattered about the city. Several stand out in my recollection. W. T. Spencer's tiny shop was so crammed full of prints that one could hardly move about. He specialized in caricatures, and sporting and flower prints. He had the reputation of having instigated a great deal of modern coloring of old prints, and he sold wholesale without warranty, but the huge portfolios were filled with prints, good, bad, and indifferent. One could pick and choose and buy cheaply, and I bought a great many Rowlandsons, and Thornton and Furber flower prints. Once I came across a set of Goya's Caprices. To him they were caricatures by some foreign artist. I bought them and took them to the British Museum for comparison. It turned out to be a complete set of superb quality, a real bargain. Craddock and Barnard were located at the time in Tunbridge Wells, and a visit to the shop of the Barnards, father and son, gave me also a chance to enjoy the charm of the English countryside. Young Osbert, even then, was a serious and intelligent student of graphic art. It is with particular affection that I recall Parsons and Sons on Brompton Road. They no longer exist, alas, but in the old days they had a vast stock. It was exciting to leaf through their portfolios: one never knew what would turn up next in the way of prints and drawings. From the eighteenth century onwards, the English had been collectors of paintings and prints, not only the noblemen on a grand scale in the tradition of the Grand Tour, but also the cultivated amateurs of moderate means, who cherished and assembled their scrapbooks of "curious prints." This vast reservoir of graphic art was gradually being tapped, and all sorts of prints appeared on the market through the auction houses of Sotheby or Christies, and in the print shops of Parsons, Colnaghi, Rimmel, Spencer, and the like.

I also visited a few artists to chat and buy: Lucien Pissarro and his daughter Orovida out in Hammersmith, or Leon Underwood in Brook Green. I spent a day in High Wycombe with Eric Gill and came away with prints and drawings. He lived in monastic simplicity as befits a convert to Roman Catholicism. He was a rare combination of sensuous feeling and stringent discipline. I likewise spent what time I could in the public galleries, at the British Museum, in the print room naturally, but also with the illuminated manuscripts, the Elgin marbles, the Assyrian and African sculpture, and at the National Gallery, the Tate, and the Victoria and Albert Museums.

In Paris I stayed at a little hotel at No. 10 Rue Croix des Petits Champs that rejoiced in the name of *Hôtel de l'Univers et du Portugal.* Walter Pach had recommended it, and it was convenient to the Latin Quarter as well as to the Louvre, the Bibliothèque Nationale, and other Right-Bank institutions. For me it was situated on hallowed ground, for right next door on the corner was the site of Aubert's lithographic shop, where people once queued up to see Daumier's *Ventre Legislatif* and *Rue Transnonain* in the window.

I liked France from the moment I landed. In the euphoria of first acquaintance everything seemed wonderful. On the boat train from Dieppe I was not put out that a large Cook's tour party had preempted all the seats: I sat in the corridor on my suit case and gazed at the landscape. I felt that the French countryside was quite as beautiful as the English, perhaps even with a touch more of *finesse*. If the French had occasion to erect a scarecrow, they made sure that it came alive by a touch of humor or art. And the tiny cottages with thatched or tiled roofs gathered around a courtyard were charming to look at if not to live in. Finally in Paris, when I saw from the taxi the lovely Tuileries gardens, the Louvre, and bridges across the Seine, I felt that my first glimpse of Paris was indeed an unforgettable experience.

Subsequently, as I became acquainted with the gardens and the bridges and all the usual sights of Paris, I would almost say that they grew on me, for often my encounter was not the result of deliberate exploration but a fringe benefit enjoyed while on another errand. But I did love to saunter in the Tuileries. The numerous statues scattered around the garden were not very interesting in themselves, but their cumulative effect was delightful, likewise the arrangement of the fountains and flower beds and especially the vistas toward the Place de la Concorde and the Louvre. Somehow the Tuileries became for me a collective symbol for all the sights and scenes of Paris.

I found the French people most attractive. They seemed to have much more zest for life than the English. I had found the English as a whole rather cold and reserved, individually charming when the ice was broken, but collectively not very outgoing. The French seemed exuberantly themselves. Of course my first enthusiasm was somewhat tempered by subsequent experience. Even then I was not entirely unaware of other aspects. My reading of French literature had revealed the fact that peasants could be mean and avaricious, and my own experience taught me that city folk—waiters, innkeepers, and taxi drivers who fatten on strangers unfamiliar with the language—could be arrogant and mercenary. But the folk as a whole were sound, and in contrast with the comparable class in England, had *esprit*. Their sidewalk cafés and puppet shows proved it. I had faith in the French people if not in their government, then the most militaristic in the world under the leadership of Clemenceau. I would say to myself that the *Quai d'Orsay* does not exist: here is the real Paris, the real France.

Paris was the art center of the world. Not only were the great masters of the School of Paris living and working there, but there also had been a background, an awareness of art all through the nineteenth century and extending back into the *ancien regime.* The nineteenth century had a distinguished record of achievement in the graphic arts from the romantics on through to the precursors of the modern movement. It was my favorite century. The eighteenth century somehow left me cold. Its solid and somewhat formal virtues do not appeal to youth but rather to maturity, as I discovered from later experience. The stocks of the dealers had not yet been depleted and there was a profusion of material from both eras to choose from. I combed the stock of Le Garrec, Rousseau, Prouté, Gosselin, Grosjean-Maupin, Gobin, Michel, and the like.

Le Garrec-Sagot was the leading firm at the time. Maurice Le Garrec had married Sagot's daughter and inherited the business. Sagot had been a great dealer before him. He had been the first to buy Picasso's etchings, and also introduced Jacque Villon, Vallotton, and others. Le Garrec was a shrewd businessman but he had a broad vision and an honorable reputation. He had had cast and published the great set of caricature busts by Daumier, having purchased the fragile plasters from the heirs of Phillipon. Always working closely with the Bibliothèque National, he published at his own expense the sumptuous set of facsimiles of the masterpieces of French graphic art as a tribute to the genius of his country. He had tremendous reserves of stock, only part of which he would ever bring out for display. Weyhe and I had a pact that if there was ever any news that the firm would be liquidated, we would fly to Paris to be present at the auction. But it never came to pass. When Le Garrec died, Mme. Le Garrec carried on, and now their son has taken over. She was a gracious lady, and the assistants, too, were always friendly and helpful. I used the shop at 39 bis Rue du Chateaudun more or less as my headquarters, and received my mail there.

Le Garrec would take me to lunch between sessions and we would talk about art and other matters. He made flattering remarks about the good taste of my selections and my industrious habits of work. No doubt he said similar things to his other clients. But when he continued with penetrating remarks on the shortsightedness of some of my American colleagues in continuing to buy the same conservative trifles year after year, I could not but agree. Once he spied Laval sitting at a table nearby, and he repeated to me the witticism on the devious French politician that was current at the time: Laval means the same thing from right to left as from left to right.

A few doors away on the same street was Maurice Rousseau, another honorable dealer who specialized in eighteenth-century engravings and early nineteenth-century lithographs. His daughter has now taken over the direction of the business, just as the sons of Paul Prouté are carrying on after their father. Once while wandering on some side streets in the same ninth arrondissement, I came across a shop with a Toulouse-Lautrec lithograph in the window. I entered and met the proprietor, an elderly man who turned out to be E. Kleinman, the original publisher of many of Lautrec's prints, as well as those of Steinlen and Forain. I bought a great many Lautrec lithographs and other things at very low prices, for they were not yet fashionable. It gave me quite a thrill to meet and talk to the man, even though he was quite matter-of-fact about the past. It brought me close to the Paris of the Gay Nineties. Le Garrec told me that I was lucky to find Kleinman in; he often was drunk and neglected to open his shop.

My major interest, however, was the art of today, and I established contact with some of the artists. One of the first was with Henri Matisse through an introduction from Walter Pach. I was pleasantly received by the red-bearded gentleman himself. He did not look at all like an artist who would paint wild pictures, and the tone of his apartment was far from bohemian. He was then living at 19 Quai St. Michel, and there was a lovely view of the Seine from his window. I purchased a group of his etchings and lithographs and even acquired a couple for myself, which he inscribed to me.

Though I liked Picasso's prints, I made no attempt to get in touch with him, probably because he was already selling his work through dealers. In fact, most of my purchases were through agents and dealers. The case of Matisse was exceptional, and later I would acquire his work through his son Pierre or through dealers such as Bernheim Jeune. I did not have time or opportunity to make many personal contacts with the artists just for the sake of contact, nor was my French fluent enough to have made them rewarding. I do, however, have pleasant memories of meetings with a number of artists—Maillol, for example. Our gallery did much with his work, and we bought drawings and commissioned bronzes from him for exclusive publication. I visited him at Marly on the outskirts of Paris—I never saw him in Provence, where he stayed in winter. His studio was not fancy; it was a real workshop. There were sketches and models on shelves attached to the walls, and bigger pieces in the corners, perhaps a big clay figure on the modeling stand wrapped in wet cloth. One or two planks of the wooden floor by the threshold had broken in, and he had never found time to fix them. One had to step carefully over the holes on entering the studio. Maillol was a simple man, almost a peasant type. He was not glib or articulate. He thought with his hands and felt sensuously with all his being. His life work was one great affirmation of fecund Earth, of sun-drenched land and the fruits thereof, of simple husbandry and pastoral pleasures, of the ample pregnancy of Nature. All this was reflected in his radiant bearded face. He was the ideal illustrator of the bucolics of Longus or Vergil. He talked of his papermaking. He was almost prouder of his handmade papers than he was of his sculpture.

Of city folk I have pleasant recollections of the circle of Pascin, Hermine David, Lucy and Per Krohg, and the elegant engraver and gourmet J. E. Laboureur. Not all of these and others like them turned out to be major artists, but they contributed to my treasury of delightful human relations. One such was the Greek engraver Demetrios Galanis, whose hobby was building organs. He took me to his tidy garret high up in Montmartre and played Bach for me on the organ he had constructed. He had one of the sweetest natures I have ever known. Another memorable occasion was a visit to the studio of Constantin Brancusi. Like Maillol, he was a peasant in appearance—he had a beard and wore a rough peasant smock—but he had a more complex personality. He carried simplicity almost to the point of madness, not only in his highly finished sculpture but also in the austerity of his studio and surroundings.

Many of the artists had exclusive contracts with dealers and one could acquire their work only through an intermediary. Thus I bought much from dealers. I remember especially Henry Kahnweiler, the early friend and supporter of the cubists. He was more than just a dealer; he was a critic of discriminating taste and farsighted intuition. And he commissioned original prints from such artists as Picasso, Dufy, Derain, Gris, and Braque as illustrations in books that he printed and published, thereby producing some of the most distinguished illustrated books of modern times. I bought Picasso and Braque and Manolo from the Galerie Simon, which was the name under which he operated. Leonce Rosenberg, never so financially successful as his brother Paul, likewise had taste and vision, and dealt largely in the cubists. He must have been Diego Rivera's dealer when the Mexican lived in Paris. I discovered about forty beautiful drawings and a number of large cubist paintings, which Rosenberg cleared out to me at bargain prices. There were numerous print dealers and publishers from whom I bought wholesale, such as Jeanne Bucher, Henri Petiet, Frapier, Billiet, and Nouvelle Essor. I remember an experience with the last named: the proprietor and his wife—Monsieur and Madame Candinier—took me to dinner and then to a night club with a floor show and champagne and dancing. Finally at dawn we went over to Les Halles and had onion soup at L'Escargot d'Or. It was my one experience in what might be called the tourist orbit in Paris. I was never thrilled by night-club life, and found its gaiety synthetic, and its tenet of conspicuous consumption fatuous. No doubt they thought me a cold fish for not responding more warmly to what they supposed all Americans gloried in. They seemed to enjoy themselves, however, and we got along well enough drinking champagne and talking—against the din—of life in Paris and New York.

I did enjoy the end: it was wonderful to see the markets at dawn.

The Weyhe Gallery had an agent in Paris, William Aspenwall Bradley. I had first known him in New York, in the circle of William Ivins and Fitzroy Carrington, as a charming but not-too-successful author and translator. He brought out an English version of *Aucassin et Nicolette* and wrote numerous articles for the *Print Collectors Quarterly*. When he planned to settle permanently in Paris, I arranged that he execute commissions and make contacts for us. He found his true *métier* there in the role of literary agent, and acted in that capacity for Gertrude Stein and for others. He also translated Remy de Gourmont and other French authors. He knew everybody in the literary and art world. Through him we established relations with Vollard and acquired Picasso, Maillol, and Renoir bronzes, Picasso etchings, lithographs by Cézanne and Renoir, and the lavishly illustrated books published by Vollard. I went once or twice to Vollard's studio. Nothing was visible. Vollard decided what would be brought out and shown, and there was a take-it or leave-it attitude in his manner toward customers. Noncommittal to the point of deceiving by half truths, Vollard was not an engaging figure. His secretiveness masked an unscrupulous mercenary drive. Of course, in the late 1920s the whole world was clamoring at his door, and he could afford to dictate terms. I believe that Bradley ingeniously arranged for our entrée by stressing our interest in Vollard's book and print publications, of which he was very proud. He could be pleasant and polite —in my experience he always was so—but I have heard tales that he could be otherwise. Vollard had an enormous stock of prints by Chagall and Rouault, for example, which he held back for future publication, but never did achieve during his lifetime. We tried to negotiate directly with Rouault to get some of the *Miserere* engravings. Bradley and I met Rouault at a café, but, being bound by contract, he could or would do nothing. I found it difficult to understand Rouault: his speech was gusty and passionate. He was a visionary and lived in an unreal world. Walter Pach told an amusing story of having received a letter from him. On the back of the envelope was scribbled a note: "I am not sure of your correct address. If you do not get this letter, you will understand why."

Bradley, as I have said, knew everybody. Once he took me to tea at Natalie Barney's where there was a big gathering to hear Ford Maddox Ford· discourse on Djuna Barnes and her work. Miss Barney was the daughter of an American concert impresario and had lived in Paris most of her life. She maintained a literary salon where such writers as Remy de Gourmont, Paul Valéry, Dr. Seignobos the historian, and Dr. Mardrus the Orientalist used to come once a week. But it was not only a literary meeting place: homosexuals and beauties also gathered there. Natalie herself was a lesbian and had several celebrated affairs. On this occasion there were crowds of people. I met a number, including Gertrude Stein, with a constant smile on her masculine face, looking like a laughing philosopher. I also saw a few old friends, Julien Levy, Gerald Kelly, and Edith Taylor. Miss Barney's place on the Rue Jacob was indeed charming and I wandered about the house and into the garden, which had once belonged to the poet Racine.

Once when I was in Paris, Bradley was engaged in checking on Paris restaurants for a translation and revision of *The Yellow Guide* for a London publisher. He sometimes took me along for lunch or dinner—an experience both educational and pleasurable. It is interesting that although Bradley had great facility with the French language, his accent was atrociously American. He was a delightful and extremely literate companion, and I spent many happy hours consorting with him around the city or enjoying the hospitality of his home on the *Île Saint Louis* presided over by his charming Belgian wife. The house in one of the oldest quarters of Paris was tastefully and comfortably furnished. It was there that I had a glimpse of French family life at its best.

There was a separate enclave flourishing in Paris, the colony of American expatriates. I would occasionally see the colonists lined up for the mail at the American Express on Rue Scribe or taking their ease during the day in the cafés. In general, I had little association with them: I never had the time, nor did most of my artist friends, who were busy all

day in their studios. Unlike the expatriate who made a career
of being a coffeehouse philosopher, my friends came out
only for an hour of relaxation with an apéritif or coffee and
fine, before or after dinner. I avoided the boulevards and the
Café de la Paix, where the tourists and playboys congregated.
I spent my time negotiating with the right-bank dealers or
exploring the shops along the Rue de la Seine, Rue
Bonaparte, or Rue des Saints-Pères. Occasionally while working my way along those streets, I might take a coffee break at
the Deux Magots and gaze at the noble church of St.
Germain-des-Prés across the street. Bradley told me it was
Santayana's favorite café. This of course was long before the
existentialists. Similarly, I used to dine at the Brasserie Lipp
only because the beer was good and the Alsatian cuisine excellent. More often I would go in the evening to meet my artist friends at the Montparnasse cafés. There was a succession
of popularity among cafés. The Rotonde was past its prime;
the Dome was the place where the other non-French artists
gathered. The French café is a wonderful institution. It was
pleasant to relax and to gossip with friends, or even to just
watch the people passing by or an Arab rug vendor trying to
sell his wares. But it was the greater pleasure when earned by
constructive work in its fitting season. My friends did not go
to Paris to live lazily off the fat of the land, but to live better
and more cheaply through the favorable exchange. I might
run into Kuniyoshi, Ganso, Fiene, Burlin, or Warneke and
share a coffee and a chat with them. I remember once there
was a rumor buzzing through all the cafés with the word that
Dr. Barnes had come to town. The artists all hoped to meet
him and bring him to their studios! Or I might have a
rendezvous—to arrange for a future date or event, a party or
whatnot—with Adolf Dehn, for instance, to watch him print
lithographs the next day at Desjobert's, or Mabel Dwight with
whom I explored many out-of-way places in the old quarters
of Paris, including on one Sunday the cemetery of Père
Lachaise. I saw much of Mahonri Young, and would often sit
with him at a café while he made sketches in his ever-present
notebook. I recall one memorable Sunday when we went to
the Louvre and showed each other its masterpieces. We had

supper at the *Place du Tertre* in Montmartre, not so infested with tourists in 1923 as nowadays. In the evening we went to the *Cirque Medrano,* a little one-ring circus, most intimate and amusing, because so simple and well done. A famous clown was performing then—Fratellini.

Life in Paris during the 1920s was pleasant. No doubt it was because we were young and gay, as the saying goes, but also because we could live well and cheaply. Whether all of the French people were as well off is another matter; those who felt the pinch of inflation and devaluation were not obvious to us. It was otherwise after the Second World War, when everybody seemed bitter and defeated. I remember visiting the old haunts, such as the *Dome,* in 1948; everything seemed drab and lifeless. But in the old days there were life and excitement. I was in Paris when Lindbergh made his historic flight. Paris went wild, and he became the popular hero. Ambassador Herrick called him the real ambassador to France. His modesty, quite apart from the daring and sureness of his flying, endeared him to the French people. After he had arrived, he was rushed off to the Embassy. He fished out of his pocket a letter of introduction to Herrick, because he was not sure that the Ambassador would know who he was without some formal papers. His straw hat became a symbol of unassuming but intelligent simplicity of equipment as contrasted with the elaborate paraphernalia usually carried around by explorers or aviators. He was feted daily and the people, including myself, lined the streets to see him pass.

To pass into Germany in 1923 was to enter a totally different world: a world of desperation, of nightmarish tensions, of poverty and starvation. I changed two hundred francs (then about $12.50) at the border and became a millionaire—in marks. One did not dare exchange more than a dollar or two at a time because the *valuta* would fluctuate wildly from day to day. A whole class of people, the middle class, was being wiped out by inflation. The life savings and the hope for security of hundreds of thousands of sober industrious people vanished over night. Only two worlds were left: that of the speculators and ruthless entrepreneurs, *Die Schieber,* and that of the proletariat, the aged poor, shading off to beggardom—the world of Grosz and the world of Kollwitz. Beggars were everywhere. Emaciated children swarmed into my restaurant in Frankfurt and begged for a pat of butter. I remember that on the boat trip home I saw an elderly German woman who had been lucky enough to get a passage through American relatives. When she was given a menu for her first meal on board she broke down and wept: "Can I really get all of this to eat?" It was heart-rending to be in Germany in the early 1920s. But one also sensed the ferment of social change. As a defeated nation, the Germans were disillusioned about militarism. Everywhere there seemed to be a wholehearted revulsion against war. *Nie Wieder Krieg* was a constant refrain. The victors, however, had no such scruples. The moment may have been crucial. If Clemenceau had not demanded even more than his pound of flesh, the vicious cycle of hate and militarism might possibly have been broken for a spell. *Peace without Victory!* This is a purely personal speculation; I did not speak to all classes, certainly not to politicians or industrialists of both sides, but merely to artists and humble folk. At any rate there had been turmoil and agitation and maneuvers close to revolution in Germany. Things were very much in a state of flux. The artists and architects, among others, began to wonder what place they would fill under a socialistic or communistic State. The Art Workers' Council (or Soviet) of Berlin—one of those *ad hoc* organizations, not necessarily class-conscious, which appear in times of crisis—circulated a questionnaire among its members in an attempt to clarify the issues. The questions and answers were published as a book, *Stimmen des Arbeitrates der Kunst,* late in 1919. It was an illuminating document, not only in the basic questions that were posed but also in the spirit with which they were met. The questions touched on art education, state support, fine versus applied art, new concepts of art exhibitions and public works, internationalism, the alienation of the artist from the people. The tone of the answers ranged from doctrinaire communist solutions to fervent pleas for a return to the dedicated service of the cathedral builders of the Middle Ages. Many other problems, such as the education of children, city planning, color on public buildings, interior decoration, the future of the framed picture, the anonymity of art works, were brought up in connection with the main theme. Among the artists participating were H. Campendonck, Karl Schmidt-Rottluff, Rudolf Belling, Gerhardt Marcks, and architect Walter Gropius and museum director W. R. Valentiner. I wrote a review of the book in *The Freeman* in July 1920.

Many of the ideas expressed in the book, especially in connection with art training, the artist as craftsman, and the arts centered around the building, were shortly thereafter embodied in the program of the Bauhaus at Weimar under the direction of Walter Gropius. When I went to Germany in 1923, I especially wanted to see the Bauhaus in operation. I therefore journeyed to Weimar—for two reasons. I made a sentimental pilgrimage to the birthplace of Goethe. I visited the shrine, saw all the mementos, and that evening I dined on venison at a quaint old inn. The next day, very much in the present and future, I spent at the *Bauhaus*. It was summer and vacation time, and thus I did not see the school in operation, not did I meet the principal teachers, Klee, Kandinsky, Feininger, Albers, or Gerhardt Marcks, but Walter Gropius spent the day with me and showed me all around. He could not have been pleasanter; perhaps it was because I was an American, and he hoped possibly that I could give him American contacts. I came away with a portfolio filled with literature and documents, as well as my modest purchases, a ceramic pot made and decorated by Gerhardt Marcks and a chess set designed along modern functional lines by Josef Hartwig. I also subscribed to the portfolio of woodcuts by L. Feininger. It was sent later as the first publication of the Bauhaus Graphic Workshop.

Of all the cities in Germany or even in Europe, Berlin seemed to me most akin to New York. The people there had much in common with the Americans in their unflinching exploitation of science and industry, and especially in the intensified tempo of their daily life. Both Berlin and New York were world capitals of comparatively recent origin. Whatever they had of monumental significance or public treasure —their museums, for example—were a recent growth, a tribute to what could be achieved by informed and unstinting application, even though late in the field. Thus I was impressed by the profusion of superb works of art of all kinds in the Kaiser Friederich Museum and the other museums of Berlin, including the Kupferstich Kabinett, one of the greatest in the world. American ideas and customs, especially motion pictures and jazz, penetrated to Berlin as they had elsewhere in Europe. The leading cafés usually had two bands; the very moment one stopped, the other started with the result that one was constantly bombarded with music. One of the bands usually played jazz. Germany, too, and especially Berlin, had its own jazz era, and its strident and heartless tone was perhaps best expressed by Max Beckmann.

Munich had much more charm for me than Berlin. The South Germans were more *gemutlich,* less arrogant than the Prussians, and more picturesque, too, for many wore the national costume of lederhosen or colorful dirndl skirts. The beer gardens were more relaxing than the high-tension cafés of the North. The city was laid out monumentally with imposing public buildings and spacious avenues. Der Englische Garten was a continual delight. The museums also were impressive, Die Alte und Neue Pinakothek, the Glyptothek (marbles from Olympia), but most impressive to me was the Deutsches Museum, that stupendous aggregation summarizing the history of civilization in its scientific and social aspects. I also heard some good music. On my first visit in 1923 I heard a performance of Bach's *Passion according to St. John,* which is presented less frequently than the *St. Matthew Passion.* It was a beautiful performance, and I was especially impressed by the joyous participation of the chorus. I remember reflecting that in the singing of a great choral work the performers must get more out of it than the audience. Even though they do not hear the work as a whole, they do by study and practice become more cognizant of its masterly structure and felicitous detail. In addition, communal singing can be a noble and spiritual experience. These observations were confirmed later by my own experience in choral singing in Philadelphia.

I found Dresden a charming city. I marveled at the baroque splendor of the Zwinger and the museum with its paintings and important print room. I met there the American-born print curator Hans Wolfgang Singer and his chief, Max Lehrs. The latter was a great admiration of mine, for he exemplified what I felt was the ideal attitude of the print curator. He was learned in the past, and alert and responsive to the creators of the present. This dual response was symbolized in Lehr's bookplate, in which a figure by the Master E. S. reaches out to a figure by Toulouse-Lautrec.

In the German print market I found relatively few Old-Master prints. For contemporary work I went to such dealers as Paul Cassirer and the Flechtheim Gallery in Berlin. Alfred Flechtheim was a flamboyant character, and, because perfectly adapted to the speculative, ebullient temper of the era, was fabulously successful. He started in Düsseldorf, but soon expanded to Berlin. He was one of the first to introduce the French Postimpressionists to Germany. He was interested in sports, boxing and racing, jazz, modern theater, Cocteau, Marie Laurencin, Picasso, everything modern, and published a lively magazine, *Der Querschnitt,* reflecting his interests and publicizing his various enterprises. I usually dealt with his assistant, a quiet-spoken, and to me much more sympathetic character, Curt Valentin, who later was to make a name for himself in New York. In Munich I also found numerous galleries and rare book dealers. I remember especialty Hans Goltz, a sympathetic personality from whom I bought much modern graphic art, especially prints and watercolors by Paul Klee. There was a great deal of creative activity in Germany then, including a vast amount of second-rate stuff. It was difficult not to be taken in by the very quantity of mediocre work, and easy thereby to overlook gems among the dross.

It was exciting, though not entirely pleasant, to be in Germany in the early 1920s. It was distressing to live in a palatial hotel suite that one could not afford at home, or eat a sumptuous dinner when one knew that other people were starving. It made one feel like a *Schieber,* though of course the *Schieber* himself had no such compunctions.

5

Mexico

My last purchasing trip for the Weyhe Gallery was to Mexico in
1930. I have been generally fortunate in that when I visited a
new region, I somehow always knew a friend or acquaintance
living there who could give me the key to an inside view. It
happened so on my trip to Mexico, and because of it I probably had more varied and significant experiences in one
month than another might have in a year. The key figure in
this instance was William Spratling. During the 1920s he had
been a professor of architecture at Tulane University in New
Orleans, had written a book on plantation architecture, and
collaborated with William Faulkner in a book on Louisiana
writers. Later he settled in Mexico at Taxco to develop what
was to become an internationally famous silversmithing industry. He had a flair for design (later winning many prizes
at expositions) and the organizing ability to train native
craftsmen and market their wares. He made Taxco famous.
When I came to Mexico in 1930 he already knew most of the
important people there, at least in artistic circles. He knew

the American Ambassador Dwight Morrow and was instrumental in bringing him and Diego Rivera together—a meeting that resulted in the commission to paint the *History of Cuernavaca* in fresco at the Palace of Cortez. Bill told me that the negotiations required considerable tact and diplomacy to accomplish. Morrow as Ambassador was reluctant to be placed in the position of favoring an outspoken even if somewhat unstable Communist, and Rivera on his part was afraid that he might lose his illusions about capitalists and even grow to like them.

Spratling met me at the train when I arrived in Mexico City, and I stayed with him at Taxco whenever I was not in the capital or not traveling about the country. The road to Taxco in those days was not quite the highway it is today. The road from Mexico City had been improved as far as Cuernavaca, but from there on it grew steadily worse. The ten miles through mountainous country were rough and hair-raising. Much of it was the original mule-path road built by José de la Borda, the eighteenth-century mining magnate, and one could still see, in places the original paving stones in patterns on the road. Since stone railings had been built to keep the silver-laden pack trains in formation, the road was just wide enough to accommodate one present-day automobile (bays were provided at intervals to allow for passing). After traversing the wild and rugged terrain I was not prepared for so charming a sight as the view of Taxco. With its cobbled streets, red-tiled roofs, and imposing Churrigueresque Cathedral (also built by de la Borda), it looked like an Italian hill town perched on the side of a mountain.

Bill was then living in a house aptly located up high on la Secunda Calle de las Delicias, the Second Street of Delights. It was set in a walled garden where orange, lemon, pomegranate, and other fruit trees grew, and orchids bloomed all the year around. Several kinds of bananas flourished, from the tiny finger bananas to the large plantains. A tame deer lurked in the shadows. The house, with its tiled floors and whitewashed walls, always seemed cool and comfortable. Don Guillermo, as he was called, introduced me to such typical Mexican food as frijoles refritos, tortillas, aquacate (sprinkled with fresh lime juice and eaten out of the shell with a spoon), and chocolate prepared in the Aztec way, not with milk but with water and a twirling stick. For a special feast we had *Mole de Guajolote,* turkey with a highly spiced dark sauce, which took over forty-eight hours to prepare.

The special occasion was the fiesta for Natalie's birthday. Natalie Scott was in the circle of New Orleans friends and had come to Mexico around the same time that Bill had. The party at her house was jolly with music and drinking. Three little children, decorated with floral wreaths, brought a live chicken as a present, tied up with green ribbons. While the music was playing and the dog was barking, the chicken became violent and the children frightened. For a moment comic pandemonium ensued. Among the serenading musicians was the guitarist Poncho, who was also the town's *milagro* painter. I commissioned a little painting from him to commemorate my narrow escape from injury through the miraculous intercession of Santa Prisca, the patron saint of Taxco. The incident occurred at a swimming pool, where I slipped and almost fell on some wet rocks. The pool was in a secluded spot on the road to Landa. Its beauty was enhanced by a tiny waterfall, and a background of tropical forest embellished with wild orchids and yellow *yoyote* flowers. A group of us—Bill, Natalie, Tom Handforth, Laura Cornell, and I—went there almost every day.

Life in Mexico was social, and we were always going to parties. Once we ventured a little farther afield. Spratling had heard rumors of a huge Calendar Stone buried in the jungle near Acapulco. He wanted to see it, and Natalie and I went along for the ride. I was to stay with Natalie at Acapulco and keep her amused while he went into the jungle with a native companion. Bill borrowed Tom Handforth's Ford and we started off. The country was mountainous and the roads were primitive. We passed through wild canyons and once almost ran into a huge rock which had fallen on the road. It took some maneuvering to get around it. We had lunch in the company of two tame egrets in the courtyard of the Hotel Bravo at Chilpancingo, the capital of the State of Guerrero, situated two hundred miles from the railroad. We crossed the Rio de las Balsas on a flat raft—a rather ticklish and time-consuming job. Finally we arrived in the *tierra caliente.* Acapulco then was a sleepy little tropical town and I was introduced to the customs of the "hot country"—the midday siesta behind mosquito-net curtains, and the *paseo* around the Plaza in the evening, when the populace promenaded in two opposing columns of men and women. The natives, of mingled Indian and Negro stock, were strikingly handsome. We spent much time at the beach, *La Caleta,* in that era completely deserted. It was a huge crescent of white sand on an inlet of the ocean and thus without breakers. The water was warm and limpid and deep blue in color; under water there was a riot of color—red, green, and purple rocks, murex shells, angel fish, blue fish with flashing green spots, and the like. We swam for hours and sunned ourselves on the rocks. For diversion we would occasionally walk to a *cantina* at the far end of the beach for a *refresco,* an infusion of tamarind root, or a *copita* of *Habanero* (rum) or best of all, a fresh coconut. We would first sip the milk through a straw and then crack the shell and eat the custard-like meat with a spoon.

After a couple of days relaxation we drove twelve miles north along the coast to the First Lagoon, where Bill hired a boat and went off into the marshes and jungle. The man who owned the boat was a real beachcomber, the only one I have ever seen in the flesh. He was an American who lived with a native woman in a ramshackle hut on the narrow strip of sand between the ocean and the lagoon. I heard later that he had been a physician in a sanatarium who through some tragic error had been responsible for the death of a patient. He spoke practically no Spanish and the woman no Enlgish. We wondered with whom he ever conversed in that out-of-the-way place.

Natalie and I went back to Acapulco to while away the time until Bill's return. We swam at the beach, we had our siesta, and we played dominoes and drank *Habanero* in the evening at a *cantina* on the square, euphemistically called "The North Pole." Natalie was an amusing and gay companion. She was perhaps too incessant a talker to be endured as a steady diet.

It was characteristic of her verbalized attitude toward life that she had several romances but no consummation of any one. I asked her why she had never married. She replied that she did not want to talk about business, or golf, or economics all her life—the subjects in which her beaux were interested. There was a kind of Southern futility about her: she was witty and charming but basically conventional and afraid of life. We had a talk about free will. It did not bother her that her life was predetermined: she was merely anxious to find out what life was going to do to her next. Bill returned the next day, weary and bedraggled, having accomplished his purpose. The following morning, after having bought pottery, fresh coconuts, and bundles of native cigars at the market, we returned to Taxco.

On my journey back to Mexico City from Taxco, I stopped off at Cuernavaca. I delivered some pottery from Spratling to Ambassador Morrow and saw the Casa Mañana. Two years later Mrs. Morrow asked me to supervise the printing of a book on their residence there. Mrs. Morrow wrote the text, Spratling drew the illustrations, and Joseph Blumenthal of the Spiral Press printed it handsomely. I also stopped in at the adjoining house of Fred Davis to look over a group of Rivera drawings that the artist had left for purchase. And finally I went to the Town Hall or Palace of Cortez to see Diego Rivera painting a fresco. I climbed up on the platform and watched him work in true fresco and admired the dexterity with which he painted in a medium that allows no corrections. He was working not from a cartoon but directly from a model, and portraying a captive bringing a tribute of a turkey to Cortez, a chapter in the history of Cuernavaca. I was introduced to an old woman who evidently had brought the model and the turkey. She was the niece of the revolutionary hero Zapata, who had issued his agrarian proclamation from this same town hall. Thus was Mexican history brought vividly to my mind.

I saw a great deal of Rivera during my visit to Mexico. I had met him several years previously in New York. Rivera had then come North with two Mexican companions on some political mission, and had brought a batch of his drawings with him to finance his and their expenses. Walter Pach met them at the station and took Diego to the Weyhe Gallery, which bought the drawings at once for cash. Pach and Rivera then went to the Metropolitan Museum of Art, where they spent the rest of the day ecstatically looking at pictures. It was not until six o'clock that Diego remembered his companions, alone in a strange land and waiting patiently on a bench in the Pennsylvania Station.

On my first day in Mexico City, Bill took me to the Ministry of Education building to see the frescoes. A concourse of school children happened to be gathered there to dedicate a puppet theater in the courtyard. The national anthem and folk songs they sang gave an added thrill to my first glimpse of the pageant of Mexico's occupations, fiestas, and revolutionary ballads. Bill then took me to the Preparatoria to see the Orozco frescoes, so different from Rivera's in spirit and execution. Rivera is a storyteller and propagandist, a masterly and inventive decorator of walls, the Raphael of the socialistic religion. Orozco is an epic painter, but without a sense of the wall. His murals are a series of superb fragments of unusual emotional intensity. In his St. Francis subjects, Orozco, professed hater of God that he was, succeeded in painting some of the few truly religious paintings in modern times. He and Rouault have much in common in their sense of tragic irony. His satiric paintings "The Last Judgment" and "The Rich Dining and the Workers Fighting" reveal a savagery and bitterness that sting like a slap in the face. It is no wonder that many people were offended.

After this introduction, Bill took me to Rivera's house in the suburb of Coyoacan, where he lived before he built his house in San Angel. There I saw Rivera and his new wife, Frieda Kahlo. The little patio or garden was filled with huge pre-Columbian idols; the house likewise was packed with hundreds of carvings from all areas of Mexico. Diego had a huge stone phallus which he brandished while showing his treasures. He also had a big Mexican hairless dog—the biggest I have ever seen and a most naked-looking creature —who begged at table and looked at one with pathetic wrinkled eyes. Diego claimed that he had been trained to annoy only the people whom the master disliked.

My first meal at Diego's was a gargantuan midday repast. It began at noon with tequila. It was my introduction to the taste and ritual of this Mexican drink. I did not find it so unpalatable as I had been led to believe: it might be called an acquired taste similar to that for oysters or roquefort cheese. The dinner consisted of innumerable courses—hors d'oeuvres, soup, macaroni (Diego ate a huge plateful), several courses of meat and fowl, red wine, bowls of salad, fresh fruit, mangoes, pineapple, stewed fruit, and coffee and countless cigarettes. Bill and I left at half past three to keep an appointment with Ambassador Morrow. When we returned at five o'clock they were still at table picking at nuts and fruits and still talking. The conversation during the meal was sprightly; much of it of course passed over my head because I knew little Spanish. Diego spoke with gusto, Malou Cabrera with the speed and rhythm of a machine gun. Malou and her future husband, Harry Block, an American whom I had known slightly in the States, were also present at the dinner. After we came back the interest of the company turned to music. Frieda sang *corridas,* which Harry accompanied on the guitar. Diego sang one song with more gusto than art.

In my interview with the Ambassador I found him likable and intelligent, even if a bit naive. We talked about the pressing need for education in Mexico and he went on to say that there was another thing even more important than schools, namely good roads. He spoke of the differences between the cultures of Mexico and the United States. We Americans, he said, have always judged Mexican culture by the border states, which actually combine the worst elements of both. We should revise our thinking. The "greaser" is no more Mexican than the "gringo" is American. I commended him for having commissioned Rivera's Cuernavaca frescoes. He recounted that he had gone over to the Town Hall to inspect them. The priests in the pictures seemed to have hard mean faces; Morrow wondered if the artist could have conceived them as more kindly people. The matter stuck in his mind and he did pursue it further, as René d'Harnoncourt told me later. Morrow had René bring Rivera for an interview. The Ambassador asked, through René, if Diego had ever known a good priest. The artist answered that he had been educated in a Dominican convent and the Dominicans had taught him to hate all other priests. Diego decided he did not like the Dominicans either. Therefore between the two he did not know a single kindly priest. (This was about the thirty-seventh version of Diego's early life!) Then Morrow said, "He is an artist isn't he? Can't he *imagine* a kindly priest?" Diego grinned and said that he could, and in fact he was planning to paint in another fresco the portrait of Bartolomé de las Casas, the apostle and protector of the Indians. Morrow beamed and said, "I want Señor Rivera to paint an extra portrait of him. This is a definite order, and I will present it to the archbishop!"

It did not take me long to feel at home in a circle of Mexican acquaintances: Bill Spratling (when he was in town), Malou Cabrera, Harry Block, René d'Harnoncourt, Allan Dawson, an attaché at the American Legation and a man of charm and intelligence, the Riveras, and the Vintons, American collectors and friends of Walter Pach. We often met at the French restaurants, Pache or Prendes, for the big midday meal, or at Lady Baltimore or Sanborn's for lighter repasts. Malou was the daughter of a well-known lawyer and minister in a previous regime. She was vivacious, intelligent, exceedingly dramatic, with hair-trigger reactions, and very Mexican. I found her fascinating, though it seems that women were uneasy in her presence. Through her I had a glimpse of life in an upper-class Mexican family. I recall a whole evening till past midnight spent in playing poker with Harry, Malou, her two brothers, and the artist Manuel Rodriguez Lozano. The game was interrupted at ten o'clock for a light supper of enchilladas, three flavors of tamales, coffee and pan dulce. Malou and her brother, Bill Cabrera, took me to the bullfights and instructed me in the art of the *corrida de toros*. Of course, during the summer or off-season, the performances did not measure up to the highest standards, but at least I gained some insight into the ritual and fine points of the game.

I recall a dinner party given at the Pache Restaurant by Warren and Helen Vinton in honor of René d'Harnoncourt. It might be considered typical of the gay round of parties at the capital. The guests were René, Frieda and Diego Rivera, Malou and Harry Block, Allan Dawson, Fred Davis, and Miss Stevenson, a newspaper woman who had come to Mexico for a month and stayed three years. The meal was an elegant repast with vintage wines and champagne. Throughout the banquet telegrams for René arrived from famous persons —all written by Helen Vinton. We went for coffee and orange liqueur to the house of Fred Davis, head of the Sonora News Company, for whom René worked. His house was a picture of himself, amiable, innocuous, and lacking in taste. The library was overloaded with books he had not read, and with dull, old-hat paintings, except for two by Rivera. There were heaps of glass and other art objects around, fine in themselves but getting in each other's way. The phonograph was turned on and we danced. The company began to do stunts. René made a speech on art in the style of Dr. Atl. Frieda and René did a marionette stunt, and as a climax Diego dressed up and impersonated a fat old woman with a *rebozo* and billowing breasts.

I did not spend all my time at parties. I had come to Mexico to purchase art—not pre-Columbian art, for I did not wish to become involved in smuggling, but contemporary art. Through Malou I was introduced to Manuel Rodriguez and bought paintings at his studio. Through him I became acquainted with Julio Castellanos and bought three paintings, all that were available, since he was not a prolific artist. I rated him as important and was saddened by the news of his early death some years later. Through Frances Toor I bought paintings by Siqueiros, who was then in jail. I met him later in New York and was overwhelmed by the flamboyance of his style and particularly of his speech. I commissioned several editions of lithographs from him nonetheless. My major purchases were from Rivera. Even though I did not buy pre-Columbian art, I improved my connoisseurship in the field by study in the National Museum, in the collections of Rivera, Spratling, and d'Harnoncourt, and by conversations with them.

Frances Toor, as editor of *Mexican Folkways,* was helpful about the sights and daily life of Mexico. She was short in stature, rather pedestrian in her ways, good-hearted and generous. At her house I met Dorothy Brown, an attractive young American girl with whom I went on a number of excursions. We formed a mutually advantageous alliance. As in most Latin-American countries, it was more expedient for her to go places with an escort. For me, not speaking Spanish, it helped to have a companion who knew the language well. She had graduated very young from college and had taught Spanish in California. She was now taking a year off to explore the art and culture of Mexico. She was a wholesome American girl, athletic, direct, fully able to take care of herself, reserved, yet free and easy with men. She confided that she was saving up for the Grand Canyon for her honeymoon because it is so stupendous that it would take one out of oneself. We had delightful times together without emotional involvement. We hired a car and drove to Puebla. On the way we stopped at Cholula, climbed up the earthen pyramid to visit the Christian shrine built on the ruins of a Toltec temple. We turned off the highway for a few miles on a bumpy road to see the church of Santa Maria Tonantzintla (mother of the Gods). It was an enchanting little church decorated with hundreds of angels of a polychrome cement composition in high relief. The idea of decorating the church in this fashion came from a little Indian village of about one hundred inhabitants. If architecture can be called frozen music, here the peasants joined together in singing a naive and charming *Gloria in Excelsis.* About a half mile further was another edifice, the church of San Francisco Acatapec which, in spite of its impressive tiled facade, was as sinister as the other was sunny. There the suspicious natives kept us under constant surveillance. There was an air of mystery about the place, an oppressive feeling that made Dorothy want to get out and away as soon as possible. It is around this church that the legend of the Green Stone was centered. René told

me the story with subtle and suggestive art. I can merely re-
peat the bare outline without the atmosphere or mystery.
There were rumors that a green stone of extraordinary qualities was hidden or guarded in or around the church. It
might have been a jade idol or it might not exist at all. One
could get no definite information about it; the natives remained as mute as clams. Some years ago a military governor
got the notion that the strange stone might be an emerald,
and sent some soldiers to get it. Twelve soldiers were killed.
Their graves can be seen: that much at least is verifiable
René also told the story of the gasoline station at Huejotzingo. The owner had a garden in the rear and kept bees.
He hired a stone idol from some one for five pesos a month
to keep the bees in order. It was another example of the obvious fact that the veneer of civilization was often thin.

We went on to Puebla, saw the sights and bought *rebozos*,
pottery, and baskets at the market. Dorothy was adept at
bargaining in the approved fashion with much good-natured
banter. On the way back we stopped at Huejotzingo, not to
visit the gasoline station but a native goldsmith whom René
had recommended. From this expert craftsman I bought
some beautiful gold earrings. We arrived in Mexico City a little late on account of tire trouble and went directly to a
marionette show based on Indian legends *(El Conejo Astuto*
and *El Sombreron)* at the Casa del Estudiante Indigina. Between the acts a native band, *El Mariachi Coculense,* played and
sang with great vigor. Afterwards we went backstage and
admired the workmanship of the marionettes, especially the
animals, at close range. I went on other tours with Dorothy,
but perhaps our most idyllic experience was our excursion
one Sunday to Xochimilco. It was an area of flower and veg-
etable gardens demarcated by a vast network of canals, a
favorite place for the populace of Mexico City. Flat-bottomed
boats with chairs and colorful arches of flowers plied the
canals. We sat side by side in one as the boatman poled us
through the quiet waterways. Parties came along singing to
the twang of guitars. Whole families passed in boats with ta-
bles loaded with food. Canoes darted up with flowers and
beer or food for sale. At the center of the area were restau-

rants with music and dancing. Dorothy and I played at being lovers on the most romantic day of their lives. I bought her a bunch of flowers. On the way back Dorothy suggested that I give the flowers to Frieda Rivera. When I replied "but I bought them for you," she said "I could kiss you for that," and she did.

I wandered about one morning in the poorer quarters of the city. The slums generally have more individuality than the elegant areas, since showplaces everywhere are usually very much the same. In the poorer sections the people mold their environment more purely according to racial inheritance, albeit always in an indigent minor key. The Mexicans have a love for flowers handed down no doubt from their Aztec ancestors. Even in the poorest tenements one sees pots of geraniums or other flowers in the windows. One is impressed in a Mexican city—as no doubt in any Spanish town—by the way in which mechanical uniformity is broken up by the separate *casas,* each forming a little community within the urban complex. In the patios of these houses—one catches glimpses of them through open doors—the children play and live, water is fetched, clothes are washed, and tenants gather for gossip. The coldness and rigor of city life are softened by a more human relationship, though always against a drab and poverty-stricken backdrop.

Having said farewell to my friends, I left Mexico City on my way to Vera Cruz. The descent from Orizaba into the *tierra caliente* is an exciting experience, a mélange of breathtaking vistas, lacy bridges over deep ravines, waterfalls, and lush vegetation. Almost a whole day in Vera Cruz was spent in the formalities of getting out of Mexico. Because of the absurd regulations, I had to chase from one official to another in the oppressive heat of the day. As I stood in line watching Mexicans crowd in ahead of me by what an Anglo-Saxon would call an unfair advantage, I reflected that from an objective point of view an orderly arrangement of people by priority of time was no more inherently equitable than an arrangement based upon privilege and special favor. I can imagine situations where either system would impose unfair hardships upon certain people. In the end we all got on the

Ward Line's *Morro Castle* before the scheduled sailing time at half past four o'clock. The ship, however, did not sail until six because it waited for an operatic impresario named Robinoff, who was flying by plane from Merida.

The sea voyage was relaxed and uneventful. The ocean was calm and the weather tropical. As I sat on deck smoking a cigar in the romantic light of a full moon, I reflected that the setting was perfect for a Joseph Conrad story. Unfortunately, I had no one with whom I could exchange confidences about life's adventures, nor could I even be romantic with a girl in an un-Conradian way. I sat at table with Herbert Feis, his wife, and Mrs. Wright and her two children. I had met Feis at the American Legation; he occasionally had moments of a puckish charm expressed in his dancing eyes, quite unexpected from the solemn authority on economics he was supposed to be. There was another person on board who was the subject of considerable conversation at our table. She was Alice Leonie Moats, a very attractive girl of twenty-two, and daughter of a socially ambitious and snobbish mother. She spent most of the day lying in a deck chair and reading listlessly. Her lack of enthusiasm for the natural pleasures of her age stimulated speculation, and Mrs. Wright bet me that I could not make her get up out of the chair and walk around the deck with me. I accepted the wager. I went over to her and overcame her indifference without much difficulty. We soon were promenading on the deck. I believe that she really was bored: she had been conditioned by her mother to be dependent upon outside stimulus. When there was no stimulus she was quiescent. I did walk around with her from time to time thereafter, but our encounters were casual. She did not bring out the Romeo in me. The boat stopped for a day at Havana, and the Feises, Wrights, and I got off and had a grand swim at La Playa. Miss Moats met us later for lunch at the Ingleterra on the Plaza; we had a delicious dish of lobster and stone crabs à la Morro (big red and black claws) and fresh coconut ice cream. I went with Miss Moats while she bought perfume and rumba records. She danced a few steps of this national dance of Cuba for me. Later a group of us hired a car and drove out into the country to a brewery beer garden and watched the Cubans dance to a sprightly jazz band. On shipboard we again fell into the rhythm of *dolce far niente*. I reflected on my Mexican trip. It had been a delightful experience. As an outsider I had lived on the fat of the land. I had known the right people, I had made new friends—René d'Harnoncourt, Malou, and Harry Block—whom I continued to cherish. I became better acquainted with Diego Rivera and his wife, Frieda Kahlo. I found Frieda most congenial and I was struck by many resemblances in personality between Diego and Rockwell Kent. It was a happy holiday with little contact with the seamy side of Mexico. To be sure, I had observed a considerable range from primitive to civilized living, but I had little personal involvement in it. And I would not have wanted it otherwise. I had no desire to live in Mexico for the rest of my life. Certainly not in the capital, and not even in the primitive regions, although the Indian types fascinated me. The children and young men and women, with their clear complexions and regular features, struck me as very handsome. The patient endurance and intense faith of the Indios were soul-stirring but also frightening. I shall never forget the Indian girl offering the flowers to her Saint in the church at Taxco on the day I left. What pure beauty and grace of gesture! Nor the old woman crooning in despair by the church of Los Remedios.

Also, I reflected, one had to come to terms with the perplexities of Mexican psychology. I had always been sympathetic to the Latin-American temperament and even admired many of its qualities. But I was somewhat appalled by the prevalence of graft, corruption, and exploitation in Mexico. I recalled in this connection a penetrating comment that René d'Harnoncourt once made while we were having dinner in Pache's restaurant. The reason why it was so baffling to deal with the Mexicans, he claimed, was because their motivations were so different from other people's. They did not regard as sacrosanct three things that most others venerated. The first was money, which was why graft was such a casually accepted occurrence. The second was a modicum of political and social ideals. They were never hypocritical about ideals;

on the contrary, they were realistic and cynical. The third was that they did not fear death. To the Mexicans death was familiar, not calamitous. In connection with the last point, I remembered something Orozco had once said to me in New York, namely, that his pictures depicting dead bodies looked different to him when he saw them in New York from when he had painted them in Mexico. I might add a fourth point of difference: the time sense in Mexico is not nearly so urgent as it is in Anglo-Saxon countries. From my brief experience, I might venture to suggest two other Mexican characteristics: a highly personal sense of honor and a genuine respect for imagination.

I also reflected on the role of the artist in society. It seemed to me that the artist—that is to say, practitioners of all the arts—had contacts with two worlds, that of the elite or "haves" and that of the underprivileged or "have-nots." Rivera was a striking example of this duality. He could associate with capitalists such as Dwight Morrow, and also preach the gospel of socialism. Artists were among the few who were not imprisoned in the bonds of class: they could enjoy the advantages of money and social position without becoming lotus-eaters and losing all contact with the grim realities. And so, happy in the friendship of artists and sharing their point of view, I lived imaginatively in two worlds as I sailed peacefully from a Latin-American to an Anglo-Saxon milieu.

6

Travels in the United States

I have lived most of my life in and around New York, with occasional excursions to New England and the Middle Atlantic States. I did, however, make two extended tours into the Far West. The first in 1928 was memorable for my discovery of the Southwest. I had written Andrew Dasburg that I wanted to see Taos and Santa Fe, an Indian dance, pueblos, and prehistoric ruins. He sent me an itinerary, which I followed, and had five days of exciting adventures. The approach to Taos was unusual. I got off the train at Raton, took a car, still called "The Stage," across the sage brush desert and up the Cimarrón Canyon to Eagle's Nest and then down the Taos Canyon to the plateau of Taos. As we climbed up and up, the scenery became more and more Alpine: pine and aspen forests appeared and the adobe hut was changed into the log cabin. Going down the other side, the flora was again transformed into the sage brush of the desert mesa. I was met at Taos by Ward Lockwood; after dinner he took me to the Taos Indian Pueblo. There was to be a Corn Dance tomorrow and the Indians were rehearsing the music. We heard it faintly but I was more entranced by the spectacle of the Pueblo in the bright moonlight. It is impressive because of its unusual three-story height, since most of the Indian pueblos do not rise beyond one. White-robed figures would emerge mysteriously from the dark masses of the structure. I could not have had a more dramatic introduction to the Indian scene.

It was arranged that Dorothy Brett would take me to the Corn Dance. We parked the car outside and walked to the courtyard where the dance was performed. The space was being taken over more and more by the cars of tourists, who pushed in to see the spectacle; hardly any room was left for the dancers. I was chagrined by the shamelessness of the tourists who so impudently intruded upon a religious ceremony. I was reminded of an incident recounted by Flandrau in *Viva Mexico:* a group of tourists parked themselves in a church, had their lunch, left the litter on the floor, and washed their hands in the holy water. His comment was, "I do not vouch for the story but I believe it." The Corn Dance had hardly begun when a dust storm came up. The air was filled with choking dust almost obliterating the dancers. Brett and I retired to our car to sit out the storm. As if by magic all the other cars backed out and disappeared. The storm lasted ten minutes, during which time the dancers kept imperturbably to their routine. We emerged from the car when the dust settled, and we were almost the only spectators for the balance of the performance. Both the dancing and the chanting were fascinating. There were strange off-beat rhythms, hard for a white man to follow. It was interesting to see how the children, outside the line of dancers, imitated the steps and thus were learning the "feel" of the complex patterns. We remained to the end.

I saw Brett in Taos again in 1939. With Howard and Barbara Cook I went up the mountain to Brett's cabin and had lunch with her. Later she and I walked over the trail to the D. H. Lawrence house and met Frieda and Angelino, her current husband. He seemed like a shrewd Italian peasant with an eye toward the tourist trade. Frieda loomed large, more a virago than a feminine type. Her scraggly white hair was cropped close and she had a booming voice. When she asked a question she looked and sounded as if her whole life depended on the answer, yet the question was trivial. I was taken to the Lawrence shrine, with its gaudy decorations in mother-of-pearl by Angelino. Somehow the whole affair seemed a sorry anticlimax to the Lawrence legend.

It was inevitable that I would meet Mabel Dodge Luhan while in Taos. I had heard much about her and was curious to find out wherein her fascination lay. She floated about in billowing white gowns as if she were an angel, a rather substantial angel. She was a gracious hostess with an engaging smile and an eager outgoing manner. Robert Flaherty was also present that evening. He was in the Southwest sizing up the possibilities of doing a cinema documentary on Indian and Mexican cultures. He had arranged with Tony Luhan to drive to Santa Fe the following morning. Since I planned to do the same thing, I was invited to come along. Flaherty wanted to see some of the churches and places off the beaten track in the *Penitentes* country—an added dividend for me. Tony drove us through Talpa, Trampas (a tiny church with a terrifying Chariot of Death), Truchas, Chimayo, and then on the highway to Santa Fe. It was an eerie experience to travel through the country of that strange sect so aggressively secretive and dedicated to self-torture. It was fascinating, too, to hear Tony singing Indian songs as he drove the automobile—surely an odd juxtaposition of old and new.

After my introduction to Mabel Luhan in Taos, I used to see her occasionally in New York when she had an apartment at Number One Fifth Avenue, or when she bought books at the Gallery. I recall one party at the apartment when Tony Luhan was present, quietly sitting in a corner amid all the sophisticated chatter. I was the only person who talked to him. Mabel used to sent out Christmas cards to me and no doubt many others. I thought she had a charming and original idea, a souvenir of the desert mesa: the cards were always the same, a sprig of sagebrush stuck in the slit of a paper folder.

I arrived at Grand Canyon Station one bright morning and

had my first view of the Grand Canyon—breathtaking, stupendous. I took a dislike to the big hotel close by: the place was filled with tourists playing bridge or staring vacantly from rocking chairs on the veranda. I decided to spend the night down in the Canyon away from frivolous tourism. As the small group of us on muleback inched around the hairpin curves on the Bright Angel Trail, I reflected that certain experiences such as the Grand Canyon have been made too easy for modern man. Obstacles should be erected for those who do not feel the sacredness of the occasion. A spectacle as sublime as the Grand Canyon should be approached only with a pilgrim's reverence. I stayed overnight at Hermit Creek Camp. I walked to the bank of the Colorado River and watched the impetuous flow of its waters, and marveled how its small size could have carved out so mighty a chasm. I was lucky in that the moon, though past the full phase, was still shining brightly. Entranced, I gazed at the cliffs above me. I was inspired to write a prose poem, which was later published in Orage's *New English Weekly.*

When God needed material to fashion men and women, He thought of the Grand Canyon. Everything He needed was there—hard rock and soft rock of many colors, water and dust. It was there that He molded the types of mankind. Because Man vaguely sensed the holiness of this creation, as well as the superhuman character of the chasm itself, he has always considered the canyon as sacred, and has named its peaks after the most exalted teachers, Buddha, Vishnu, Zoroaster, and the like.

At twilight its aspect completely changes. Innumerable shapes take form for a brief moment and then are lost in the darkness: shapes and forms and faces, fantastic, misshapen, ridiculous, cruel, bestial, yet deeply related to the essential nature of man because made of the same materials. These are the models and molds which God did not use when He fashioned the types of man. How little difference there is between the used and unused models, only those know, who have had a glimpse of man's hidden nature.

As the sun thins away and the moon ascends, one is dragged down into the bottomless pit. Monsters and death's heads leer and glare monotonously in this colorless, soundless world. Creatures of the abyss, frozen with terror or racked with pain, lurk amid the shadows. All night long this titanic Dance of Death goes on, deep down five thousand feet below the surface of the earth.

It is well that the dawn comes once a day.

The next morning in the bright sunshine, pleasantly relaxed in our Western saddles, we jogged along the valley
floor upstream for about ten miles toward another trail leading to the top.

On my next trip around the United States, in 1939 on a
Guggenheim Fellowship, I visited almost every state to gather
data on printmaking in America. I went to the studios of
many graphic artists and took notes on their work. I made a
special point of inspecting about fifteen of the regional cen-
ters of the Art Project to get a general idea of their impact
throughout the country. My reaction on the whole was favorable, although I had some reservations on administrative de-
ficiencies. The organization had been set up at short notice
as a relief measure, and retained the spirit of its hand-to-
mouth existence, especially in the assurance of its duration.
Few long-range plans could be made: the threat of liquida-
tion was always hanging over the heads of the artists and
administrators. Furthermore, as in other bureaucratic relief
organizations, it attracted "finaglers" and politicians among
both personnel and dependents. Yet, in spite of these hand-
icaps, the potentialities of the idea transcended the scope of a
purely charitable enterprise. The Art Project could be and
was an investment in creative talent. Many distinguished artists of today served their apprenticeship on the Project. It
also acted as a stimulus for the development of regional
schools throughout the country and thereby counteracted the
centralization of activity in the New York area. It encouraged
not only artists but also the appreciation of art in backward
communities. Because of sponosred loan exhibitions and allocations to schools and libraries, many people looked at real
works of art for the first time in their lives.

Much of my research throughout the country was routine
fact-finding. But I did have some memorable experiences. I
recall some talks with Jonathan Daniels, the newspaper editor
at Raleigh, about the spirit of the South and the reaction to
his recent book on the subject. We were talking about the
American Dream: he felt that for most Americans it was the
sweepstake ticket, something for nothing. I had a pleasant
visit with Walter Prescott Webb and J. Frank Dobie in Austin,

Texas. The author of *The Great Plains* gave me some insights on the local background, such as that life in Texas is dynamic because it is the vortex of three cultures, Southern, Mexican, and Western. I clicked at once with Frank Dobie; he was a salty character with a cowboy's common sense. He told the story of how the politicians outsmarted themselves, or why the University of Texas had such a rich endowment. It seems that the University was a land grant college and the Texas legislature had allocated a huge area of rich grazing land for its support. In the following decade the politicians got to work and managed to trade, bit by bit, the rich land for worthless scrub land. But later, oil was discovered on the scrub land and the University struck it rich.

In Los Angeles I paid a visit to the Disney studios. I had met Jo Grant, one of the higher-ups on the staff, in New York and he provided the entrée. I was talking to him and examining the sculptured models used to fix the type of a character such as Mickey Mouse or the ostrich ballet dancers, when word came to join Disney in the "sweat" room. We viewed the first sketches for what was later issued as *Fantasia*. There were colored "stills" and portions of sequences already synchronized with music. The plot of the music always came first: the pictorial plot and drawing were always synchronized with the music. The conjunction of Stravinsky's score of *The Rites of Spring* with the story of the birth of the world seemed apt in an illustrative way. I understand that Stravinsky has since repudiated his connection with the combination, but at the time the studio affirmed the musician's enthusiasm and wholehearted cooperation. I was especially taken with the Dance of the Hours, using ostrich, hippopotamus, elephant, and alligator characters. It was funny, satiric, and completely beguiling. Later I had a forty-minute interview with Disney in his office. We sipped tomato juice and talked. I found him much more intelligent, dynamic, and modest than he had appeared in company. I asked about his beginnings. He had started making animated cartoons in Kansas City. They were quite bad, he admitted. He went to Hollywood, and, looking for an idea that would be different, projected live people against or with cartoons, such as Alice in Cartoon Land.

When sound began to be used in moving pictures, he experimented with sound effects. His first real successes were Steamboat Willie and the Skeleton Dance (*La Danse Macabre* by Saint-Saens). I asked him about Mickey Mouse. He replied that he never drew Mickey Mouse; he had stopped drawing around 1926, and he felt he could not claim credit. Under Jo Grant's questioning, however, he admitted that he had created the type. He went on to say that he never coudl draw very well anyway, that there were a number of fellows there who could draw much better than he. All he did was to make suggestions.

From further conversation supplemented by comments later by Jo Grant, I began to get a picture of the organization. There were about six to ten idea men (of whom Grant was one) who thought up the theme and determined its form and the types of characters involved. The theme was elaborated by a vast number of assistants, animators, background men, camera technicians, musicians, adapters, and the like. The idea was tested and whipped into shape by collective criticism in weekly editorial and executive sessions. It actually was a cooperative enterprise. Disney presided over the whole, "making suggestions." Grant said that Disney was a stimulating force and kept everyone on his toes, often pitting one man against another. He was an executive in the truest sense, creating by working on and through other people. In the training of assistants the apprentice system was used, and it took at least two years and usually more to develop a capable animator. One had to have a special aptitude, namely, to see everything in terms of motion or character, to break down an action into component and essential parts. Grant said that suggestions from the staff were welcomed, and that artists could work up into positions of greater responsibility. On the other hand, the gossip among outside artists in Hollywood and elsewhere was that Disney was a ruthless exploiter of talent. It is obvious that the job of animator was not suitable for a creative artist. But for a person who had no great aspirations the task might be a comfortable and occasionally exciting way of earning a living. The work was not repetitious.

Disney said that they were all sick and tired of Mickey Mouse and The Three Little Pigs, and were looking for other types and novel modes of expression. Disney had a penchant for new enterprise: he was dynamic and always the keen business man. This was in 1939. Since then he has built up a vast empire in the entertainment industry. He had no consistent taste: he used available human agencies and their tastes were variable. Some of his achievements were inspiring, others were banal and directed toward the lowest common denominator.

In Los Angeles I found new friends among the artists, Paul Landacre, Fletcher Martin, Herman Cherry, Denny Winters, and Eula Long. The three men took me to the station to see me off on my way to San Francisco. I was about to step on the train when they said, No, we can't let you go like this: we will drive you ourselves. After a quick telephone call to their wives we were on our way—an example of the carefree camaraderie possible only with artists. We stopped at Santa Barbara to see Donald Cullross Peattie, and I introduced Paul Landacre to him as an appropriate artist to illustrate his forthcoming book, *Flowering Seed,* with woodcuts. Next day we worked our way up along the coast, with glimpses, in sunshine or through swirling mists, of the surf and sea gulls. Paul and Fletch stopped to sketch the colored rocks and fantastic canyons. We went inland through the Redwoods and back to the coast at Big Sur and later to Point Lobos and the Monterey Pines. We had lunch at Carmel and then visited Edward Weston. He showed us his photographs while his young wife with starry blue eyes entertained us with an unending flow of limericks. As we plunged into the shifting fog-banks, illuminated only by the yellow sodium vapor lights on the last lap of the highroad to San Francisco, I reflected on what a glorious adventure these last two days had been. The trio had been perfect companions, full of fun and banter, yet sensitive to beauty and nature. How different from each other they were: Paul, the lame wild petrel, lovable, weak yet strong; Fletch, big, Rabelaisian, ex-sailor, sensitive to music, exceedingly male, antagonistic to the female yet drawn to her, appraising the figure of every woman; Cherry, a tragic comedian and introvert, always "wisecracking" to hide emotion.

San Francisco was older and more cosmopolitan than Los Angeles. It had more art museums, although they were cluttered with politics and maneuvers for prestige. Grace McCann Morley of the Memorial Museum was helpful in showing me around. At the World's Fair, then in progress, I was especially impressed by the Federal Building. A section of it was devoted to an Indian exhibit arranged by René d'Harnoncourt. It was a model of what such an exhibition should be, stressing social, historical, ornamental, and environmental factors, all of it imaginatively installed. The rest of the building was devoted to a survey of government activities in the best sense, that is to say, without benefit of politicians. There were instructive displays on conservation, the right of citizens to a job and a minimum living standard (with horrible examples of one third of the nation in poverty or slums), the effect of inventions on civilization, maps, weather reports, Coastal Survey, lighthouses, aeronautics, Bureau of Standards, Department of Agriculture, and the like. All in all, it could be put in a class with Boulder Dam as an example of worthy government enterprise. On my last day I met the photographer Ansel Adams. I took to him at once as a sympathetic friend. I spent the rest of the day with him and regretted exceedingly that I could not accept his invitation to spend a few days with him in the Yosemites.

I had met, through Douglas Haskell, Frank Lloyd Wright when he had come East for lectures and the like. While I was in Wisconsin I took advantage of the occasion to visit him in Taliesin. Wright showed me around the complex of buildings; we watched the apprentices at work on projects. We talked about Japanese prints and he showed me his woodcuts by Shunsho and Hiroshige. We had lunch seated on oriental rugs under the big tree in the central court. I talked to his wife, Olgavanna, who had been a dancer-initiate executing the sacred dances under Gurdjieff in Paris. I did not care much for the furniture that Wright had designed: he was, I felt, a better architect than interior decorator. I was especially impressed by the strong roots he had in the soil. Perhaps this stemmed from his Welsh ancestry, but in any case it was obvious in what he said and wrote, and in the pride he took in the "agricultural combine" (recently acquired), which was then in operation in the fields in front of the house. There are charming vignettes of rural life in his autobiography, and his allegory on footsteps in the snow is a delightful and profound prose-poem. Beneath the mantle of the prophet and spellbinder was an earthy personality.

7

The Philadelphia Museum of Art

At the beginning of the year 1941 I took over the direction of the Department of Prints and Drawings at the Philadelphia Museum of Art. As I reviewed my qualifications for the new job, I wondered how I would manage without having ever worked in a museum before. I decided, however, that the know-how I had acquired as director of the Weyhe Gallery would be sufficient to sustain me until I could become familiar with museum routine.

As was my custom, however, I did put down on paper some of my ideas regarding the purpose and proper use of a museum print department. They were later published in part in a Museum Bulletin. A curator—true to his name—must care for his collection and guard it against theft, damage, and deterioration. Efficient administration, however, is not the only task of the curator. Stagnation is apt to ensue if there is no expansion. The *raison d'être* of a print department after all is the extent and nature of its holdings. It is important, therefore, that there be growth in quantity and in quality. The aim is an ever-increasing collection of masterpieces in all schools, even the unfashionable, together with, in equitable proportion, the works of young and living talent.

In the field of public relations, a print department has a threefold obligation of service to the outside world, namely, to the general public, to the collector, and to the artist. It has a duty to the public to arrange stimulating exhibitions with popular and timely appeal. The average layman is more interested in pictorial subject matter than in formal or aesthetic values. Although this fact must not be ignored, it is not an excuse to cater to sensationalism or the lowest common denominator. Much can be done to raise the general level of taste through education in appreciation—not necessarily by lectures in professional jargon, but by labels, for instance, explaining in simple language what to look for in a picture, or by making some specific allusion to the art work at hand.

The obligation to the print collector is in terms of advice and stimulation. The print department should be a place that will educate his eye for authenticity and quality of impression, that will supply him with standards of judgment and appreciation. Similarly, for the artist the print department should be a place where he can see what has been done before and find additional sources of technical knowledge. The museum should also help living printmakers by purchasing their work.

Within the walls of the museum itself, a print department should have close ties with other departments, and cooperate with them in research or display. For instance, an old engraving of a painting might furnish a link in its identification and authenticity. Similar services might be supplied for the decorative arts, textiles, costume, and the like. Two departments might collaborate in presenting a major exhibition of a painter or sculptor who was also a strong graphic artist (as I actually did with Corot, Lautrec, Maillol, Matisse, and Picasso). A print exhibition could also present the contemporary background or memorabilia of the exhibiting painter (as I did with Courbet and Eakins). The print department and the library are the only two places that have direct links with all other departments in a museum.

It was with such guide lines in mind that I started out to build up a token print collection into a flourishing print department. I shall not attempt a detailed account of major acquisitions or a roster of all the exhibitions from month to month and year to year. Such information may be found in the Museum Bulletins and elsewhere. I will say that the print department, with a very small staff, staged many more exhibitions per year than the rest of the departments combined. I also came up with more suggestions for acquisitions than other departments. In the early 1940s many bargains were to be had: the boom in art had not yet begun. I had enough experience to recognize a bargain when I saw one. Whatever works of art I was able to buy during my tenure could not have been purchased without the encouragement and support of my director, Fiske Kimball, and later of his successor, Henri Marceau (as I have written elsewhere). Meanwhile, I was becoming acquainted with my colleagues on the staff, with trustees and other officials, and being initiated into the daily routine of a big museum. Again, I shall not elaborate except to signalize the two trustees most active in the support of the print department. The first was Staunton B. Peck, a gentleman of the old school. He was an engineer and industrialist who by some invention essential to the working of a link-belt conveyor had amassed a fortune. He was a dedicated print collector, ever searching for beauty and quality of impressions within the area of his interest, prints made during his lifetime. His outlook was conservative and did not extend beyond the achievements of Whistler and the British School, such as Haden, Cameron, and Bone. He was a good sport, however, and supported me in my quest for more advanced and wilder-looking examples of the art of today. At his death he bequeathed his excellent collection and his entire fortune to the print department.

The second trustee was Lessing J. Rosenwald. Although his major ties were with the National Gallery of Art in Washington, to which his stupendous collection of fine prints was committed before I came, he took an active interest in the affairs of the Philadelphia Museum of Art. Indeed it was he who, by his pressure upon the trustees to establish an active print department, was responsible for my appointment as curator. I found him very congenial. He had a great passion for fine books and fine prints covering a broad spectrum. He had, like Staunton Peck, started with the British School, but he kept on studying his collection and learning much from it. He soon began to reach out, backwards and forwards, toward other and possibly more exciting modes of expression in graphic art. He was resolute in maintaining a high standard in quality of impression and condition. He was interested in many things and might be impressed by their beauty or aesthetic importance, but he would not add them to his collection unless they lived up to his standards of quality and condition. There is an engaging modesty in Lessing's manner—and deceptive too—for he knows more than he ever admits. I often sought his advice regarding acquisitions and museum procedure. Early in our association he called me aside and said, "No doubt you often have targets—special prints you have found and would like to buy. I would like you to tell me about them; I might help you to hit the bull's eye. I won't say that I will do it every time, but I would like to know." Another time he called me on the telephone in his unassuming way and said, "I have just bought a big collection of Toulouse-Lautrec lithographs; some are duplicates of subjects I already have. Would you dare to have them?" "I most certainly would; how many did you say there were?" "I believe there are between twenty and thirty." "I'll be right over!" Actually there were thirty-eight Lautrec lithographs. Notable also was his gift of the famous *Recueil Jullienne*, Paris 1735, bound in red morocco with the arms of the Marquis of Bute, with other additions including over one hundred proofs in etched and *avant-lettre* states—one of the world's greatest collections of prints by and after Antoine Watteau.

Although Lessing was friendly and cooperative, I was always reserved and never presumed too much. My instinct told me that he was a rich man who was constantly exposed to the designs of beggars and schemers. I did not wish to be classed with them. The advances had to come from him. I did not mind begging for the museum if given the slightest encouragement, but for personal advantage never. Several people did come to me and say "I hear you are a good friend of Mr. Rosenwald. Will you introduce me to him? I have a proposition I would like to put before him." Needless to say, I was evasive or refused outright. Eventually Lessing and I reached a state of mutual confidence: we really became friends. It has been a rewarding experience. In a somewhat different sense he was and is a great friend of the Print Department. His many and distinguished benefactions were memorialized in an exhibition entitled *Rosenwaldiana,* in 1961 on the occasion of his seventieth birthday. He in turn wrote a warm and very laudatory foreword to the catalogue of my *Curatorial Retrospective* exhibition (1964), which assembled a number of art works acquired by the department during my incumbency.

I have always been sensitive to the moral issues involved in a conflict of interest. For that reason I resolved that I would not buy prints for myself when I became a curator. Before I came to Philadelphia I had acquired a sufficient number of art works to decorate my home. Henceforth the Museum would be my collection; I channeled my acquisitive instincts for the public interest. I adhered to my resolution with very few exceptions: during my twenty-two years of service as curator I purchased about a half-dozen prints, most of them since given to the Museum. On one occasion I purchased a print from a dealer who offered to give it to me. I demurred, saying, "I will take anything you will give me for the Museum, but I insist on paying for a private purchase." I never would accept a gift from a dealer. I did accept works from artists who were my friends, for they were given without *arrière pensée.*

The largest single addition to the museum collection during my term was the transfer in 1956 of the holdings of the Pennsylvania Academy of the Fine Arts in foreign prints and drawings to the Philadelphia Museum of Art. The Academy, in addition to its foremost specialty, American art, had in the course of its long existence accumulated a huge collection of extraneous material that had become a burden to maintain.

It consisted of over sixty-five thousand prints and perhaps a thousand drawings by foreign artists of the past (and a handful of the present), all uncatalogued and occupying, in their huge metal cases, a sizable space in the library. No one on the Academy staff had any expert knowledge of prints. A large majority of the collection was made up of reproductive engravings of indifferent quality. Owing to legal restrictions it was not possible to sell any of it—not that it would have realized any great sum according to the outside appraisal that was made. Altogether, from the viewpoint of the Academy, it was a white elephant. It occurred to John Frederick Lewis, Jr., then President of the Academy, to sound me out on the practicability of transferring the whole thing to the Philadelphia Museum of Art. It could be done only on the basis of a permanent loan, since the title could not be transferred for legal reasons.

After sampling the collection I came to the conclusion that it was decidedly worth while. After numerous conferences with the Academy Director, Joe Fraser—John Lewis had decided that the negotiations should take place between the two of us rather than at the presidential level between himself and Ingersoll—the transfer was consummated. The Museum agreed to take over the collection, catalogue, and care for it, thus relieving the Academy of the responsibility and giving it some much-needed space. The Museum also agreed to catalogue the Academy's collection of American prints (which contained some rare early Americana) after it had been separated from the foreign material and to return it to the Academy. The Museum's contribution to the exchange was largely in terms of services, although it did offer a token collection of sculpture by Benjamin Rush and a group of American paintings on similar terms of permanent loan to the Academy. The huge collection of prints and drawings, though weighted down with reproductive engravings and duplications of inferior impressions, has admirably supplemented the Museum's own holdings. It did contain many rarities and out-of-the-way prints, hard to come by, and greatly extended the range of historical coverage. A description of the collection and its contents appeared in the

Museum Bulletin for Autumn 1956 on the occasion of the inaugural exhibition of selections from the Academy Collection. I felt that its acquisition was a real triumph since, in one single operation, it gave the Philadelphia institution a stature as a study collection unusual in America and existent only in some of the European print cabinets. I have always been grateful to John Lewis for having the idea, and to Joe Fraser for his friendly cooperation in carrying it out.

One of a curator's ever-pressing tasks is soliciting gifts by cultivating people. It usually leads to frustration, but at times there can be a bit of serendipity attached to it. I recall one such instance. In June 1946, Mrs. John D. Rockefeller, Jr., whom I used to see occasionally in New York, wrote me a note asking for advice about a collection of engraved portraits of Franklin that she had. When I visited her in New York she told me she had been thinking of depositing the collection somewhere in Philadelphia; would I advise her what institution would be best qualified. I rose nobly to the occasion and offered the hospitality of the Philadelphia Museum of Art. She agreed—perhaps it was what she intended to do all the time. In the course of conversation it turned out that she also had an excellent collection of Japanese prints that needed a home. At the end of the interview, I left with the promise of the Japanese prints as well as the Franklin portraits. Furthermore, Mrs. Rockefeller, inspired for the moment by the needs of the Philadelphia Museum of Art, recollected that her friend Mrs. Anne Archbold of Washington also had Japanese prints; she would suggest to her that she give them to Philadelphia. She did, with the result that two choice collections of Japanese prints were added to the Museum's holdings. The two groups, together with later gifts by Mrs. Emile Geyelin and Mrs. S. S. White, 3rd, are the cornerstone of the Museum's *Ukiyo-e* collection.

Another instance of serendipity on an even larger scale occurred in connection with Alice Newton Osborn. I had first met Frank and Alice Osborn in the 1920s, through Egmont Arens. They both were painters, and I sometimes would meet them at bowling parties with the Laurents and

Kuniyoshis. (Peggy Bacon made an amusing drypoint of such a party.) They often came to the Weyhe Gallery to buy books and see exhibitions, and once I sold Frank a huge collection of *Imagerie Populaire,* the personal, working collection of one of the pioneer authorities on the subject. Frank had a private income—a fact that set him apart from the general class of artists leading a hand-to-mouth existence. He did not feel the urgency to be a great painter; he could afford to indulge in fancies, and explore the possibilities of experimental ventures. At one time he created a series of table lamps out of found objects—pulleys, marine gear, and the like. They were charming and ingenious. At another time he investigated the resources of airbrush painting and made delightful drawings with undersea and dreamlike effects. I put on an exhibition of his airbrush drawings at the Weyhe Gallery in 1929. Alice Newton had studied music but, not finding complete fulfillment in piano playing, had taken up painting before she met Frank. They were a devoted couple. They left New York and built at not great cost a big house out of the culls from the marble quarries in Manchester, Vermont. It turned out to be a mansion cleverly and beautifully designed for gracious living. And indeed he and his wife did lead a life of cultivated leisure. They collected paintings and Americana, furniture and *objets d'art* in an easygoing way. Books and music added zest to their life. They traveled; they set off for Europe whenever the impulse moved them. Frank had a private plane—he had been a flyer in the First World War—and would often take a little spin before cocktails.

This happy way of life was tragically ended by Frank's sudden death from pernicious anemia as early in 1948. Alice was heartbroken; her whole world collapsed. She and Frank had been very close; now she was alone and desolate. My wife and I went up to Manchester in February to console her. We went up again later that year, and somehow we got into the habit of visiting her for a few days every summer. I suggested that she give up the big place and get away from the memories. But she could not bring herself to make the break. For several years she did spend a month or two in New York during the winter to see plays and visit exhibitions. We would occasionally meet her there and take her to dinner. But her trips to New York became less frequent; she stayed in Vermont and became a hermit. It was sad to see her withdraw more and more into her shell. She, who had been warm and outgoing, became ingrown and suspicious. She had riches but could not enjoy them. She lived like a pauper in a palace. The elegant china accumulated dust in the closet while she made do with a hand-me-down cup and plate. When we came in the summer it would take a couple of days before she would thaw out of her solitary and pinchbeck routine and become human again. Then I would chat and gossip with her, hour after hour, about all the artists we knew. I had a good memory for names and a large acquaintance among artists. She would live again briefly, as it were, the good old days of her life with Frank. How much this meant to her I did not realize until later. With Laura she would chat about clothes and materials, and show her old gowns made by Worth and other couturiers of Paris, or her collection of old lace.

We discussed art and the art market. She asked my advice as to what she should do with the art works she contained in the house. Although she tended to suspect everybody of trying to take advantage of her, I believe she trusted me, since I had made it very clear that I had no personal axe to grind and that we liked her for her own and Frank's sake. We never accepted a gift from her. As far as the Museum was concerned, I laid my cards on the table. If, as she said, her relatives had not the slightest interest in art and did not need the money, I could assure her that the Philadelphia Museum would be delighted to accept anything she wanted to give during her lifetime for income tax deduction, or else to bequeath in her will. She said she would think it over. I did not put on pressure, but I did expatiate a bit on how comforting it was to know that one's treasured possessions would be properly taken care of, and how gratifying it was to have one's name live on in a kind of donor's immortality. I was careful to prove my reliability by never making any wild promises and by always doing what I said I would do. Eventually, while she was still alive, she gave the collection of about 2,000 *Imagerie* and other prints, also a large painting by Kuniyoshi and various watercolors for tax deductions. I never knew the provisions of her will nor how rich she was. After her death I was informed that in her will she had left to the Museum her oil paintings by Cézanne, Bonnard, and Renoir, her important group of watercolors by Demuth, together with as many other objects as I might care to choose. She set up a perpetual trust, and left one third of the annual income to the Museum. She even bequeathed to me a small personal annuity. Serendipity indeed!

In terms of their major interest, there are, one might say, two kinds of print curators. One is the connoisseur or collector type, who is concerned largely with rarity and condition and quality of impression. He seldom makes personal judgments as to what prints are important and worthy, but is content to follow the lead of the "authorities." He is more impressed by the tangibles of state and condition than by the intangibles of aesthetic response. Such types are often found in the large printrooms that already have sizable collections. Because they have ample funds for purchase, they are likely to be the darlings of the dealers who buy and sell "masterpieces" and are ever conscious of rarity. The second type of curator is more adventurous and more involved with history and the social and aesthetic significance of prints. It was to this class that I belonged, both by temperament and by the situation that I faced. I was more or less a "writing" curator—as were William M. Ivins, Paul Kristeller, and Curt Glaser, for example—and could readily make my own critical estimates. I had little money to spend and could not afford to buy rarities at a high price. I found I could buy a number of out-of-the-way but historically important prints for the price of one standard "collector's" print. I tried to spot worthy contemporary prints before the rise in the market, and in general search for important works in unfashionable and therefore inexpensive categories. The ability to recognize a bargain comes from long experience. Because I had the experience and the good fortune to operate in a rising market, I was able to impress my superiors by my foresight and persuade them to give me more money to buy more "bargains." I also had the courage to venture into uncharted fields, such as photography (Stieglitz, Atget, Weston, Ansel Adams). Although I could not compete with the old established print rooms in the extent and quality of their Rembrandts and Dürers, for example, I could assemble a fair sampling of works by the great printmakers from the fifteenth century to the present, and also concentrate for greater coverage in certain special areas such as French eighteenth and nineteenth centuries, impressionist, postimpressionist, and expressionist works, and especially in American prints 1910-1950. In this latter category I envisioned the complete oeuvre of such strong graphic artists as John Sloan, Edward Hopper, John Marin, and Rockwell Kent, together with an adequate representation of works by Arthur B. Davies, Adolf Dehn, Wanda Gág, Louis Lozowick, Yasuo Kuniyoshi, Reginald Marsh, and the later Hayter group (Lasansky, Peterdi, and Misch Kohn) and other leading printmakers of the 1950s, Shahn, Baskin, Yunkers, Frasconi, Summers, and June Wayne.

I likewise began collecting prints in special categories, such as medical prints, flower prints, engraved maps, *imagerie populaire,* caricatures, early lithographs, and the like. The Ars Medica collection was initiated in an unusual way. An executive of Smith, Kline and French Laboratories (William du Barry) called up the president of the Museum (R. Sturgis Ingersoll) and asked how to approach the Mauritshuis in the Hague with a view to borrowing Rembrandt's painting of the *Anatomy Lecture of Dr. Tulp* for promotive exhibitions around the United States. Ingersoll replied, "You don't have a ghost of a chance to borrow that picture, but why don't you commission our curator of prints to buy a collection of medical prints which could be sent around the country under your auspices." The suggestion bore fruit. The pharmaceutical house advanced the money and gave me a free hand. I began to study medical history and gather the material. When the collection covering various aspects of medical practice and history was complete, I arranged it as a traveling exhibition by installing groups of prints related to a single theme on twenty-one separate panels. The show traveled around America and even to England for several years. The Smith, Kline and French Laboratories behaved throughout with exemplary propriety. They exerted no pressure for commercial exploitation, they donated the prints to the Museum, and they even financed the publication of a handsome and informative catalogue. Before the catalogue was printed I asked them to show my text to their medical staff to eliminate any possible errors in medical phraseology. They did so and returned the manuscript without changing a word—which I considered a high compliment.

I had earned the confidence of the trustees and executive staff, and when Henri Marceau became Director in 1955 I was appointed Vice-Director. I served in that capacity until my retirement in 1963, becoming Acting Director whenever Marceau was ill or absent on vacation.

In addition to my duties at the Museum, I had opportunities for public service in related but extracurricular fields. For instance in 1943 I was asked by the Office of the Coordinator of Inter-American Affairs (located in the Department of Commerce, Washington) to select twenty collections for exhibition purposes, consisting of thirty prints each, from a huge mass of graphic art left over from the WPA Art Projects. The prints had been allocated to the Coordinator's Office for distribution to cultural institutions in Latin America. I wrote a brief introduction for the multiple exhibitions. In due course I received the translation, which had been made at the Office. Although I did not consider myself a Spanish scholar competent enough to savor all the niceties of style, it was obvious to me that the translation was stupidly literal and pedestrian. I felt that if the enterprise was intended as a gesture of good will, it should at least be said gracefully. I therefore asked Katherine Anne Porter, whom I had met in Mexico, to recommend a Spanish-American writer who could make an idiomatic translation. Thus it came about that Diómedes de Pereyra produced his idiomatic and charming version, which did not seem like a translation at all.

In the following year, 1944, I worked on an even more ambitious project of cultural exchange for the Office of War Information. I was commissioned to assemble a collection of contemporary prints illustrating the setting and life and culture of the United States for exhibition and circulation among, presumably, the allied and neutral nations of Europe. I purchased four units of sixty prints each—within the limits of the budget allotted ($900 per unit)—and wrote an introduction of 1,500 words together with notes on each print. Since the OWI was a hush-hush organization, I had to obtain clearance; my title was Exhibit Picture Editor, Overseas Operations, News and Features Bureau, Pictures Division, Exhibit Section. The only person with whom I had any contact was my immediate superior, F. A. Whiting, Jr., Chief, Exhibit Section, Overseas Branch. What I remember chiefly about the experience was the vast amount of paper work, the number of forms and vouchers I had to sign. Bureaucracy flourished from beginning to end. Characteristically—as far as bureaucracy was concerned—I never knew for whom the exhibitions were destined nor what became of them. Many years later I happened by chance to see the catalogue of an exhibition, *Amerika I Bilder, Nutidsgrafikk fra U.S.A.* (America in Pictures, Contemporary Graphic Art from U.S.A.) arranged in 1947 at the National Gallery in Oslo by United States Information Service. My introduction and notes all were there, translated into Norwegian. At least one show had not vanished completely. I still believe it was a good show for the purpose.

In 1954 Harry F. Guggenheim appointed me, as I have told elsewhere in this book, a trustee of the Guggenheim Museum in New York. There was an interregnum at the Museum: the Baroness von Rebay was due to retire immediately, and I was to help find a new Director. He was James Johnson Sweeney. In the interim I practically ran the museum with the aid of a business manager, for none of the trustees were knowledgeable in museum affairs. Sweeney was not easy to work with, a prima donna in his way, but he had the guts to stand up to the Baroness and to Frank Lloyd Wright, both also prima donnas. He was self-centered, a shrewd politician, and could turn on the charm when he wanted to, but he was impractical and unable to formulate a consistent policy or to carry things through. He moved by whim, but, to give him his due, he had a marvelous eye for quality and could install an exhibition beautifully. Many fine works of art were acquired during his incumbency. Harry Guggenheim was easier to work with, being able, intelligent, and understanding; his wife, Alicia, supplied the sensibility for art that he did not possess. Later, Fred Hauk, Harvey Arnason, and Dan Rich came on as trustees, and there was not so much pressure on me. I found Sweeney's successor, Tom Messer, thoroughly congenial, an excellent Director, with all of Sweeney's sensibility and a more practical bent, even though I do not always agree with his opinions. He was and is a valued friend.

It has been my practice, when given an assignment, to ask myself first of all, what the purpose of the job is and to whom it is addressed. My experience as a consultant with the Carnegie Study of the Arts of the United States could be cited as an illustration of the point. Let me recapitulate the history of the project. Some time late in 1955 the Carnegie Corporation made a grant to Lamar Dodd, an artist and professor of the history of art at the University of Georgia, to initiate and administer a survey, in two-by-two-inch slides, of every aspect of the visual arts in America, from Indian artifacts to contemporary art, architecture, and design. The material was divided into eighteen categories, and a specialist in each was asked to submit a list of from 250 to 500 objects (with their locations) of which color slides could be made, and which in his judgment would best record the development and achievements in his field. The consultant was also required to furnish a two-thousand word introduction to the subject. The project when completed would provide a corpus of over 4,000 color slides covering every aspect of American art as a visual teaching aid for schools and colleges and as a reference work for libraries here and abroad.

By the beginning of 1956 plans were completed and work was under way. I was invited to supply the section on American prints of the eighteenth and nineteenth centuries, and William S. Lieberman of the Museum of Modern Art was chosen to select the prints of the twentieth century. On first thought, I would have preferred the modern assignment because it seemed more exciting and I knew more about it, but on reflection I became reconciled to working in the earlier field because it would give me an opportunity to fill in a number of gaps in my scholarship. I therefore accepted and set to work. I made the rounds of the museums, libraries, historical societies, and dealers specializing in Americana. I had some ridiculous and exasperating encounters with what I call "historical society psychology"—a drive to conserve and preserve objects so intense that even the slightest outside exposure is resented and, if possible, prevented. I covered institutions in the Atlantic States from Washington, D.C., through New England. I made my lists and submitted my introduction. In mid-September I received a letter from Martha Davidson, who was coordinating editor of the project:

> I have just finished reading your essay and with such interest and pleasure that I felt impelled to dash off a note of thanks to you despite the thousand and one things I have to do at this moment of moving into a new home. In truth, your essay is so perfect an example of what we had envisioned for the Carnegie Study that I am going to suggest to Lamar that we send copies of it to those other Consultants who have not yet submitted theirs—if we have your permission to do so. The essays which have arrived to date are of such a disparate nature that editing alone would not help to bring about the uniformity which we desire.

I replied that I had no objection other than a slight qualm of modesty, since I was reluctant to spread myself all over the landscape, particularly where art historians are concerned, not being an orthodox one myself. She replied in a letter dated October 2, 1956:

> But you *would* be surprised if you saw what some of our "orthodox" art historians are capable of doing! Thanks for the green light. A carefully worded letter will accompany your essay, and I hope that no feathers will be ruffled, for you sake as well as ours.

I had finished my work, and now the editorial board took over to coordinate the lists and texts for publication in a reference catalogue, and the photographers and technicians started to produce the slides. About two years later, on May 14, 1958, I received an urgent call to attend a meeting of the editorial board at the Whitney Museum. There I learned that Bill Lieberman had left them in the lurch. By various excuses he had put off delivering his introduction and detailed lists until now, when everything else was ready to go to press. They had just received a letter from him informing them that regretfully he could not furnish the material since he was leaving for Europe. Lloyd Goodrich asked if I could help them out of their predicament, and, if I would, how soon I could deliver the essay and the lists, because the whole book was being held up. I replied that I would do the best I could. But there was another complication. Although Lieberman had not submitted any annotated list, he had indicated which prints in the Museum of Modern Art should be photographed for slides. Since they had been processed into slides I was asked to base my essay on his selection. Because I had no respect for Lieberman's taste, this was a galling assignment for me. To be sure, Lieberman probably had as little regard for my taste as I for his (as some bitter wrangling on juries revealed), but this fact was irrelevant, since he never had to clean up a mess that I had made. A compromise was reached with the board: I was to use whatever I could in good conscience accept, and they would make slides of whatever prints I nominated. I delivered my manuscript and list in a little more than two weeks' time!

In 1960 I undertook another assignment, which was no doubt related to my previous commissions, since it was also coordinated by Lamar Dodd. I was invited by the U.S. Information Agency to record a thirty-minute talk on modern prints for the Voice of America in a series called *Forum*, or survey of the arts and sciences in America. It was a difficult assignment because I had to speak eloquently and persuasively about an invisible subject, very much as if I had been asked to talk about color to the blind. I did my piece and again earned the commendation of Lamar Dodd. I never knew when or where the series was broadcast, although I suppose that it was in Europe. I never had any response from the void into which my voice was launched, but about nine years later I received a letter prompted by the printed text that had been issued by the USIA in connection with my broadcast. It was from a student at the University of Mindanao, the southernmost island of the Philippines, in what I suspect was very primitive jungle country. It was a touching "fan letter" from a person who had never seen an etching or any kind of print. He asked for titles of books, and I sent him not only books but also a roll of prints in various media. I never heard from him, and assumed that he never received the objects, since the post office refused to insure parcels to that destination. Some three years later—the ways of the Oriental are slow—I received a letter expressing gratitude for my gift.

I have written elsewhere about my connection with the Philadelphia Print Club, with the Print Council of America, and with the jury of selection in awarding Guggenheim Fellowships to artists. I could go on recounting further activities both inside and outside the walls of the museum, but such stories should perhaps be more properly reserved for a third volume of autobiography. I might, however, review one other extracurricular activity, namely, my literary production during the period. Owing to my strenuous schedule as curator and vice-director, I was only an occasional or weekend author. I had literary aspirations, but wrote little on my own initiative and mostly on demand (press releases, reports, and articles for the Museum Bulletin, which I edited for a while). I had come to Philadelphia with a guilty conscience. My appointment to the Museum followed so closely upon my tenure as a Guggenheim Fellow that I had no time to finish my projected book on American prints. My obligation to the John Simon Guggenheim Foundation was partially fulfilled by the publication of *The Artist in America* in 1942. The book consisted of twenty-four close-ups of typically American printmakers, serving as a first volume, to be followed by a regional survey of graphic art in the United States (which never did appear). *The Artist in America* was published by Alfred Knopf in a very handsome format. For the first time a book of mine was embellished by beautiful typography and tasteful design. It was fairly successful in reviews and sales—books on prints are seldom best sellers—and went out of print after a few years. I remember one amusing incident. About a year after it was published, Alfred Knopf asked me if I had a friend in the State Department. Apparently he had been getting repeated large orders from the department. It turned out that the book was being sent to all the official libraries of American books abroad. Fortunately, it did not attract the notice of Cohn and Shine, who later searched the libraries for subversive literature on behalf of Senator McCarthy. In 1946 Herbert Bittner asked me to write an introduction to a book of Käthe Kollwitz's prints and drawings. It was to be a short introduction, but it grew larger in the writing. Bittner was a good sport and printed it without deletion. The work proved popular and ran through four printings before Dover issued a handsome revised edition in a large paperback. Among other commissioned books I might mention *The Expressionists,* prompted and published by George Braziller, and two booklets on the prints of Mauricio Lasansky and Misch Kohn, issued by the American Federation of Arts. After my retirement from the Museum—(and thus not really to be included within the scope of this chapter)—I began writing on my own initiative and have achieved four books: *Multum in Parvo, The Complete Etchings of John Marin, The Appeal of Prints,* and the first volume of my autobiography, *My Own Shall Come to Me.*

I shall conclude my brief sketch of the Print Department in the past with a word about its future under the direction of my successor, Kneeland (Ding) McNulty. While at Princeton, McNulty became interested in prints and rare books through the inspiration of Elmer Adler, who conducted an extracurricular seminar on the subject there. Ding's interest eventually grew into a choice of vocation. Through the good offices of Elmer Adler he was enabled to spend two years (1947-1949) as an apprentice in the Philadelphia Museum print room. He went on to New York, received a master's degree in Library Sciences from Columbia University, and served a stint in the print and arts division of the New York Public Library under Karl Kup. In 1952 he returned to Philadelphia as assistant curator in the print department, and has remained there ever since. He was my choice as successor, and I deliberately tried to share with him my knowledge and experience. I trust and believe that some of my advice was acceptable and became part of him. He was appointed Staunton Peck Curator of Prints and Drawings upon my retirement at the end of 1963. It was a pleasure to work with him, for he was a loyal, decent, cooperative colleague, dedicated to his profession. His temperament, his taste, and his approach to the problems of curatorship are quite different from my own—which is as it should be. I am not so egotistic as to want a slavish replica of myself to follow in my footsteps. In the 1940s, when I first started, my staff consisted of one secretary; I did everything by myself. I worked under Fiske Kimball, who also believed that a small staff could work miracles. Nowadays one sees everywhere a proliferation of subordinate functions that can not be performed by a single person. McNulty is of course more geared to the needs and techniques of the present that I am. The Print Department has expanded greatly, almost as if it were a tiny museum within a big one. (It has a staff larger than many small museums throughout the country.) McNulty considers his function to be the coordinator, within this enclave, of a group of specialists in graphic art, old and modern prints, medical prints, art photographs, drawings, paper conservation, and the like. The department is buzzing with activity and still growing. What more could one ask for?

PART II

Profiles

8

Randolph S. Bourne

Randolph Bourne and I were close friends in college. Later, in 1914-1915 we shared an apartment. I was thus in constant association with a figure who has since become a legend in the American literary world. After his untimely death in December 1918, I wrote an article at white heat summing up my impressions of him. It appeared in *The Modern School* magazine for January 1919. I had intended my essay to be a warm appreciation yet a balanced and objective portrait of the man. But some of his friends, knowing of the break in our friendship after 1915, chided me for speaking ill of the dead, assuming that certain sentences in it were motivated by malice. One in particular, Alyse Gregory, wrote me a long letter, a beautiful tribute to R.S.B. and friendship, but based upon utterly mistaken premises as far as I was concerned. Some thirty years later, having come across my essay again, she wrote me "I have read it through carefully three times, and each time admire it more. I wish it could be reprinted somewhere." I am not quite so enthusiastic about my essay as

Alyse apparently had become. The style now seems to me a bit extravagant and one or two judgments appear questionable. I believe that I would have written it differently had I undertaken it today. Some of Bourne's own writings have not stood the test of time too well. Some are carelessly written—more journalism than literature—and some of the content seems dated and inconsequential. The vitality of Bourne's reputation lies less in his contribution than in his personality. The richness and pungency of his responses in his brief and tragically limited life have kindled popular imagination, and transformed him into a symbol and culture-hero.

After I left college to live on my father's farm near Kingston, Randolph spent several months in the summer of 1912 with us there, and wrote a number of the essays that appeared later in his book *Youth and Life*. In September of the same year Randolph, Roderick Seidenberg, and Vedder Van Dyck came up to the farm to celebrate my birthday. The day after, Vedder was stricken with a splitting earache. The other two returned to New York with him and delivered him to St. Luke's Hospital. Randolph wrote me on October 3rd:

> Whether it was the effects of the birthday party, or a reaction from Vedder's suffering, R.S. and I came back to my room Sunday night and talked one of the most brilliant talks that we ever had. It was really quite wonderful and impressed me so much that I started to make an article out of it, with what success remains still to be seen. It started with Catholicism, of course, and ran gently into Protestantism, discussing the two ideals, the two conceptions of a church, the appeal of the two bodies to young men, ending up with an extraordinarily acute psychological analysis of Mr. Babbitt as the typical non-Catholic and Vedder as the typical Catholic. Never was religion treated so sympathetically by a Jew and Infidel before, never was such comprehension of ideals and motives and purposes exhibited by outsiders, and, best of all, never did R.S. and R.S.B. react to each other so harmoniously, so stimulatingly, so lucidly. Altogether a high and elevating experience. If you don't believe me, ask him.

When Randolph was awarded the Gilder Fellowship for travel abroad in 1913, he wanted me to go with him, but I could not. After his return as a war refugee in 1914, he and I decided to take an apartment together. It actually was a model tenement, the Phipps Housing Development at 325-335 East 31st Street, about a block or so from the East River. It was a four-flight walk-up and consisted of two bedrooms and a larger kitchen-dining room, opening upon an inner court. It was plain living; we supplied the high thinking. We lived there for a little over a year.

We had wonderful musical evenings, when he would play the piano, or Edward Murray would come with his violin. We would have little dinner parties. I had become interested in cooking through my camping experiences, and it was part of my philosophy to be self-sufficient in the business of living. My mother gave me recipes and instructions. I found that it required considerable organization to have all the dishes cooked and ready at the same time. After a few failures, I did manage to produce a tolerable meal, and even baked cakes for tea. After all, I was a chemist of sorts, and cooking was a branch of chemistry. Randolph sometimes would invite young girls from Barnard or elsewhere for tea. I remember one vividly, Freda Kirchway. I thought she was wonderful —intelligent, strong, and handsome—but I was too shy to say much to her. I still have a vision of her face illuminated by the match I offered to light her cigarette. I remember also Alyse Gregory with her warm responsiveness; no doubt there were others. But many visitors, men and women, came while I was at work.

It was in many ways an exciting year, yet it had its measure of petty annoyances. Since Randolph was hopelessly impractical in everyday affairs, the responsibility of the household fell upon me, that is to say, I saw to the laundry and cleaning, the food and supplies. This in itself was not too onerous, but there were other considerations. I sensed a subtle change in our relations. Some of the earlier carefree camaraderie was gone. He was now a successful author; he was making many new friends and traveling in circles that I did not share. This again was not decisive, for I, too, was exploring new orbits, and we still had much in common. But somehow I began to have the feeling that I was being used. There is no point in raking up all the details of our estrangement. After 1915 we parted, never to meet again.

I went to his funeral in 1918. I wrote down my impressions at the time:

> The funeral—a desolately ironical thing it was. What a master ironist Death can be. After his death, Randolph's particular flavor of life, his tangible reality, his outlook and philosophy, ceased to exist. He was gathered back into the bosom of his family, back into the middle class from which he sprang. In short, he was buried from an ugly church downtown in Bloomfield with the ritual of a Presbyterian funeral service. Everything about it was commonplace; even Norman Thomas, who delivered the eulogy, was disappointing. There was not even good music—and Randolph loved good music. Everything was mockery except the weather, which was dreary, desolate, pouring rain. About forty people in all were there—Randolph's sister, who was surprised that I recognized her: she just knew she was looking so wretchedly; Jim Henle, rather overwhelmed by grandeur of the Presbyterian funeral service; MacMahon, rather stiff and pompous and looking more and more the professor; Edward Murray and his jolly mother; Gerald Thayer, conventional and reverent; Ridgely Toreence, dignified and sympathetic.
>
> Somehow it was not the thing I had expected of Randolph. I never thought of him in connection with age or death. This is the first death that has come to me among those I have known well, and it haunts me. There is the feeling of sadness and regret: scenes of the past constantly flash across my mind. There is the constant wonder why the force and vitality that was Randolph should have dissipated into nothingness. There is the question as to why the power of his practised hand, all the preparation and training and culture, should suddenly be broken, before it had come to the fullest fruition—or had it come to the fullest fruition? Then there is the recollection of his charm, his music and conversation, the lightness and deftness of his responsiveness (when he wished it so); the recollection also of his malice, ruthlessness, unscrupulousness, the tragedy of his warped body and thwarted desires.

Let me continue in this elegiac strain—after an interval of fifty years. For those who knew him, and especially for me, as I look back over the years, Randolph was a brave soul striving against great odds. When we said that his being a hunchback made no difference to us, we meant it. But we did not—in our normality we could not—realize what a difference it made to him. I remember the morning after he had had his first experience with sex, how his face lit up as he said, "I have had an experience which nothing can diminish or take away from me." Most of us were understanding and tolerant of this and other problems of handicap, even though we could not fully comprehend how inexorably his waspishness was conditioned. Perhaps we could have been even more understanding, but we were not. What he did and what I did can not now be changed. But, with more compassion now, I can choose to dwell upon the high spots of those exciting early years, and attribute the rest to the *Sturm und Drang* of youth.

9

Rockwell Kent

Rockwell Kent, *in his autobiography*, commented as follows on his first meeting with me:

> It is the silly playful way of elders, who have known us in our childhood, to tell us—to compensate us, so they say, for how we look today—that we were in truth lovely babies. Just so, and with the somewhat elderly, most scholarly and distinguished, bearded Curator of Prints at the Philadelphia Museum of Art in mind, I may remark that, aged about twenty, beardless, blue-eyed and crowned with a true glory of blond hair, young Carl was as angelically beautiful a youth as ever trod our earth, his beauty being eloquent of such unearthly purity of soul as shamed a sinner such as I. I virtually told him so, and warned him against knowing me. "There is nothing that you can ever do" the young man answered me, "that can affect my friendship."

I have described my first meeting with Rockwell elsewhere in this book. After our first brief encounter late in 1910, I did not see him again for about six years. I had left New York to work on a farm and he had gone to Minnesota, Newfoundland, and other places. From Winona he had sent me a Christmas card of his own design, a standing *Madonna and Child,* the madonna looking very much like his wife, Kathleen. I was touched that he remembered me. Marsden Hartley, who was present at my first visit to Perry Street, remembered me also, and wrote me a postcard at the farm:

> Kent was kind enough to let me read your nice note to him. Your letter indicates that you are at peace with that which is around you, and that it is beautiful. I think it fine that you can go in suddenly among dumb beasts and feel the poetry they contain. You have my best wishes. I hope to meet you again sometime. I would appreciate a line from you.

I met Rockwell again on Monhegan Island in 1917. For the next year I saw much of him both at his studio on Twelfth Street, and at his home in Richmond Terrace, Staten Island. It was then that our contacts ripened into friendship. Since he was older than I by eight years, my relation to him was that of a youthful admirer. In the quotation from his autobiography, Rockwell had combined two incidents, our first meeting at Columbia College and my declaration of friendship. The latter took place six years thereafter. I was indeed a youthful and uncritical admirer. (How necessary uncritical admiration was to him I did learn much later). We were both idealists and we had many interests in common. I would be with him at the studio, and we talked while he drew or painted. He was having a hard time supporting his growing family. Because his paintings did not sell, he was forced to earn a precarious living by architectural renderings, by illustrations for magazines under the name of Hogarth, Jr., and by decorative paintings on glass in combination with framed mirrors. In the autumn of 1918 he went to Alaska with his eight-year-old son, and we maintained our friendship by extensive correspondence. Scattered through his letters were fervent wishes that I were present to share the delights and wonders he so vividly described. Many passages from his letters to me were later incorporated by him in the text of his book *Wilderness.* We were very close in spirit during this period. The exhibition of Alaska drawings held at the Knoedler Gallery after his return in 1919 was dedicated to me;

and people have professed to see a certain resemblance to my features in drawings such as the *North Wind* and *Superman,* and in later lithographs such as *Roof Tree* and *Pinnacle.* The connection, if it exists, between my image and the characters in the drawings, has been idealized into something beyond portraiture. The wood engraving *Forest Pool,* however, was suggested by a photograph of me taken at Monhegan. He also made a carefully drawn pencil portrait of me in 1920 at Arlington, Vermont. Likewise, he made a psychological portrait of me in the form of the design for my bookplate.

Believing that he had great potentialities as a printmaker, I kept prompting him to try cutting in wood, and sent blocks and tools to Alaska. He made a few tiny, experimental wood engravings while there, but his first large block, *Blue Bird,* was engraved after his return to New York in 1919. He went on with wood engravings and then lithographs with such proficiency that in 1936, when the magazine *Prints* conducted an elaborate survey on the practitioners of graphic art, Kent came out far ahead of the others as the most widely known and successful printmaker in the country. Not that popularity is necessarily a criterion of excellence. Few artists have experienced such fluctuations in the public estimate of their work as has Kent, from extravagant praise to fanatic denunciation, usually based on nonaesthetic considerations or a misunderstanding of the real import of his prints and paintings.

His return from Alaska with drawings and paintings marked a turn in his fortune as an artist. His two exhibitions, arranged by Marie Sterner, at the Knoedler Gallery were a success, critically and financially. His first venture into authorship, *Wilderness,* with an introduction by Dorothy Canfield Fisher, received wide acclaim. His earlier paintings, which he had turned over to a dealer in a moment of desperation for less than forty dollars a piece, began to sell. His wood engravings and lithographs, as they were made, reached another kind of audience. But, although Duncan Phillips, Henry Clay Frick, Ferdinand Howald, Adolf Lewisohn, and others, bought paintings, the actual financial returns were still not very great. He therefore conceived the idea of incorporating himself. He wanted to get away from the city and establish himself in a country place, preferably in the mountains; he wanted enough money to live on for a year or so in order that he might devote all his time to painting. Other artists had made arrangements with dealers for a guaranteed income or had borrowed money from a bank on the basis of future production. Kent did it in a more dramatic way: he sold shares in himself for a limited period to a few patrons, such as George Putnam, Mrs. Caroline O'Day, and Mrs. Harry Payne Whitney. He did not thereby commercialize his art, as has often been alleged. After a few years he paid back the shareholders and liquidated the corporation. The certificate, incidentally, was a handsome and characteristic design executed by the artist; I was given one as an honorary, nonpaying shareholder. With the money, he bought an isolated farm on a spur of Mt. Equinox, above Arlington, Vermont. It was to be his home for many years. I have many pleasant memories of the place. Dorothy Canfield Fisher lived nearby in Arlington, and in fact found the farm for Rockwell. She and I often talked about our mutual interest, education.

I had procured a Washington handpress for Rockwell, and when his studio was set up, we would print wood blocks and line cuts. I learned to ink blocks and perform the meticulous operations of "make-ready." When he planned to build an additional wing to the house, we went into the woods and cut oak timber for the beams. Logging is always exciting, and a wonderful rhythm is established when two people manipulate a crosscut saw. Once when a felled tree was caught and held by the branches of another tree, he climbed up with an axe, chopped off the branches, and stepped to safety just as the tree finally crashed. The lithograph *Roof Tree,* executed five years later in 1928 and dedicated to me on the stone, was a reminiscence of the building operation.

I remember an amusing incident once when Rockwell and I were having an outdoor supper in an upland pasture. We were engaged in cooking over an open fire when a flock of sheep, led by a rather aggressive ram, appeared. They were a bit too curious and insistent, and walked all over our camping place. We assumed that they were merely innocent creatures motivated by curiosity, and decided to ignore them. When Rockwell bent down on some culinary chore and presented his rear, the ram saw his chance. He suddenly charged Rockwell, gave him a terrific butt, and knocked him sprawling. Our mood changed at this treacherous attack; we were no longer tolerant and understanding but fighting mad. We routed the flock and pelted its leader with sticks and stones. We finally drove him off; he was tough and took a lot of punishment. In the telling afterwards, the incident became an epic fight between man and beast.

In the decade of the 1920s, Rockwell was perhaps more "social" than at any other period of his career. He often went out in society with black tie and dinner coat, and moved, in New York or at Long Island estates, in the circle of the Ralph Pulitzers, the Watson Webbs, the Whitneys, and Gordon Abbott and his wife, Katherine, who later became Mrs. J. Cheever Cowdin. It was in that circle that he met and married Frances Lee, one of the Lees of Virginia. He had in the previous year been divorced from his first wife, Kathleen Whiting. In the fall of 1926 Frances and Rockwell were installed in a pleasant apartment at 3 Washington Square North. Rockwell was very busy at the time trying to make money to acquire another permanent home out of town, the place in Arlington having been given to his first wife. He made advertising drawings for N. W. Ayer; illustrated *Candide*, Chaucer, and other works; designed bookplates; contracted to make all the illustrations for *Adventure Magazine* for a half year; served as editor of *Creative Art;* and made numerous lithographs and wood engravings. He hired two assistants, Ione Robinson and Dehli Gág, to color the de luxe copies of *Candide* in his studio. And he still had time and energy left over for sociability. I did not see very much of Rockwell during the social years.

In 1927 Rockwell purchased a large farm at Ausable Forks in the Adirondacks. He drew up plans and built a house during the following year, on a site having a lovely view of the mountains, including Whiteface. His architectural training served him in good stead: he was able to cut costs by knowing how to specify standard fixtures, moldings, and dimensions. He built a charming and comfortable house, admirably suited to his needs. The central unit was a huge living room, the width of the whole building, and thus with windows on two opposite sides, and containing a spacious fireplace. This was flanked in one direction by his private living quarters, including an office and drawing studio. On the other side was a kitchen and a dining terrace (later glass enclosed) facing the view. At the farthest end was a bar, where guests could carouse far into the night without disturbing the host, if he should have work to do. There was a second floor over the central unit, a corridor leading to bathrooms and guest rooms facing the view. The living room was papered with maps of regions he had visited or explored, and everywhere there were bookshelves filled with books. Rockwell moved into his house in 1928 and it remained his home until it burned down in 1969. It was christened Asgaard (Abode of the Gods) after his return from Denmark in 1929.

Even before he left New York he had started to work on *Moby Dick*. I had first suggested to him that Melville's great work might be an ideal vehicle for illustrations by him. I had introduced him to Alfred Knopf at lunch at Moriarity's, the elegant speakeasy at 109 East 61st Street, in the hope that the house of Knopf might undertake such a publication. Unfortunately, Rockwell's idea of adequate illustration for Moby Dick was considerably larger than Alfred's, and nothing came of it. Later I put Rockwell in touch with Bill Kittredge of the Lakeside Press, who was looking for an artist to illustrate *Two Years before the Mast* as a sample of the fine printing that the Press was prepared to execute. It ended up by Rockwell's persuading them to do *Moby Dick* instead, in three lavishly illustrated volumes. His work on the drawings was interrupted by his first voyage and shipwreck on Greenland in 1929. It was there in Greenland that he met the two great explorers, Peter Freuchen and Knud Rasmussen. His wife Frances met Rockwell in Denmark upon his return from Greenland, and they stayed at Rasmussen's house, where he finished the *Moby Dick* drawings. Weyhe bought the whole set of drawings, and the gallery had an exhibition of them in March 1930. The three-volume edition came out in November of the same year.

On January 24, 1930, an event took place that perhaps marked the ultimate in expensive literary cocktail parties. It was said to have cost well over three thousand dollars. It was given by Bennett Cerf and Donald Klopfer at Random House, then at 20 East 57th Street. The invitation called it "a so-called tea or inspirational orgy for the spiritual benefit of Rockwell Kent, from five to eleven o'clock." The party lived up to its name: there was dancing, not to mention gaiety of all kinds, and, as often happened during Prohibition, the company became quite happy and wild. Everybody was there, almost a thousand people. The invitation contained a typographical hoax in the sentence "This edition, privately printed, is limited to 99 copies of which this is No. 1." Actually four hundred copies, all with the same text, were printed and sent out. But many people assumed that they were being specially favored by receiving No. 1, even though it was obvious that the numeral was printed along with the rest of the letterpress.

This was the period of Rockwell's greatest popularity. He was a famous man; his exploits made the first page of the newspapers, whether it was impounding an ocean liner or forcing a railroad to restore service. Reporters would meet him when he returned from his Arctic or Antarctic explorations. His name was familiar to countless people throughout the country, but not always in the role of artist. I remember the reaction of the *Times* art critic, E. A. Jewell, to Kent's widespread popularity. "Don't we all know it *ad nauseam*," he exclaimed. He resented the fact that the artist had avenues of publicity outside the art critic's field, and that he, Jewell, was not the sole arbiter of his reputation. At any rate, if Kent was a VIP, a very important person, he at least was genuine. He was no "stuffed shirt" seeking unmerited acclaim; Rockwell did certain things for reasons of his own, and the publicity just happened to follow therefrom. He moved into the limelight as if to the manner born. He was gracious, natural, and quick-witted—always master of the situation. He had a marvelous public presence. For me, being with him under such circumstances was an instructive experience.

As one who was both famous and affluent, Rockwell could afford to indulge in a passing fancy—such as taking up with "Prince Romanoff." He first met him at Moriarity's speakeasy—an adventurer totally without funds, but determined to get to Hollywood by hook or crook. Rockwell was amused by his absurd pretentions and invited him to stay at Ausable Forks for a spell. The artist was busy then, making drawings to meet a deadline for the publication of *N. by E.,* and the Prince would be useful in exercising his thoroughbred horse, which Rockwell had no time to ride. When I visited the farm in August 1930, I met Michael Romanoff. I was sure that he was an imposter. Romanoff did not say so directly, but allowed people to infer that he came from Russian royalty. I felt that he was familiar with the forms of elite behavior but that such familiarity was not instinctive but acquired. There was just that shade of exaggeration or lack of habitual ease that betrayed the *parvenu.* I told Rockwell so, but he laughed and said, I am sure he is "a phony" but I don't care; he amuses me. Romanoff stayed at the farm for a few months until he was asked to leave. He departed, taking a few odd trinkets and photographs with him. Rockwell was able to trace his progress toward Hollywood by the spurious checks he cashed on the way. He had taken to impersonating Kent, even to autographing copies of his books, and the memorabilia he had filched were useful in bolstering the deception. The checks were never for large amounts, and Rockwell did not contest them. Romanoff finally did get to Hollywood, and eventually opened up a fashionable restaurant. He prospered and had at last found his proper *milieu.* There was an amusing sequel to the relations between Kent and Romanoff. Many years later, when Rockwell happened to visit Hollywood, he was taken by some friends to the Romanoff restaurant for dinner. It was a luxurious meal with all kinds of drinks and extras, and Rockwell, to the astonishment of his host, insisted on paying the bill. He paid the check, forging Romanoff's name—and the check was honored.

The Adirondack home became the scene of many gay parties. There were several years when Canadian friends, including Col. Billy Bishop, the flying ace, were the most frequent visitors. The Canadians were a hard-drinking lot; one man in particular used to measure himself against a whole bottle of whiskey per evening. Most of us had no such special ambition, but we drank more than enough. Much drunken philosophy was expounded in the bar! Rockwell never allowed anyone to outdrink him, and, with tremendous will power, he was able to carry his liquor. He and I usually had a pact to meet at five o'clock the next morning for a plunge in the cold waters of his pool, then breakfast and a few hours in his painting studio (hidden among the pines) for work and talk.

One of the high points of the Kent saga of the 1930s was the wedding of Barbara, the first of the Kent daughters to be married. She married Alan Carter, a musician and professor at Middlebury College, and he became a valued addition to what we called the Kent Clan. I went up to Asgaard with Egmont Arens the night before and found a merry party in full swing. Besides Rockwell and Frances, there were, among others, his mother, old Mrs. Kent, his daughter Clara, Mae and Dan Moran, Stanley Marcus, Louis Untermeyer, and Poppoff, a Russian engineer and associate of Sikorsky in airplane work. At the bar Jack Lowry was drinking steadily and accumulating momentum to shine on the morrow with his "Poopy" story. The secret of his success was the infectious laugh with which he punctuated every few sentences. In the end he had everybody in hysterics. Louis Untermeyer compared it to the *Congressional Record,* where the sentences themselves are ordinary, but the inserted cheers and laughs are impressive. Rockwell, Egmont, Mae, and I took a dip in the pool, and went to bed about three o'clock. The next morning more and more guests came, the rest of the Kent children, including the bride, and their mother, the groom and his family, Judge Byron Brewster, and numerous others. At about six in the afternoon the ceremony took place in the open. Judge Brewster pronounced Alan and Barbara man and wife, while a quartet was playing Mozart. Punch was served and everybody was merry. Alan Carter picked up a violin and played a Gypsy melody. Poppoff sang a Russian wedding song, bringing a glass of punch to each of the principals in turn with ceremonious courtesy. After a buffet supper the happy couple disappeared, and the carousing continued. There was activity in three separate places, and I circulated among them. In the study I found Judge Brewster reading Lounsbury's famous will to old Mrs. Kent; in the music room Louis was playing the piano, Kathleen the violin, and Rockwell the flute; in the bar, drinking, smoking, and storytelling were in full swing. People wandered off into the night and returned casually. Around two o'clock a party went off to the Ausable Hotel, only to find it locked. Back they came to upset Frances's sleeping arrangements. Two hours later another departing contingent was assembled with great difficulty. One girl was missing; I found her swimming in the pool. A checkup revealed that the musician, Carl Bricken, was absent; he was found in the kitchen washing glasses. He climbed into the car, which I had been holding back, and off they sped into the night. Frances and I found another person stretched out in the grass. He was picked up, dumped into a car, and carted off. Only the judge and his wife, Poppoff, Egmont, Frances, Rockwell, and I remained. Everybody was mellow. Rockwell told the judge that Egmont and I were his oldest friends. The judge gave us his card to help us with traffic policemen. The judge told stories. Time passed. Mrs. Brewster was asleep on a chair in the living room, and Frances on the couch. Rockwell disappeared. At six in the morning, Egmont and I left, while Poppoff and the judge were telling each other what swell guys they were. We walked toward the studio as dawn was breaking, and breathed in the invigorating morning air.

I have perhaps exaggerated the bacchanalian aspect of the occasion. There was at this party, as in many others at Asgaard, much merrymaking not necessarily stimulated by alcohol. For me, the outstanding personality at the wedding party was old Mrs. Kent, Rockwell's mother. It was the first time that I became really acquainted with her, and discovered her charm and independence of character, and the *joie de vivre* that animated her in spite of crippling arthritis. It was only in this last phase of her life that Rockwell respected his mother. He had become alienated from a way of life in which she had grown up, and which he felt she represented, but now she emerged as a personality rather than a symbol of background. I jokingly told Rockwell that now I knew from whom he had inherited his charm and integrity. She was very forthright in her opinions, and was the only one in the family who was able to stand up to Rockwell in argument. When Mrs. Kent heard that Frances was getting a divorce from Rockwell, she wrote Frances and congratulated her on having taken the step at last.

Rockwell's life was punctuated by a series of excursions to distant places—Newfoundland, Alaska, Cape Horn, the West Coast of Ireland, Greenland, and the like. The motivation of these journeyings was, no doubt, complex: in addition to the lure of adventure, there might have been the need, in some instances, to escape from emotional entanglement. Whatever the reason, they served as an outlet for exuberant energy: life for Rockwell was never dull. Having discovered Greenland by being shipwrecked on its shores, he returned with his son, Gordon, for an extended stay in 1934. Walter Riegals, art director at General Electric in Schenectady and a great admirer of Rockwell, arranged for a broadcast to Greenland by his friends in New York. He organized a national radio hookup as well as a short wave broadcast on the evening of September 23rd at the Hotel Lexington. It was quite a party, and Mr. Rochester, the hotel manager and our host, served a very elegant supper with champagne. There were brief talks and messages by Frank Crowninshield, Louis Untermeyer, Bob Flaherty (just back from the Aran Islands), Frances and the two children, Kathleen and Clara. Stefanssen told a folk tale in Eskimo for the benefit of the native listeners. I was asked with scant warning to say a few words. Fortunately, I was in an articulate mood and came up with an appropriate greeting without stage fright. I recalled to Rockwell that he had told how the Eskimos had no conception of art, and that, when he returned from a painting expedition on his sled with a finished painting, they congratulated him as if he had brought home a seal. And so I asked him if he was having good luck hunting. It was my first broadcast, and I was much interested in all the operations of radio transmission. I was amused when our host, the hotel manager, was called upon to say a few words, that he pulled out a paper and began reading: "Unprepared as I am at this unexpected opportunity to deliver a friendly greeting to you in the Arctic night. . . ." All together it was a gay party and an exciting experience. Several persons told me later that they had heard the broadcast and that my voice carried well over the radio. The irony was that Rockwell never heard a word of it; his radio had gone out of commission about a week or so before the event.

Early in the summer of 1935, Rockwell sent from Greenland the manuscript of *Salamina* to Harcourt, Brace and Co. for publication. Donald Brace asked Louis Untermeyer and me to read the proof, since Rockwell was so far away. We both made several corrections in the manuscript, not many; I can remember only one of them now, one that any conscientious editor would have made, regarding the text of a Walt Whitman poem that had been quoted. We altered it to conform with the final authorized version. The book was in press when Rockwell returned from Greenland unexpectedly. He was indignant that we had tampered with his text and ordered the corrected passages to be reinstated. In the regular trade edition the following note appeared:

> In this book all the mistakes of grammar and punctuation are to be attributed to the perverseness of the author who, unexpectedly returning from Greenland, put back some of those errors that his friends Louis Untermeyer and Carl Zigrosser had carefully eliminated from the proofs.

The roster of Rockwell's friends and acquaintances varied from time to time according to whether they were in or out of favor. Either they did not live up to his impulsively generous estimate—presuming too much on a friendly relation they did not understand—or else his interests changed and the ties between him and them no longer endured. For me the challenge never took place. I remained his friend, and became, by virtue of duration, the friend of the family as well. I came to know and affectionately admire his three wives, Kathleen, Frances, and Sally. It is a commonplace observation that the wives of great men generally are unheralded and uncelebrated heroines. It is true of Rockwell's wives, even though he did voice his appreciation of them at times—not, however, at all times, nor with full understanding. He made great demands upon them: they must be wife, companion, household manager, hostess, amanuensis, and secretary for voluminous correspondence. Brimming over with energy, he could and did wear out two wives. I salute all three for their loyal and unselfish devotion.

The activities in his public career continued unabated. I recall that early in 1939 he made the principal speech at the annual dinner of the League for Mutual Aid. W. C. Handy also was there, and told about composing the *Memphis Blues*. His daughter sang the *St. Louis Blues* to his trumpet accompaniment. Afterwards Rockwell, Frances and I went to the "21" nightclub to meet Lewis and Kendall Milestone at their invitation. I had met Milestone before at Asgaard (Frances Kent and Kendall Milestone were sisters); he was of course the director of many distinguished motion pictures, *All Quiet on the Western Front, Front Page, Rain, Of Mice and Men*. Knowing of his Russian birth and leftist sympaties, I asked him how he managed in Hollywood. He got along tolerably well, he replied; he had certain technical skills and experience that few of the Hollywood directors had, and, besides he did not demand such exorbitant fees. He went on to talk about Clifford Odets and his Group Theatre venture and about Stanislavsky's experiments in the spontaneous acting out of roles. It was my first and only visit to "21," and I gathered the impression that it was a place where celebrities went to be seen. As if in confirmation, another cinema director, Anatole Litvak, who had bought things from me at the gallery, came over to shake hands with us.

A week later, there was a dinner in Rockwell's honor at the Town Hall Club. First a small group, Untermeyer, Stefanssen, and I gathered at Rockwell's for cocktails. And then to dinner. Louis Untermeyer got up to make some facetious remarks to accompany pictures of Rockwell's early life, but the projectionist ran the slides too fast and Louis was not able to deliver all his witticisms. Heywood Broun also spoke, and of course Rockwell, fervently, on the prospect of a union of artists. Later our little group went to Café Society and stayed till after three in the morning. Unlike "21," Café Society was noisy: there was a jazz band and jitterbugging on a dance floor about twelve feet square. The insistent rhythms, the strident outbursts of trumpet and saxophone, the dervishlike flopping of the drummer, the frenzied tapping of feet, induced a kind of hysteria in the dancers. As Untermeyer said, only those who were completely and satisfactorily absorbed in their own work could withstand the obsessive call to release their pent-up energies in frantic agitation. In the intervals, guest artists performed: the two-piano team, Mead Lux Lewis and Albert Ammons, played boogie-woogie fortissimo, equally obsessive in their performance. It was the first time I had heard boogie-woogie, and it was fascinating in a strange way: the right hand improvised against a consistent faster rhythmic pattern by the left hand. The performance was quite spontaneous and exciting, as in the best of jazz. During a quiet spell, Earl Robinson sang folksongs with guitar accompaniment, including his own *Joe Hill.* He was a charming soft-spoken man. He was interested in art, and we talked about Daumier. About six months later I was to hear his electrifying *Ballad for Americans* as sung by Paul Robeson over Norman Corwin's radio program.

In 1955 Kent's autobiography *It's Me O Lord,* appeared. As with most autobiographies, it is in fact an *apologia pro vita sua* and contains the usual amount of inaccuracies, half-truths, and evasions. In saying this I do not minimize the obvious merit of the book. It is a marvelous projection of a personality and a record of a full life lived on many levels. The book *is* the man. But from the fullness of my knowledge I can not accept his legend entirely at its face value, nor refrain from expressing my sympathy for some of those who have experienced his disfavor. Recently, when I told Rockwell that I was planning to include a chapter on him in my memoir, Leonard Boudin, who happened to be present, jokingly ad-

monished me to be merciless. My aim, however, was not to
be ruthless, but to be understanding, and to be open-eyed
enough not to distort the value of a relationship that once existed in the past. I had already written one pen portrait of
him in *The Artist in America*, 1942, and he had sent me a most
enthusiastic letter of appreciation. My portrait was not entirely a panegyric and contained some critical comments. I
was not prepared, therefore, for Rockwell's reaction to my
new portrait, which was intended as a supplement to the
first, when I read it to him in 1967 in a first draft (I usually
check with the subject for factual errors). He begged me so
earnestly not to publish the work that I had no choice but to
comply. I did not promise never to publish it, revised of
course, but to postpone it until a later date, which might be
after his death. I was surprised by the vehemence of his solicitude. It was not until 1969, when I saw how he reacted to
the destruction of his home, that I realized the true significance of his attitude. After his house had been struck by
lightning and burned to the ground with most of his possessions and memorabilia, his immediate response was to re-
build it in the same form and shape as it formerly had been.
To be sure, it was not an exact replica: the second story was
missing, which was used exclusively for guests. He could live
and function on the first floor and not be aware of much difference. He wanted to blot out the memory of the calamity
and live as before. The intensity of his determination could
be revealed by asking how many men at the age of eighty-six
years would start rebuilding a home as he did. He had terrific will power and an unshakable belief that he could accomplish anything that he decided to do. This feeling of in-
vincibility carried him successfully through most of his life.
Whatever he could not meet and overcome—he was very
competitive—he would obliterate and act as if it had never
existed. Had he lost his faith, the whole structure of his life
would have crumbled. Hence the urgency of his desire to
prevent a few negative assessments in my pen portrait from
impinging and challenging his assumptions. I might say in
extenuation that at the time of the reading his hearing had
been seriously impaired, and he may have misunderstood my

words. I really had not intended to be malicious, nor do I believe that I was: I was aiming at a balanced assessment. It may also be that as he grew older he felt less secure and needed more and more reassurance.

Why did I have the impulse to blurt out my own balanced view when I sensed vaguely that I might disturb him? It was because I wanted to change the quality of our relationship. When I was youn,g I admired him uncritically. As I grew older, I saw him as a human being endowed with certain frailties that I was prepared to accept. I felt, however, that to acquiesce invariably was dishonest: I had my own opinions and was not just a yes-man. I viewed him now in perspective: my regard was tempered but also deepend. I admired him with more understanding. Such a new dimension in friendship was a more worthy tribute to him and to me than uncritical admiration.

Thus the bonds of our friendship were never broken—but they were strained on occasion. One sore point was Rockwell's intolerance of modern art, to which I was in a large sense committed. When we both were young, we saw eye to eye. I championed the art of his generation against the old fogies of the Academy. Being instinctively in favor of the underdog and realizing that change was the normal course of events, I continued, as time went on, to champion a newer generation. He could not, or would not. Of course, it was much easier for me than for him. I was above the battle, whereas he was committed to his own expression, which he had achieved with considerable effort. I can respect an artist for sticking to his convictions and not following the fashions. But he need not be intolerant about it. Not all young artists are charlatans or fools; they have their ideals just as the older generation had. It was not, however, Rockwell's temperament, when he had convictions, to refrain from expressing them forcibly on all occasions. I found it expedient, therefore, to avoid, as far as possible, arguments on certain issues, debates in which neither could convince the other, and which could lead only to the aggravation of tempers for no good purpose.

This did not, however, alter the plight he was in: he felt

himself increasingly alienated from and ignored by the art world of his own country. He who had enjoyed enormous popularity and acclaim now found that his art was rejected and reviled, often for reasons that had nothing to do with his art, namely, his politics and his radical activities. It was not enough that a few, including myself, still valued what he had achieved. He had lost his following and his public. But by rare good fortune, he found another audience, even greater and more appreciative—in the Soviet Union. He was an honored artist behind the Iron Curtain. His paintings hung in the Hermitage and the Pushkin Museum; influential critics, such as Andrei Chegodaev, have written books about him. His own books have been translated into Russian and Czech, and beautifully printed in editions of from fifty to seventy thousand copies. In some instances more than one edition has appeared, bringing the totals into the hundreds of thousands. He introduced Melville's *Moby Dick* to the Slavic world. His big retrospective exhibition of paintings was seen by over a million visitors. The magnitude of such a response should have the virtue of soothing quite a number of rebuffs for an artist without honor in his native country. Obviously the Slavs liked his work and his type of "realism." He in turn had established friendly ties with numerous Russian artists, since they and the people in general were warmly responsive. It is small wonder that Rockwell was active in promoting Societ-American friendship. He was awarded the Lenin Prize in 1967.

I am not suggesting that he liked the Russians only because they liked his art. He admired them also for aiming to establish a workers' republic. He had been a socialist since his youth, but he was never, I am certain, a member of the Communist Party. One might call him a fellow traveler, but with an American slant; in other words, he endorsed Soviet policy as expedient for that country but not necessarily applicable to conditions in his own. As a grass-roots American, he was at times critical of the American Communist Party, although he accepted the drives of the Soviet Union with a little more equanimity than most of his fellow Americans. He was active in promoting peace, in thawing out the cold war, and in establishing a basis for peaceful coexistence between two great nations.

I am a great advocate of peaceful coexistence, and I feel that the principle applies equally to nations and to individuals. During the 1940s and 1950s, Kent was becoming more and more engaged in political activities, which included speechmaking and membership in many propaganda organizations. His right, and even duty as he saw it, to engage in these operations was not to be questioned. But when, in his proselytizing zeal, he tried to convert his friends—not to mention his relatives—to aggressive action, the ties of friendship were bound to chafe. I am sure that there was nothing personal in his attempts at indoctrination. For a man of his temperament, matters were desperately urgent, and everybody was grist to his mill: "he that is not with me is against me." Our differences, such as they were, stemmed from the difference between an active and a reflective temperament, or could be explained by "the things that stick in one's throat." Every one of us encounters in life certain issues that seem inconsequential and that we can tolerate or ignore with easy grace, whereas there are others that we simply can not swallow: they stick in our throat and move us to indignant judgment and perhaps to action. The things that raised Rockwell's hackles did not necessarily have the same effect on me.

Rockwell's father had been a lawyer, and he himself has always had a great interest in court trials and questions of law. He might well have become a successful lawyer. He also had the ability to think quickly on his feet, and, through his sure sense of crowd psychology, to be an able and persuasive speaker. All these special skills enabled him to make a good showing at several judicial inquisitions during the 1940s and 1950s. On October 31, 1939, I recorded a luncheon conversation that I had with him:

He spoke about Martin Dies and his Un-American Committee. He had written a letter (much longer than was published) to Dies, also a telegram telling him to listen to Rockwell's broadcast. He sent a copy to Ruby Black, who called up the U.P., and they got permission from the Committee to publish it. That is why the letter got into the papers at all. Rockwell is angling to be examined by Dies, and his line will be that all his life he has taken exactly the same stand, namely, union card, membership in Socialist party, and the like. The communists are merely taking up, at a much later date, an American tradition—Life, Liberty, and the Pursuit of Happiness. He wants to see if he can break the newspaper bias of Dies publicity. Prof. Harry Ward of the League for Peace and Democracy had no chance at all. He can't forgive Browder for saying that the League was a subsidiary of the Communist Party. In general the leadership and publicity of the Communist Party are most inept. Why not admit that the Hitler-Stalin Pact was a surprise, instead of assuming an omniscient air. Nobody is manly enough to admit a mistake—witness the spectacle of Kaufman trying to wiggle out of the revelations of Mary Astor's diary. He spoke with approval of Granville Hicks' document in the *New Republic* resigning from the C.P., and also said that Kyle Crichton stopped writing for the *New Masses* because of inept leadership.

His contretemps with Senator Joseph McCarthy was more dramatic and somewhat more perilous. He was called before the Seante Committee in connection with the contents of official American libraries abroad. McCarthy treated him with a little more respect than usual, probably because Rockwell showed at once that he was not afraid. He scored a hit at the very beginning by announcing that he came to the hearing voluntarily. "What's this!" exclaimed the Senator, bristling at any slight to his authority, "You came by subpoena." Pulling the paper out of his pocket and handing it to the Senator, Rockwell said "The document is not legally binding: it is not signed." This threw the Senator into confusion and he went into a huddle with his assistants, Cohn and Shine, and bawled them out. Eventually he resumed the proceedings with the sheepish explanation, "Anyway the duplicate was signed." Later Rockwell asked permission to read a statement. The Senator refused; "We won't have any lectures by you, Mr. Kent." Rockwell popped right back, "You won't get any lecture from me: I get paid for my lectures." In the statement that he was not allowed to read, Kent charged that the Senator was a leader in conspiracy to overthrow our form of government, if need be, by force and violence. Furthermore he likened McCarthy to Hitler in his book-burning activities. He concluded as follows, "let me say that I intend to avail myself of every legal and Constitutional right I may have before the Committee. The cards are stacked. I will not play the game." He handed out copies of the statement to members of the press later, but only one paper, the *York Gazette,* printed anything about it, or about another statement on the very plausible reasons for invoking the Fifth Amendment. The latter statement ended as follows:

> One of the earliest non-conformists to refuse answers to his inquisitors was Jesus. In the twenty-third chapter of St. Luke we read:
>
> "And Pilate asked him, saying, Art thou the King of the Jews? and he answered him and said, Thou sayest it."
>
> Herod then, "questioned him in many words; but he answered him nothing."

Rockwell was one of the few during the shameful McCarthy era who had an impregnable position, and was therefore able not only to defend himself but also to counterattack.

I have often wondered what was the impulse that prompted Rockwell to be a nonconformist. He had many qualities that might have ensured him riches and conventional success. That he did not worship the "Bitch-goddess" with all his heart and soul, was to his credit, although he had flirted with her on a few occasions. But why did he not choose the easiest way? The motivation was probably complex. In personal matters he might, under the sway of power emotions, be driven to contravene the conventions, knowing full well that he was doing wrong. In social questions, the drive might have in it a large measure of altruism, a sympathy for the workers and the underprivileged, but also a modicum of defiance, a revolt, especially in his youth, against the easy comfortable circumstances of his family background. The note of controversy often recurred in the pattern of his life: he was "agin' things" and he was easily moved to indignation. Indeed, as someone said facetiously, "he joins causes so that he can hate legally." As a young man he went to Newfoundland expressly to paint. It was not very long before he had reacted so aggressively to the stupidity and prejudices of the natives that he was deported as a German spy. Many other examples of his contentiousness could be cited: he was always standing up for a principle and he loved a good fight. In later years, animated, I would say, more by altruism than by defiance, he espoused many unpopular causes, and reaped the inevitable ostracism and obloquy.

Rockwell Kent could be described as an extrovert of great versatility and tremendous will power. But underneath that alert and poised exterior, there lurked a bundle of irrational impulses and paradoxes. His mother has said that his childhood was plagued by terrifying nightmares and even by somnambulism. I imagine that, as he grew up, he was able to curb some of his unnatural fears by a rigid censorship of the will. But one occasionally had glimpses of the abyss—was it fear of death and dissolution?—in his art, as in the Newfoundland painting *The House of Dread,* the lithograph *Nightmare,* and that extraordinary self-portrait head that once appeared on the cover of the *New Masses.* Being human, he had his share of petty traits of character—cantankerousness and egocentricity—that are more apt to annoy than to alienate. But more worthy of record are the contradictions and paradoxes that add spice to a human personality, such as, for example, the spectacle of an untamed individualist acting as apologist for an autocratic, collectivley orientated society. Or his gesture in mimeographing and distributing to his friends a report of comments (rather doctrinaire, they seemed to me) by members of the Soviet Academy of Arts—all this from the man who once claimed to despise and ignore all criticism. Such inconsistencies are both endearing and amusing.

In an autobiographical fragment Kent once spoke of the challenges that had shaped his early life. I would go further and say that reaction to challenge has been the dominant leitmotif of his whole life, and that the competitive impulse has been its mainspring. What has given his career its special flavor was the variety of the challenges and the vigor with which he reacted to them. The good fairies endowed him at birth with many extraordinary gifts—too many, perhaps, for his own good. He never subordinated all his faculties to the attainment of one long-range or exclusive goal. He was an actor of many roles but he never completely lived any one. He began as a painter and attained a good measure of achievement. Later he ceased to be a compulsive or dedicated artist: he found other vehicles of expression, such as writing, and the intensity of his communication was to that extent diluted. He went on to other activities and fulfillments as an explorer and world traveler, as an illustrator and editor, as a farmer and builder, a lecturer and public speaker, as a union executive and political figure, and as a fighter for social justice. Rockwell always believed that the living entity is greater than its various achievements ("Vaster is Man than his Work"). It is understandable, therefore, that the artists might not give the supreme accolade to his paintings, nor the writers to his books. It may well be, as a corollary, that his title to immortality will be as a heroic all-around personality—among the later great affirmations of individuality, before mankind sinks to the level of *Massenmensch*. He died in March 1971, within three months of his eighty-ninth birthday.

10

Roderick Seidenberg

My friendship with Roderick Seidenberg dates back to college days. After we left school we continued to see each other: most of my tramping and camping adventures were in his company. He had been enrolled in the Columbia architectural school in 1906 as a young and brilliant scholarship student. He entered at seventeen without having taken the preliminary two years' college course, a special exemption having been made in his case. After Columbia he earned his living as an architectural draughtsman, and eventually advanced to the status of designer. His design for the exterior of the Hotel New Yorker was perhaps his major architectural achievement. Around 1926 he was invited by Ralph Walker to join the firm of Vorhees, Gmelin, and Walker in a designing capacity. The firm had great prestige in the profession, and Roderick knew that if he accepted he woudl have to live and think of nothing but architecture for the rest of his days. By this time, however, he was not sure that architecture was his only vocation. He had discovered other interests in himself, a liking for abstract ideas, a bent for mathematical and philosophical speculation, and an itch to write. He therefore declined his friend's flattering offer, and continued to practice architecture, but without total commitment.

Randolph Bourne and Roderick Seinenberg often met in college and thereafter. Both were devoted to conversation: Roderick enjoyed the clash of minds and Randolph needed the stimulus of new ideas in his writing. They were of different temperaments. Roderick was the more integrated personality. His opinions came from inner convictions: they were basic and did not change. Randolph was more of an intellectual chameleon. He was a professional writer, a publicist in the best sense; he saw issues in terms of their effect, the pragmatic approach. His attitudes changed from time to time. As a matter of fact, in the last years of Randolph's life, he approached Roderick's position on many issues, on absolute opposition to war, for instance.

In August 1914 Roderick and I went on a two-weeks' camping trip in the Adirondacks. When we left civilization there were headlines in the papers about an assassination in Sarajevo. We climbed mountains, explored deserted lumber camps and isolated ponds, avoiding all habitations. When we returned to civilization two weeks later we found all of Europe plunged into war. We talked much about the developments overseas and the issues involved. Roderick felt strongly that conscription was basic to the conduct of war: without conscription war could not exist. He even wrote letters to the *New York Evening Post* on the subject. (He has continued the practice of writing letters to newspapers ever since!) In the summer of 1917, the war was in full swing here also. Roderick was called in the first draft, and in April of 1918 he was sent to Camp Union. He resolved to take his stand as an absolute conscientious objector for political and philosophical reasons. His experience, by reason of his uncompromising stand, reveals most clearly the broad implications of war and conscription and their impact upon the individual. All in all, Seidenberg spent over two years in army barracks and prison—a longer time than military service overseas. He spent weeks on end in a solitary cell on bread

and water, standing nine hours a day with his arms shackled
to the bars. He endured this and other punishments, but the
military authorities could not make him give in. He never
compromised his convictions. He thus might look toward the
future with foreboding, but he could view the past without
shame.

Seidenberg always had a vague impulse to write, but he
had doubts about his ability. His early style was involved and
overwritten, too much hedged in by qualifications, possibly
from reading too much German philosophy. When he saw
the blank paper he stiffened up, feeling that he must say the
last word at all costs. But he kept on trying. He wrote from
the army barracks in Utah in 1919 asking me to send him a
book on the art of writing. When he read it he was disappointed, saying that it was a bit like "feeding your Pegasus
with patent medicine." His style later did become less involved, though it always retained a complex form appropriate to his abstruse and skeptical point of view. He had one
asset that compensated for a paucity of literary graces: he
had ideas—too many sometimes for his own or his readers'
comfort. He always had a respect for style. Even when his deliberate writing was tied up in knots, his letters were relaxed
and well written; his epistolary style had color, idiosyncrasy,
and verve.

One of the organs of publication that afforded Roderick
encouragement, practice, and an outlet was *The Freeman*. The
weekly, edited by Albert J. Nock, had been started shortly
before his release from prison. When he arrived in New
York he discovered it with delight. Here was a magazine really to his liking. It had style and an independent point of
view. It punctured absurd pretensions with humor and irony.
It was concerned with fundamentals—barring a few quirks
such as the Single Tax. It was unashamedly literate but never
pompous. Somehow he got started writing book reviews for
the weekly. The editors seemed to like his work. He wrote
short articles on general topics, which they printed as
editorials—a tacit compliment. He wrote considerable dramatic criticism. One wonders whether the continuance of *The
Freeman* might not have led to a closer association between it

and Seidenberg. Its demise after only four years' existence was felt by all of us to be a real calamity. According to Lewis Mumford, the editors of *The Freeman* told him that they considered Seidenberg one of their promising young authors. *The Freeman* experience in a sense turned Seidenberg into a professional writer.

As the Depression of 1929 gained momentum, he could no longer make a living by architecture. He had saved a little money, and he decided he would spend all his time in writing. He had some ideas he wanted to expound on paper. He had for a long time been concerned with the impact of the machine upon our civilization. As early as 1922 he started a paper on collective organization. He hoped to publish it in *The Freeman*, but it suspended publication before he finished it. He sent the completed manuscript to Bertrand Russell. The latter, however, replied that he did not believe that the threat of organization was a major problem. There are indications that Russell later changed his mind. Seidenberg used to recall an amusing story of a weekend at Art Young's place in Bethel, Connecticut, during the mid-twenties. On a Saturday night Roderick had entertained the company with a long diatribe on the evils of the Machine. Sunday morning, feeling wakeful, he was up before the other guests, and pushed a lawn mower around over the front lawn. Art Young in his nightshirt opened his window and yelled out: "After what you said last night, how dare you use that machine; get right down on your knees and chew the grass off with your teeth!"

The more Roderick thought about the machine and collectivization the more he realized that it was really part of a more fundamental problem—the meaning of organization in the abstract, and its implications for biology and physics, history and sociology. He was fascinated by the challenge posed by Henry Adams in his famous *Letter to the American Teachers of History* over the application of the laws of thermodynamics to the processes of history. He studied Henry Adams's several papers on the subject. His purpose was to analyze his methods and mistaken assumptions, and in addition those of other historians, such as Spengler, who also had tried to find a meaning in history. (His analysis of Toynbee came later.)

Through Dr. G. V. Hamilton, the research analyst, he received a grant of one thousand dollars to enable him to write a book. On September 8, 1932, he wrote Dr. Hamilton a long report. The synopsis he enclosed was the germ of the book *Post-Historic Man,* published eighteen years later. In the interval, he worked on it during whatever leisure he could spare from earning his living. He did a vast amount of reading—in physics, mathematics, thermodynamics, biology, evolution, history, and related subjects—all the data he needed to corroborate and reinforce his lines of argument. He wanted to make sure that his premises were correct and unassailable. Upon those he would build his argument by means of strict logic. He revised and expanded the original outline. He added new sections, new insights; he discarded ideas that would not hold up under criticism. I wish to stress above all the long and careful gestation of his ideas. The book is not an idle, armchair speculation: his conclusions were arrived at doggedly and reluctantly. It was literally a life's work—an objective critique of our civilization. During these years Roderick and I had many discussions about his thesis. I recall that he and I took a walk along the Hudson on Thanksgiving Day 1932. It was then that he told me of his new insight, namely, that the growth of intelligence is not a phase of history, but that on the contrary the emergence of history is a step in the growth of intelligence. It was a brilliant generalization—perhaps the most startling of his many speculations.

The book was finally finished in 1945 and was accepted by Harry Hatcher, American editor for the Oxford University Press. Some time after the manuscript had been delivered and the contract signed, Harry Hatcher had a falling-out with the Oxford University Press and resigned. Action on the book dragged; polite inquiries regarding its progress were answered evasively. Finally, after a delay of over a year —galling to any author, but doubly so to a person of Roderick's temperament—there was a showdown in the office of the Press. Apparently any acceptance by the erstwhile editor was suspect, and the officials of the Press had sent the manuscript to another reader for evaluation. They proceeded to read to Seidenberg the report. They did not give the reader's name, but he saw the words Columbia University on the letterhead, and he suspects that the reader was one of those sociological historians whose research consists of interviews with people, and to whom any speculative approach was anathema. It was a scathing and devastating report: it started out by saying "Any high school graduate could have written a book as good as this," and concluded with: "Only a crackpot could ask the kind of questions asked in this book." "Under the circumstances, etc., etc.," said the officials. But Roderick refused to be intimidated, and cited the obligations of a contract. They countered: "True, we are bound by contract to publish the book, but there is no specific date in the contract; the date is indefinite and might remain so." Upon a threat of a suit in September 1946, the Oxford Press paid him one thousand dollars to release them from the obligation to publish the book. It was a gratifying award, though it did not really make up for the humiliation and delay. Two whole years had passed and still the manuscript had not found its way into print.

There was an amusing sequel to the Oxford University Press affair—one of those odd coincidences which sometimes occur. In 1953 when the announcement appeared that Seidenberg had been awarded a Guggenheim Fellowship, an enterprising junior editor at the Oxford Press wrote to congratulate him on his award and to express the hope that he would allow the Press to see the manuscript he was to write on his grant. The young editor obviously was not aware of what had happened earlier. Roderick was gracious; after recapitulating his experience with the Press, he ended up by saying that he would be glad to submit the manuscript, but he warned that for this book he would charge the Press two thousand dollars for the privilege of breaching the contract.

After the Oxford Press debacle, Roderick started submitting the manuscript to other publishers. It was a depressing, time-consuming business, for each publisher took a long time to decline. The duplicate copy of the manuscript, however, elicited cordial and encouraging response from Lewis Mumford, Waldo Frank, and Reinhold Niebuhr. Finally Roderick wrote me that the work had been definitely accepted by the University of North Carolina Press, and it was formally published on September 30, 1950. The dust-jacket comments were by the three writers mentioned above, and by the Nobel laureate, Herman J. Muller, and by myself. Here is my comment, which was abreviated in the printing:

> This truly challenging book, by reason of its abstruse and subtle style, demands great concentration on the part of the reader; but his rewards are correspondingly great, for its interpretations give a new if somewhat disturbing meaning to daily events in science, art, and religion. With tough-minded logic and almost extra-terrestrial detachment, the author gauges the inevitable drift of our civilization into the future. His analysis of the concept of man's individuality, his evaluation of the implications of organization, and his vision of a post-historic era (a term coined by him) are breathtaking in boldness and brilliance of speculation. Few will accept, many will reject the startling conclusions proposed by the author; but there is no reader whose outlook will not be modified in some way by the study of this seminal book.

The critical reception of the book was disappointing. There were favorable reviews by Prof. Crane Brinton and Waldo Frank, and a shallow, patronizing critique by Prof. Robert Strausz-Hupé, the *riposte* of "the Establishment" in the historical field. The *London Times Literary Supplement* gave it a serious notice, but the *New York Times Book Review* did not review it at all. It was generally ignored—it was not even worth castigating. In a way this neglect was understandable. The author was unknown: he had no academic connections, no standing as a writer or historian. In a milieu where publicity and advertisement count for so much, he should not have spent almost thirty years in a disinterested quest for truth and perfection; he should have devoted more time and energy to building up his reputation. It was naive of him to believe that his book—bristling with ideas though it was--would obtain a hearing by its own intrinsic virtues. It could, however, serve as a gold mine for little minds to quarry from, and not always with due credit. The opus nonetheless had a few champions, notably Lewis Mumford, who tried to spread the word. Crane Brinton, ten years later, in *The American Scholar* cited *Post-Historic Man* as the most neglected book published in the last twenty-five years.

Post-Historic Man did, however, bring about one tangible benefit to its author; it was largely instrumental in obtaining a Guggenheim Fellowship for Seidenberg in 1953. Through the opportunity furnished by the grant, Roderick, not without some delay and travail of authorship, wrote and eventually published late in 1960 his second book, *Anatomy of the Future*. The reviews again were meager; and again a few isolated champions appeared, such as Prof. Hugh Wilson of Princeton and Prof. Paul Tillit of Rutgers. The few other reviews generally were vicious, usually with some references to the author as a psychopath. It is curious, indeed almost incomprehensible, that his two books should have drawn upon themselves such venomous attacks, even to the extent where critics stooped to innuendos about the author's character. Why the vindictive bitterness about a study that is quite impersonal about a purely abstract matter? Equally incomprehensible is the neglect, the conspiracy of silence to which his thesis has been subjected. Why did not someone demolish his arguments instead of ignoring them? Owing to the nature of the problem, only the physicists and biologists, and possibly the sociologists and historians are in a position to controvert his analysis. I, who am not trained in any of these disciplines, can speak only for those who are concerned with the individual and with human and cultural values. As an individualist I look with apprehension at the acceleration toward collectivization of the world over, and therefore welcome the widest possible discussion of the problem and any feasible solution. Of course, there have been crises in the world before, just as there have always been people who view them with alarm. But this crisis is different, as Seidenberg pointed out—at least to my satisfaction. Seidenberg was a humanist at heart, but he was also enough of a realist to be aware that humanist values are being more and more ignored and repudiated today.

The Anatomy of the Future seems a bit more readable than the first book because the treatment seems less abstract. In the earlier chapters he recapitulates, to a certain extent, the main points of his hypothesis that the history of man is bound up in the conflict between instinct and intelligence, that organization is a function of intelligence, that its expansion is accelerated by our complex machine technology and the population explosion, and that mankind is destined to follow an apparently irreversible course leading to the complete collectivization of human society and the consequent suppression of the individual. In other chapters there are reflections on such topics as modern art, the concept of time, the contribution of Sigmund Freud, the implications of predictability, paradox and mystical expression, nuclear annihilation, the perimeters of the future, and the fallacy of organizing to combat organization. All of these ideas are pertinent to any estimate of our present social structure and its implications for the future. One would hope that the ideas might arouse some concern, not necessarily among the heedless masses but certainly among a responsible minority. But how can one penetrate through the barriers of ignorance and apathy to strike the chord of a common humanity? One of the difficulties is due to the breakdown of communication. Our vehicles of information and dissemination—electronic speech and the written word—have been expanded into universal scope and almost instantaneous dispatch, but because they are directed almost entirely toward the sensationalism of the moment, they tend to distort and even suppress other ideas of more serious and humane import, considerations of moral and global responsibility, sober reflections on the meaning of life in the past and the future.

I have gone to some length in projecting the background and vicissitudes of Seidenberg's studies of the present and future in the hope that that author and especially his ideas may become better known. He had always been reticent about personal affairs and indifferent to personal publicity. Nonetheless, he was concerned that his abstract ideas be understood by the world at large, and if possible be accepted. He found it hard to realize that abstract ideas seldom can speak for themselves without the aid of personality. He did have personality, of a peculiarly charming kind, but it was apt to shine more in the circle of his intimates. His conversation could be highly diverting, filled with original and amusing turns of speech and spiced with wit and humor. Like all creators, he was nervous and restless when not involved in a project; his active mind had to be occupied, if not in work, then in talk, scrabble, or chess. On the big and abstract issues, of course, his mind was keen and his judgment sound. And likewise in architecture he was alert and practical, through training, if for no other reason.

His inventive mind would occasionally come up with some eminently practical and far-reaching ideas. In chess, for instance, it is well known that the potentialities of the game have been almost exhausted and codified by the great masters. Various suggestions have been offered for changing the rules to rejuvenate the game. One of the most popular solutions—namely, to add another row of squares to the board—has the disadvantage of rendering all other chess boards obsolete and therefore entailing considerable expense. Roderick's suggestion was merely to transpose the positions of the knight and bishop—a move that would necessitate an entirely new strategy of play.

He also had a bright idea for a major relief project during the Depression, namely, to convert our units of measurement, the pound, the foot, and the like, to the metric system. It is a conversion that the country sooner or later must face; the longer the delay, the greater the cost. The Depression would have been the ideal time to accomplish the turnover, since industry was at its lowest ebb. The actual conversion on all documents, books, and machines in the country would have required the services of a vast number of people in a constructive enterprise, the worth of which nobody could deny. But he could not find a receptive ear.

Still another constructive idea was concerned with the site of the United Nations complex of buildings. In 1946, when various solutions were being proposed, Roderick suggested Blackwell's or Welfare Island in the East River as a possible site. It had much to recommend it. There was ample room for building and future development. It was owned by the city, which could transfer it to the UN by a simple procedure, and thereby avoid huge outlays for ground at inflated real-estate values. It was occupied only by a hospital which could have been easily moved elsewhere. The island site was also a tangible symbol of extraterritoriality. Roderick called up Ralph Walker to see if the American Institute of Architects would give the idea some publicity, but he met with an indifferent response. Lewis Mumford, hearing about it when it was too late, thought it would have been a splendid solution of the UN problem. The body politic, however, seldom listens to the counsels of perfection.

I could continue to discuss other aspects of Seidenberg's thinking, for example, his reflections on Jewish culture, and to relate other events in his career, such as his experiences as a conscientious objector, as the supervising architect for a housing project built by Americans in Moscow in 1929, as the editor in chief of the art and architecture sections of the American State Guides issued by the Writers' Project of the WPA, not to mention his experiences later in conducting preceptorial seminars at Princeton, Sarah Lawrence, Rutgers, and elsewhere, and his participation in symposia at the Wenner Grenn Foundation and the Center for the Study of Democratic Institutions. Such matters, however, could best be told in a more detailed exposition of his life and thought than is possible here. I shall merely say that our amicable intercourse, the relaxed give and take between friends, was stimulating and gratifying to both of us for over sixty years. He died in his eighty-third year on August 27, 1973.

11

Ridgely Torrence

My acquaintance with the poet Ridgely Torrence lasted but a few years. I cannot therefore say that I knew him well, but I doubt if any one did, except possibly his wife, Olivia Howard Dunbar. One could never penetrate the gentle but nevertheless effective barrier of reserve; one could only speculate as to what lay beyond, in the way of exquisite sensibility and creative fervor, or lack of it. As a poet his reputation seemed to be taken for granted. He was not prolific and I was never able to find or read much of his poetry.

In social intercourse he was a delightful conversationalist. There was a fascinating art to his narration, a subtlety of selection and suggestion, an air of candor and restraint, nay, even a sense of deliberately minimizing the wonder of his tale—yet how he stretched and strained the props of credulity! When listening to his stories, I found it an intriguing game to try to distinguish where reality ended and fancy began. It was not that the substance of his tale passed the bounds of probability, but that the coincidence of attendant details almost staggered belief. It is a pity that an evocation so unique and charming should be cast in such an ephemeral form, and exist only as a personal recollection, and in the end vanish completely. I remember once, when I visited him at the MacDowell Colony at Peterborough, that he showed me a deadly *Amanita* by the roadside. He rhapsodized about its white and sepulchral beauty, its shy virginal purity, the symbolism of its death cup. He discoursed at length on its properties and history, how the minutest particle, if eaten, meant certain death, how man with all his knowledge and science has never been able to devise an antidote, how it was the favorite expedient of the Borgias, and how much havoc they wrought with that unobtrusive but deadly mushroom.

In a different vein, he once wrote me:

> So you are at Monhegan. I was one of the early settlers, but I have not been there for nine years. In fact I am one of the ancient bards of the island. Did you never hear me chant the *Saga of Cass Bracket and the Horse Mackerel?* Or *Ed Bracket and the Miraculous Draft of Sword Fish?* Ask some of the islanders about the ancient tales. They will give you the facts, but of course none but I, and one other ancient minstrel, John Alden of Portland, can sing the mighty songs. And even I am not so great as John Alden. Dan, the Lighthouse Keeper, may have a saga built around him some day, but at present his story lacks the heroics which charge the exploits of the others.

He would tell droll stories, sometimes spiced with a touch of malice, for instance, when he told about Mabel Dodge at the beginning of her interest in Tony Luhan, the Taos Indian. Because Tony was married, delicate negotiations had to be completed before he could leave the Pueblo and live with Mabel. Torrence summed it up: "And so Mabel rented Tony from his Indian wife for so much per month." Even more malicious was his story about Mary Austin. She was asked how she felt after she had completed her book on *The Man Jesus*. She became starry-eyed as she answered, "I had such a lonely feeling."

Torrence was a pacifist, a genuine nonresistant, one of the few I have ever known, one in whom the instinct was ingrained beyond relapse. For him in wartime, the country and the times were out of joint, and he would speak of going into voluntary exile in the spirit of the noble philosophers of old. I never dared to ask him to what place he would retire in our era of global involvement. I published a fable by him with a Christian-pacifist slant, entitled *What Became of Jack the Giant Killer* in the November and December issues of *The Modern School* in 1917, Torrence related that after Jack had killed the giants he went on to perform other good works. In due course a new giant problem began to develop, for Jack had overlooked a few who were asleep during his crusade, and now they were throwing their weight around. As a result of his adventures in pursuit of the new giants, he gained the startling insight that the giants were vicious because they were frustrated and prevented from doing what they really wanted to do. If their troubles could be cured they would not trouble others. Therefore Jack did not kill them but followed the maxim "Strike at the pain and not at the sufferer," and turned the bad giants into good ones. And presumably he and they lived happily ever after.

While I was editor of the *Modern School Magazine,* Torrence lived at 107 Waverly Place, formerly the home of William Vaughn Moody. Writers and poets would gather there every so often, and Torrence sometimes invited me. My memory is vague about whom I saw there, but I seem to recall Louis Untermeyer (full of energy and puns), Arturo Giovannitti (who had a rhapsodic presence), Edward Sapir (anthropologist and author of a book on Language), William Carlos Williams (affable and unpretentious), and on one occasion, Robert Frost. I did not take any notes, but I did jot down something Frost said, which now seems hardly important enough to record. When I left Greenwich Village and resigned as editor of the *Modern School Magazine,* I began to see more of artists than of poets.

The work by Torrence that has left the most lasting impression upon my memory was his *Three Plays for a Negro Theatre.* Torrence always responded to any suggestion of dumb suffering in bird or beast, and similarly his sensitive imagination entered sympathetically into the inarticulate aspirations of the Negro race toward a better life. The three one-act plays were one of the first instances of drama based on Negro themes and intended for performance by colored people. I remember well the opening night of the production, directed by Robert Edmond Jones, on April 16, 1917. Between the act, J. Rosamund Johnson directed the Clef Club and Chorus in musical interludes arranged by him from Negro spirituals. The opening playlet, *Rider of Dreams,* was a comedy of character, dramatizing a poet and dreamer going astray in a world of harsh and unsympathetic facts. *Granny Maumee* was a tragedy played against a background of race brutality. The tension mounted as blind old Granny Maumee, of royal African blood, left the room to dress herself for the reception of her great-grandson, the first male issue—the intervening generation having been in the female line—who was intended to be the instrument of her revenge for the burning of her son at the stake. She returned as a Voodoo priestess in scarlet, and the frenzy of her exultation carried her back to origins more horrible than are glimpsed in our civilized life. When the infant was presented to her, second sight came to her and with it disillusionment, for the babe was white, the product of a white man's rape. She proceeded with the incantation of revenge, but in the end the Galilean conquered and she died breathing forgiveness.

In the musical prologue to the final play, a faint singing was heard that gradually swelled into the magnificent chorus of *Walk Together Children.* Its sweet and haunting cadence invoked the mood of the Christian martyrs marching to their doom in the Roman Circus. The drama took place on the day of the Crucifixion and told the story of the Passion of Simon the Cyrenian, an African prince. He was prepared to lead an insurrection and rescue Jesus from martyrdom. Persuaded by a vision that Christ's ministry was not of this world, he renounced violence and took up his Master's Cross. I discussed the plays with a number of Negroes at the time. They all deprecated Granny Maumee's raising the issue of race hatred. The pendulum has swung far in the last fifty years!

In connection with a change of attitude among the Afro-Americans, I am reminded of a conversation I once had with Paul Robeson concerning Negro spirituals. Negroes, he said, were turning away from the spirituals as too passive and pacifist an expression of racial aspirations. The new mood was more militant and could be expressed only in the more strident tones of the blues or jazz. His own voice was not suited to the blues and he regretted that he could not thereby give voice to the new temper. Paul Robeson is a forgotten man today, yet in my estimation he was a noble and gifted man. As a singer of spirituals and of Earl Robinson's *Ballad for Americans*, he was unsurpassed. His performance in the title roles of *The Emperor Jones* and of *Othello* will never be forgotten by those fortunate enough to have had the experience. He was a courageous and tireless spokesman for justice and the enfranchisement of his race.

12

John B. Flannagan

There is a theory about the origin of art that is exemplified by the oyster that creates the pearl. Art—in this case the pearl——comes about through irritation and pain and suffering. Heinrich Heine put it in another way when he wrote: "out of my great anguish, I make little songs." If the theory has any plausibility, it is borne out in the life of John B. Flanagan. Out of his pain and woe he created pearls of great price.

He had a tragic life. Since he was so secretive about his origins and early life, it is pointless to dredge up all the painful details. One need merely say that he spent a most unhappy childhood in one institution after another, always with an ominous feeling of fleeing from harassment. He who so desperately craved security was deprived almost entirely of a mother's solicitude and care. This unhappy experience helped to harden his attitude toward life. He became his own worst enemy. Because he was more than cruel to himself, he could be cruel to those who loved him. And yet he was so vulnerable, so easily hurt. Only a Dostoevsky could adequately portray the complexities of his psyche or enumerate the malign forces that frustrated his daily life. Alcohol was the chief villain of his personal drama. He turned to it for support and security, but it was a treacherous crutch, for it turned him into a pathetic but disgusting beast. The descent into the depths was periodic but temporary: he also ascended to superb heights of creation. And there were times when he could be relaxed and normal, a witty and amusing talker, a delightful companion. He had a keen mind and was more than a match for several analysts who tried to "straighten him out." He knew enough of the professional jargon to lead them astray. One of them asserted confidently that John would never commit suicide: he was not the type. It turned out that the doctor was wrong. John had had two operations for brain tumor, which left him in a condition where he could no longer engage in strenuous stone cutting. When the malignancy continued and a third operation was in prospect, John felt that he had had enough. Thus his life unfolded to a tragic denouement.

His art was not tragic: it was pure and self-contained, profound yet simple. Flannagan once described his credo in a letter:

> My aim is to produce sculpture as direct and swift in feeling as drawing—sculpture with such ease, freedom, and simplicity that it hardly seems carved but rather to have endured so always. This accounts for my preference for field stone: its very rudeness seems to me more in harmony with simple direct statement. There are often necessary compromises, but the shape of the stone does not determine the design; more often the design dictates the choice of the stone. I would like my sculpture to appear as rocks, left quite untouched and natural and, as you have said, inevitable. Such qualities of humor or the grotesque or whatever may be found therein, are for the most part accidental and subordinate to a conception purely sculptural.

In the above he hints at one of the two central themes he once elaborated to me in conversation as being dominant in his attitude—a passion for anonymity. The work itself, and not the artist, was important; the ultimate end, and not the instrument. The work was enduring and timeless, the artist merely human and temporal. Why should there be this modern cult of the so-called creator; do we know who *created* Egyptian or Assyrian sculpture, who carved the Cathedral of Chartres?

> In the Middle Ages the unknown man carved the numberless statues of Romanesque and Gothic cathedrals, and covered chapel and refectory walls with unsigned frescoes. But with the approach to modern times, when the stupid craze for signatures came in, the unknown man ceased his activity and was content to rest. An immense throng of vain fellows, of men who had a name or sought to make a name, began to paint, invent, carve, write. They had less genius than the unknown man and they also had less modesty; they proclaimed to all the winds that they, and none but they, had done these things. They worked not only for their own joy or for other's benefit, but that the world might know that they, and none but they, had done the work.

Very few of Flannagan's sculptures are signed except insofar as they are signed all over. He was medieval in his disinterested and truly mystical passion for humility and anonymity. St. Francis of Assisi was one of his great heroes. He undoubtedly would have felt at home in the Middle Ages, and he might perhaps have led a happier life in the age of universal faith.

The other theme he stressed was what he called the philosophy of pity. This philosophy also had reverberations in his personal life, but in his art it was related to his sympathy for all living things, particularly the humbler animals (St. Francis again)—his *feeling into* whatever subject he approached, "the intense feeling of identification," as he put it, "with which I take up each stone to work upon it." Or, as he wrote in his notes: "Embrace all living forms, each for its plastic adjustment to a theme—living for warmth. No narcissistic worship of humanity—contra, the stately dignity of the Mountain Goat, the ironic pensiveness of the apparently thoughtful Monkey, and (in his greater moments) the timeless yet rebellious patience of the Ass." There is an all-too-human logic in this attitude, which he subtly analyzed in *The Image in the Rock:* "Many of the humbler life forms are often more usable as design than the narcissistic human figure, because humanly we project ourselves into all art works using the human figure, identifying ourselves with the beauty, grace, or strength of the image as an intense wish-fulfillment;

and any variant, even when necessitated by design, shocks as maimed, and produces some psychological pain. With an animal form, on the contrary, any liberty taken with the familiar forms is felt as amusing—strange cruelty."

His work was executed with unbelievable intensity. When the fury of creation descended on him—and it really was creation, for he never copied from a model—he worked quite literally night and day without a pause. "Creation is revelation," he said. The physical labor of direct carving, intense and exhausting though it may be, was merely the stripping away of extraneous material, revealing the image that he had projected in the rock. There was no floundering around in conception or execution. His aesthetic intuitions were immediate and absolute, and his hand with practiced cunning made them concrete. But there were fallow periods, and they were the very bane of his existence. He who had such spiritual need for certainty, fell prey to devastating uncertainty and doubt. He would lose faith in himself, his past work, and his future inspiration. He would fall into the depths of despair, an awful inchoate dread, the dark night of the soul. In this vein he once wrote me: "This past summer has been one of constant strain—a tension that has kept me drawn as taut as a violin string. Believe me I am trying but I am not always successful. Always I am seeing with the vividness of an hallucination the wraith-like figure of a child that seems irrevocably lost; and the only way I see to dissipate my own feeling of being equally lost myself is to give you a show expressing everything I have to say just now. After that I'm safe." "All artists," he said on another occasion, "are close to madness; it is their art that keeps them sane." In another mood, however, he could write serenely:

I feel like a different person. It was a case of going stale before I left, but now I find there is still something eager left in me—so much so, that I don't even feel the need of a drink any more, but feel more intensely just one steady abiding purpose—such as it is—to make images out of rock. There is here a certain quiet I have sought for a long time. There is peace in the unhurried and simple existence of life here, so that I, in relishing it, feel out of place in the highly mechanized drift of our time, and have found where I belong.

Paradoxically enough, Flannagan was both apart from and of his time. He stood apart from it in that he was essentially a mystic and not a time-server, in that he aligned himself with spirit rather than mechanism. He was modern by reason of his intelligent and profound grasp of the problems of the artist today. What he admired about the Middle Ages was the functional relation, the give and take between the aritst and society and between art and architecture. Today, he felt, both these relations were to a large extent ignored. He saw the necessity of reestablishing these values. In his application for his Guggenheim Fellowship in 1931, he cited as one of his chief aims a study of the "coordination of sculpture and architecture as expressed notably in 13th Century Gothic, the ultimate purpose being the simplification of sculptural design and structure so as to be effective in the severe architectural scheme prevailing now." And in a note more recently written: "Just as all really effective art has been an expression of the psyche of its time, so the simplification prevalent in the best contemporary art is quite in step with the severity of our architecture. It would seem also that the very austerity of that architectural style necessarily demands discreet sculptural relief, (i.e. support)."

He was always interested in the application of sculpture to building; but, not knowing the right people, he never really had a chance to put his ideas into practice. The nearest he came to it was perhaps the *Design for a Skyscraper Court*—the big *Mother and Child*, now in the Fogg Art Museum. He made the design for Rockefeller Center at the instigation of Diego Rivera. When Rivera became *persona non grata*, Flannagan's design also went into the discard. Nonetheless, Flannagan decided to execute it on a large scale. It is illuminating to cite his analysis of the problems involved in a monumental sculpture to be placed in a court surrounded by high buildings. Since it was a statue in the round, he reasoned, it must necessarily be designed to compose well from every angle where it would be seen from the ground, but beyond that it would be seen from above from many windows in the adjacent skyscrapers. Therefore it must be designed to function or compose well from every angle above as well as on the

ground. This complicated set of conditions he solved trium-
phantly in what is in my opinion one of the most important
sculptural monuments in America today.

He was modern, too, in his consistent preoccupation with
abstraction. It was always fundamental in design, but he
fused and modified it with other factors. "Pure abstraction is
dead," he said;

> make it come alive by the use of living form. Warm the cold
> geometry of abstraction with a naturalism in which the superfi-
> cial and accidental have been eliminated by their union with
> pure form. A withdrawing from the too close view of things in
> order to see them in their atmospheric content. Use abstraction
> to achieve a finality, but, in humanizing it with immediacy, retain
> it always in a stateof becoming, rather than being. A thing
> should never be finished—should rather always be in a state of
> *becoming* (no end: an evasion or overcoming of time), completed
> each according to his own psyche by whoever has eyes to see.
> Use the apparently accidental to avoid formal hardness and the
> spontaneous to avoid emotional hardness. A fine composition
> has the calm ordered elation of a mathematical solution, instead
> of mock-heroics or maudlin-nostalgic-associational emotionalism.

It is obvious that with such a profound conception of the
basis of art, consistently avoiding any formula or superficial
mannerism, Flannagan could be only a lone creator and
never the founder of a school. Yet, as has happened with
John Marin, imitators have managed to discover a bag of
surface tricks without ever penetrating to the animating spirit
within. Thus Flannagan has not been without influence as a
pioneer of direct carving in America.

He was no escapist. Long ago he spoke of "disciplining myself to think and see and feel so naturally as to escape the
precious or the esoteric. My aim is the achievement of a
sculpture that should fulfill a definite function in the social
consciousness of many instead of a limited few." He accepted
the realities of today, science, social consciousness, and the
like. Escapism he associated with the romantic attitude and
he abhorred it. "Science honest—Romance evasion and dishonest. Honesty liberates, cutting away romance and
sentiment—deals with hard realities instead of dead
moralities and high sentimental purities." In a letter to Curt

Valentin enclosing the manuscript of the *Image in the Rock,* he wrote: "Here is my credo—some weekend reading—I hope it reads well—it has clarity for those who make the effort toward intelligence. For the others, the Escapists, have their comic strip and Walt Disney. This statement has nothing of that *flight from reality,* the *romantic,* and neither have I." His work was always keyed to the sculptural needs of today: over-life-size statues, when he had the opportunity (and the *Mother and Child* at Cambridge and the *Gold Miner* at Philadelphia demonstrate with what success he solved the problems of plastic monumentality); sculpture designed for gardens and the out of doors, and small pieces designed for the home. Since he was working for the general public and not for artists exclusively, he chose themes of general appeal. The design, the sculptural form, was of course fundamental with him, but he vitalized it with living subject matter. Over and above the tactile organization of his lines, planes, and masses, there seems to brood the mystery and glamor of a living thing. Thus he created character and psychological values as well as aesthetic forms.

Flannagan had an unusually developed plastic sense, a preconception of three-dimensional form. In a way he was a sculptors' sculptor, for only they can truly appreciate the daring and rightness of his simplification of planes, the solidity of his masses, and the inner logic of his forms. He was a great technician. His knowledge of the idiosyncrasies of wood and stone and metal, or the mechanics of the sculptor's craft, was unsurpassed. But he had gone far beyond mere technique, which he called "hardness—the display of obvious skill and an overdone imitation of the surface aspects of reality." He believed in understatement, a disdain of ostentatious skill or manual facility. He once wrote, "It takes an artist to be a really good craftsman; all that these shop-trained guys know, are things one *can't do;* but we artists say *can do* with imagination."

"Thinking with his hands," as he used to call it, he could in other respects be more receptive to psychological overtones, promptings of the unconscious, suggestions of age-old dreams and fantasies. He has described one such instance as the Dragon Myth. In the following note he alludes to the *Design for a Skyscraper Court:* "As a boy I very rarely saw my mother, and I think that the whole psychological story of what that means to a child is implied in this piece, which is a consistent architectonic statement as well."

He was a searching observer of nature. Endowed with a tenacious visual memory, he would require but a glance or two at an object to add its structure to his wide knowledge of human and animal forms. He never worked directly from a model. If he ever used a model it was for study and practice to keep his hand in. On such occasions he would pose the model for a minute or two, walking around her and observing intently, and then say that is enough. Once when this happened, the model was found later in the kitchen washing the dishes and saying that she wanted to earn her fee somehow. He grasped, intuitively perhaps, and he managed to convey in his work, the essential nature, the significant gesture of an animal, the cattiness of a cat, the dogginess of a dog, the womanliness of a woman. His drawings have this same rightness and precision of simplification. But apropos of drawing, he once wrote: "Preparatory drawing seems much like doing one's thinking on paper and then carving the conclusion. I prefer to think the thing out first and last in stone or the medium for which it was intended."

Flannagan had an innate feeling for style. It was apparent in his talk and in his writing, which often had an epigrammatic quality. But it was most evident in his art. He sensed the scope and limitations of sculpture and worked within them. Sculpture is an austere art, one that requires mature planning and sustained effort in its execution. Therefore he chose themes of a generalized, universal, and symbolic nature—woman, man, child, animals. Furthermore, there are distinctions between the various branches of sculpture: carving or the art of cutting away in wood or stone; modeling or the art of accretion in clay; chasing or the art of working metal. Their forms and conventions are different, and he respected them. The great bulk of his work was in direct stone carving, but he also worked in wood at the beginning and in metal toward the end of his sculptural career, when he could no longer work in stone on account of his illness. His name is so closely associated with achievement in stone carving that it might be well to quote two passages showing his approach to metal working. The first is an analysis of the bronze *Rag Doll:*

> I have used a smooth finish in order to emphasize the form, and because it is truer to the character of the metal. Bronzes lately seem a little inclined to a tricky clay texture. An obvious contradiction. Finally the theme itself demanded, I felt, a suave touch. The doll is introduced principally to enrich the linear composition by allowing a bit of the grotesque to dramatize the charm of the childish figure. Further, the juxtaposition of the child and this inanimate shapeless mass of the doll, should vivify the main phase of the motif—the child. The work should feel easy, unstudied, and natural; carried out definitely within the limits of an utilizing to the utmost the quality peculiar to the material used.

> I am quite excited over developing this method of doing things in metal. It's so artistically right when the artist himself can carry his work on through the various processes alone. It's pretty definitely certain that I can do things about the size of those small bronzes that Maillol has done—say six or eight inches tall. I'm using silver just now because it's easy to handle. I'm experimenting with various silver alloys—working for color—it's handsome stuff and I hope to carry on with brass and aluminum as well. Bronze may be too difficult without equipment for it.

He also was interested in combining metal and stone.

Flannagan had artistic integrity. There was no dross of imitation or secondhand feeling in his work. He often spoke of "a realism of feeling rather than a painting or carving of realism." In this sense his sculpture was pure and unalloyed. He was one of the most original of modern sculptors: he revealed very little outside influence. Every one of his pieces was conceived from within, and grew into an organic and self-contained whole. He never worked with an eye to fashion or the main chance. For ever ten pseudo-artists who function only because conditions are favorable (politics or bally-hoo), and because there are other creators whom they can imitate or capitalize on—for every ten of these, there is one artist who can not help being an artist under any conditions, no matter in what age or country he was born. Flannagan was one of those rare artists.

As a sculptor Flannagan was self-taught. He studied painting for three years at the Minneapolis Institute of Art, working his way by typing and odd jobs. Among his fellow pupils at the time were Adolf Dehn, Wanda Gág, Arnold Blanch, and Harry Gottlieb. In New York he worked for a while as a night watchman, and also shipped to sea as an able-bodied seaman. He worked for a year on the farm of Arthur B. Davies, who encouraged him to go on with his art and offered to stake him to a year's study abroad. Although he tells of early childhood impulses toward sculpture that were frustrated by his environment, it was not until the early 1920s that he actually began to work in a plastic medium. The earliest works were transitional, carved panels and screens, a kind of painting in relief. Some of these were shown, I believe, at Montross and the New Gallery in 1922 and 1923. The earliest wood carving in the round was experimental and tortured, somewhat more linear than plastic in conception. It was around 1926 that he began to find his personal style and work in stone as well as wood. He ceased working in wood after 1928. He exhibited at the Whitney Studio Club and the Whitney Studio Gallery every year from 1925 to 1930, and it was there that he had his first one-man show. He had shows at the Weyhe Gallery in 1927, 1928, 1930, 1931, 1934, 1936, 1938, and at the Buchholz Gallery in 1942. He went to Ireland in 1930-31, and again in 1932-33 as a Guggenheim Fellow. The rest of the time he spent in this country. In 1935 he finished the large *Mother and Child* now in the Fogg Museum and in 1939 he completed his other monumental piece, the *Gold Miner* in Philadelphia. In 1934 he started working in metal, and continued to apply himself off and on until his death in January 1942.

Flannagan did not work in the Graeco-Roman tradition. He despised it, especially in its later Salon manifestations; and he once delivered a lecture in which he demonstrated, to his own satisfaction at least, that sculpture does not consist solely of ideal figures, sweetly modeled and smoothly polished. His work belongs rather to the great anonymous plastic tradition, the art of Egypt and China, of pre-Columbian America, and of Romanesque and Gothic Europe. He would have liked nothing better than to have had his work merge in this great nameless tradition, but it seems more than likely that his desire for anonymity will not be granted him. In his notes on the Unknown Man who carved the Romanesque and Gothic cathedrals, from which I have already quoted above, Flannagan continued as follows: "In our public squares we behold—unfortunately—numberless equestrian and pedestrian statues of men who have merely written a tiresome tragedy or given a lucky sabre-thrust. The Greeks had at least the profound and prudent idea of raising an altar to the Unknown God. Should not we forgetful moderns erect a monument to the Unknown Man?" Flannagan's oeuvre might well be considered as a monument to one Unknown Man.

13

Marcel Duchamp

Marcel Duchamp was the enfant terrible of modern art, the Dad of Dada, and the Grandpappy of Pop. He achieved notoriety in America at the Armory Show and also perpetrated some of the most sardonic spoofs or hoaxes ever made in art history, from the "urinal affair" to his final legacy. His influence on modern art has not yet been completely explored. He anticipated numerous trends in the current outlook of art today.

I first met him in the 1920s through Walter Pach, as I recollect. It must have occurred before Duchamp's prank with the Society of Independent Artists, which seemed to me to have been designed especially to get Walter's goat. Walter Pach, who was very earnest and ponderous about "art" and also very proper about morals, was an officer of the Society, which had been founded to provide exhibition facilities to anyone, without restriction or censorship. Marcel submitted a procelain urinal as a piece of sculpture under the pseudonym of "R. Mutt" for exhibition in the Annual. He thereby put to test the Society's slogan of no censorship, and created a scandal that almost broke up the Society. The piece was rejected, and some of the executive board resigned.

Many of Duchamp's actions—quite apart from his deliberately Dada experiments—were baffling and enigmatic. For instance, after he had been painting for only a few years, he announced that he was through with art and would paint no more. His early work, to be seen in the Arensberg collection, shows little aptitude for painting: it was really quite mediocre and banal. Then suddenly—overnight as it were—he changed to the cubist style for which he became famous. Thereafter, having produced a series of masterpieces in quick succession, he broke off at the height of his powers, in order to spend his time playing chess and devising a method to break the bank at Monte Carlo. He disappeared from the painting scene. Occasionally pictorial reports of his leisure activities would appear. John Sloan made an etching of a picnic party that Sloan, Duchamp, and other madcap friends had surreptitiously arranged on the top of Washington Arch in Washington Square. Florine Stettheimer painted several picnic scenes that included Marcel as a merry participant. Incidentally, Marcel also executed several miniature paintings for Carrie Stettheimer's famous Doll House. One could not help wondering why he gave up a successful painting career to flirt with triviality.

After Duchamp had stopped painting in oil, he did make some elaborate studies for a kind of painting or construction on huge sheets of glass, culminating in the work entitled *The Bride Surrounded by her Bachelors, Even.* He was struggling with a new concept: painting not to be looked at but to be seen through. His object apparently was to do away with the canvas plane of a painting by making it transparent, thus allowing the sparse forms—predominantly linear and in perspective—to float freely in space. The Big Glass and one of the smaller studies were purchased by Walter Arensberg. When he moved to California, he was afraid that the glass might be broken or damaged in transit. He therefore gave or sold it to Katherine Dreier. She lent it on one occasion to the Museum of Modern Art, and, sure enough, it was damaged in transit. One area was cracked, fortunately not broken, but nonetheless the illusion of transparency was destroyed by a raylike pattern of cracks. Duchamp, always ready to play up the creative possibilities of chance, claimed in a Dada *beau geste* that the work was not ruined but much improved. At her death Katherine Dreier left the glass to the Philadelphia Museum of Art, again to become part of the Arensberg collection. There it remains, hopefully never to be moved again.

A number of Duchamp's preliminary studies and sketches for the Big Glass, many of them on odd scraps of paper, were gathered together and carefully reproduced in exact size and shape. The reproductions were assembled in a handsome box and published in a limited edition. A sophisticated cult was beginning to grow around the name of Marcel Duchamp. Since he no longer produced great works, little scraps from his hand became precious. He may not have actively initiated such notions, but with his contempt for contemporary art values, he was not averse to gaining some advantage from them. He lived comfortably and happily upon past glory.

Many years later, in 1954, I had lunch with Marcel Duchamp at the Philadelphia Museum. It was a leisurely lunch and somehow he got around to talking about himself and his point of view. What he said seemed so significant that I jotted down some notes of his conversation in my journal. We started with general talk about modern art and the fantastic prices that were being paid for paintings. Then he went on to speak of himself:

> If I were young, I would not want to be an artist. There is so much confusion now, and so little future. Take cubism for instance: it was great while it was young and new, and there was some mystery in it. Now every layman knows the tricks, and there is no *élan* in it any more. In fifty years there will be no more art except painted decoration in connection with architecture. Such manifestations will be anonymous—what's wrong with anonymity, anyway?—as it used to be in ancient and oriental art. Art, real art, has to have some drive, such as a belief in God or even just a sense of fun. Nowadays even the sense of fun is gone, too.

Marcel had little regard for color reproductions, even Skira's. (I recall that I once consulted him about a color reproduction of one of his paintings, which I considered too inferior to use. He said, "Put it in anyway; it doesn't really matter.") He had no great respect for the younger French painters; as for the old masters of the *École de Paris*, they had already said their say.

It is easy to understand, in view of such disclosures, why he stopped painting so suddenly and completely. He never seems to have enjoyed the satisfactions of the painter's craft, nor felt the spell of sensuous color. Painting was purely an intellectual problem to him. After he had successfully met the challenge, he became bored, and preferred to play chess or engage in other games of the mind. He had a mordant sense of humor. Having come to the conclusion that there was no future to art and painting, he never missed an opportunity to disparage it and undermine its prestige with the public. Hence his impulse to play up the aesthetic significance of "ready mades" (for instance a porcelain urinal as a plastic form) or to establish the validity of an art produced by *fiat* (painting a mustache on a reproduction of the *Mona Lisa* and submitting it to an exhibition as a work of art).

His painting *Nude Descending the Stair Case* is typical of his mature style and is probably his most famous work. The artist's aim no doubt was to delineate successive movements simultaneously, and to impose the whole upon a multifaceted cubist structure. Such a task obviously demanded an intellectual approach and solution. There are three versions of the subject, not including a tiny drawing, the germ of the idea. All four are in the Arensberg collection. The first version, smaller in size than the others, is more cubist than futurist in emphasizing a single figure. The second version expresses fully the original idea and was the one exhibited in the Armory Show. Because it had been bought by F. C. Torrey of San Francisco, Walter Arensberg commissioned Duchamp to make a third version. This he did by taking a full-sized photograph of the second version and adding some brush work in ink and watercolor. Later Arensberg had a chance to buy the second version from the original owner, thus gaining possession of all three paintings.

Later, Marcel's restless mind continued to be innovative only in little things. He played around with typography and designed title pages and slogans (a rose is a rose is a rose). I recall an unusual booklet of essays by Henry McBride that Marcel designed and produced. He came up with an amusing idea. The booklet was in loose-leaf form and was bound together by three rings. The letterpress started out in very small type and gradually grew bigger with each succeeding essay, and ended with one letter filling a whole page. I sold a number of copies for him at the Weyhe Gallery. The Van Pelt Library of the University of Pennsylvania has the copy that he and Henry McBride inscribed to me. Duchamp also had a flair for installing exhibitions. Among other projects, he set up the opening installation of the Arensberg Collection at the Philadelphia Museum of Art. It has since been rearranged.

For many years before his death, Duchamp apparently worked in greatest secrecy on one last fling, another *magnum opus* or final message to posterity. No one knew about it except his wife, and no one else suspected such apsirations in Marcel. After his death, the choice of the most worthy recipient of the great work was announced. The Philadelphia Museum of Art became the lucky institution, largely because so much of his work was already contained there in the Arensberg collection. As it turned out, the work is in the form of a diorama, visible only through two eye-holes or peepholes in a door. The ensemble consists of three-dimensional objects situated in front of a painted scenic background. The chief three-dimensional object is a female nude lying in some grass, executed with the utmost realism and placed in the most alluring position to emphasize her sexual function. The result or aim is to confront the average man unexpectedly with his secret erotic fantasy: the sexual wish that seldom is actually conscious or capable of by-passing the "Censor" into consciousness. Such happenings are bound to produce emotional shock in varying degrees, but only to men, since this *jeu d'esprit* has little significance for women. Duchamp left specific instructions for the set-up of this spectacle. He stipulated that no reproduction of the tableau should ever be made. It must always be seen through the peephole because he counted on the shock of surprise. This was the ultimate *blague,* his final joke: to transform all men into Peeping Toms. No doubt he is chuckling in his grave.

14

Alfred Stieglitz

My association with Alfred Stieglitz began at "291," his gallery on Fifth Avenue, around 1913-1914. My first glimpse of him was under slightly embarrassing circumstances. I had visited an exhibition at his gallery during lunch time. The place was open, but nobody was in attendance. I looked at the show and also at some numbers of *Camera Work* that were lying around. One took my fancy, a Steichen number containing, among other things, a portrait of Anatole France, one of my favorite authors. I wanted to buy it, and decided to take it and leave the money (at the printed price) in its place. As I left the rickety elevator clutching my *Camera Work,* several men were waiting to get on. I had a flash that one of them was Stieglitz, but I was not certain; if he saw me, as I was sure he had, he might suspect that I was walking off with the quarterly until he found otherwise upstairs. In my confusion I hurried off without saying a word.

It turned out that he was Stieglitz, and I talked to him on later visits. I saw, for example, John Marin's New York etch-

ings and expressed my admiration of them. Stieglitz made
much of the fact that someone from the conservative house
of Keppel should like such wild and unorthodox prints. Our
acquaintance gradually ripened into friendship, though I was
never one of the "inner circle." Our entry into the war in
1917 forced the closure of the gallery, thus constricting
Stieglitz's public life to a certain extent. The relative isolation
during the period from 1917 to 1925 (the date of the opening of the Intimate Gallery), was increased by the circumstances of his personal life, his meeting with Georgia O'Keeffe
and the consequent estrangement of his first wife, whose fortune was larger than his own. It was a period of intense creative activity by both Stieglitz and O'Keeffe, an absorption in
each other and a mutual stimulation toward hitherto un-
realized heights and profundities. In addition to a series of
superb portraits, he embarked on a photographic projection
of Woman, all women focused through one, that was unique
in history. She, encouraged by him, revealed unknown facets
of feminine sensibility in what were also extraordinary works
of art. As he said, at last there was an artist who painted as a
woman, not as a man. Although in straitened circumstances,
they felt that they were on the crest of a wave. I remember
that in 1921 Stieglitz sent me from Lake George a tiny
photograph showing the head of a laughing Greek peasant
and a portion of the *Venus de Milo* (from the statue in the
parlor of the family mansion there), with the comment
"Venus is on the job making Art Converts. Long live the Art
Makers!" In the summer they lived at Lake George, in the
winter in two rooms on 59th Street. He told me that he paid
forty-five dollars a month for rent and spent a dollar and a
half a day for food. Later the building was sold, and they
moved to the top floor of his brother Leo's residence on East
65th Street. I continued to keep in touch with Stieglitz during this period and was sometimes invited to see a new crop
of photographs. I remember one such occasion in 1924 when
I brought with me Ananda Coomaraswamy, who wanted to
meet Stieglitz. I recall the scene upstairs in the doctor's
house, and also his characteristic way of showing his photographs. We were seated in front of an empty chair, on which

he leaned a mounted photograph. He would watch us intently to gauge our reaction, then he would try us out with another photograph, standing all the while. He conducted a kind of psychological test, since he knew from previous experience what the reaction to each stimulus was likely to be. We saw many prints that day, for Coomaraswamy's response was discerning and enthusiastic! It was a significant meeting, because it was the beginning of the negotiations that led to the gift of twenty-seven Stieglitz photographs to the Boston Museum of Fine Arts, the first acquisition of his photographs by any museum. Four years later, in 1928, some friends presented a group of his photographs to the Metropolitan Museum in New York. Their acceptance gratified him, but he told me on various occasions that he felt that his photographs were treated with greater care and respect in Boston than in New York.

In 1915 *Camera Work* had published a symposium on the question "What is 291?" Seven years later a similar survey was assembled in the occasional periodical *MSS* under the title "Can a Photograph have the Significance of Art?" I contributed a few paragraphs to it. Stieglitz wrote from Lake George in August of 1922 how hard it was to induce people to make good on their enthusiastic promises. He found my contribution capital and went on to ask if I intended to come to the Lake as I had intimated. "The weather has been rather uninviting for traveling. But you are beyond all weather, undoubtedly."

I did sometimes go to Lake George and the cottage on the "Hill," whenever I could get away for a day or so. I loved the place and the simple regime of country life. Occasionally there would be other guests—I enjoyed getting to know people such as Gustave Eckstein and Becky Salisbury—and once I came up with Wanda Gág, whom Stieglitz and O'Keeffe liked and about whose health they were concerned. But best of all, I liked being alone with the two of them. With him I could talk endlessly, and with her I could ramble happily in the great out-of-doors. O'Keeffe is a complex personality and can express many moods. One of her moods is a simple and unaffected response to nature. Some of the pleasantest memories in my acquaintance with her are of walks with her at Lake George, of the shared exhilaration of physical exertion, of a common delight in things that grow, and of expansiveness of spirit under the great vault of heaven. I have encountered other features of her character with which I did not feel so completely in accord. I therefore treasure my glimpse and experience of the outdoor aspect of her personality. And I believe it was an important element in her total endowment. It must have been active in her early, lonely Texas phase. It did not have much outlet at Lake George. Stieglitz, for all his absorption in clouds and trees, was not an outdoor man. For him nature was a means to an end, not something to be enjoyed for its own sake with animal pleasure. At Lake George, too, there was family—a way of life cut and dried. Once on a later occasion O'Keeffe told me that she had engaged a housekeeper, had given the full responsibility to her and refused to check her bills—to the horror of the family. She had wanted, she continued, to buy a house of her own at the Lake, but in the end decided to get one very far away at Abiquiu in New Mexico. She never could go alone, driving a car for instance, because of his ever-present fear that something might happen to her. Stieglitz always waited up for her return. She remonstrated: but I drive alone in New Mexico. Yes, he replied, but I am not there to wait up for you! At any rate, New Mexico must have given her a chance to be free with nature in her own way.

When I was at Lake George in August of 1924, Stieglitz took some snapshots of me with a Graphlex camera. In reply to my acknowledgement of the receipt of the prints, he wrote:

> Those prints are for you. As tokens of good will. Promisory notes for a *real* portrait some day. I agree with your "criticisms." It was impossible under the conditions—with the camera out of gear too—to do justice to you or myself and above all to photography. These prints are merely very good little photographs as photographs go. O'Keeffe is painting some large canvasses. And I continue on my path. Yes, I have photographed a rainbow."

On the same topic, O'Keeffe had written:

What Stieglitz has said with the snaps of you is very fine
—really beautiful.

Stieglitz's Intimate Gallery in the Anderson Gallery building was active from 1925 to 1929. Then because Mitchell
Kennerly had sold the building, the gallery had to move, and
later was transformed into "An American Place" at 509
Madison Avenue. With his usual procrastination Stieglitz had
left a lot of books and other belongings in the old building.
On the last day of tenancy I went over to bid the old place
goodbye and found Stieglitz in despair. What was he going to
do with all the junk that had to be disposed of before six
o'clock? he was going to give the janitor five dollars to cart it
out to the city dump. The "junk" consisted largely of a reference library on the history and technique of photography,
which he had collected for over half a century together with
bits of memorabilia. I said that the reference library was too
rare and too valuable to be destroyed: I was sure that the
Metropolitan Museum would be glad to have it as a gift, and
offered to store the books until the negotiations could be
completed. Stieglitz acquiesced gratefully. I took a dolly,
loaded the books on it and pulled it over in several trips to
the hallway of 794 Lexington Avenue (fortunately not far
away) where the material was stored until the Metropolitan
called for it four days later. There were a few items not related to photography, such as incomplete sets of the works of
Heinrich Heine and August Strindberg in German and the
big copper bowl that was a conspicuous decoration at the
"291" Gallery. These I kept for myself. Years later, in a conversation with O'Keeffe, she wondered what ever had happened to the big bowl from "291." I told her that I had rescued it and would be glad to give it back to her. No doubt it
still exists at Abiquiu.

I intervened in another transaction involving the disposal
of a part of the Stieglitz collection. I found him one day
cleaning house. Photography, he claimed, was a dead issue;
nobody cared about quality; photographers now worshiped
other gods. Over the years he had collected about three
hundred photographs, historical masterpieces from David

Octavius Hill and Margaret Cameron to Steichen (including the famous portrait of J. P. Morgan), Käsebier, White, Coburn, Strand and a host of others. Why should he be burdened with them; they meant nothing to him now. He would get rid of them, he might even tear them up. He disclaimed any interest in his legend as a photographer. But that was only a pose. I knew that he would not do anything drastic: he wanted somebody else to do something about the photographs. And so I played the game; I advanced serious arguments against precipitate action. Even if they no longer meant anything to him, they were historical documents. It would be an act of vandalism to do away with them. I offered to find out if the Metropolitan Museum Print Room would take them over. Of course they would, pending official acceptance by the Trustees. I had a note from Stieglitz dated May 20, 1933: "It rests in Peace! The Trustees have said yes. Many thanks." No doubt he was referring to the same incident on the occasion of my next visit to him when he said, "In your quiet practical way you understand me better than almost anyone."

Around the same time there was talk of a book, *America and Alfred Stieglitz,* a collective portrait that was scheduled to come out the following year. I had not been asked to contribute but I was prompted to write an essay. It became my deliberative if somewhat enthusiastic appraisal of Stieglitz; the present essay can be considered as a more personal supplement to it. It appeared in the periodical *New Democracy,* and was reprinted in *Twice-a-Year* and in my book *The Artist in America.* I sent a copy to Stieglitz. He replied with a note in April of 1935:

> You can imagine my great surprise when I opened that copy of *New Democracy* and saw your essay on me printed in life-size! It reads well. Very well. I am glad to see it in print. I have shown it to various people. They think it fine. Many thanks.

Henceforth Stieglitz looked at my literary endeavors with a kindly eye. In November of 1937 I brought him an advance copy of my book *Six Centuries of Fine Prints.* He asked me to inscribe it and said that he had never expected to see me between covers. In 1941 I read to him—for possible correction of fact—my portrait of John Marin from my forthcoming book *The Artist in America.* He was enthusiastic and said it was the best thing he had ever read on Marin. When I said that it was limited to his prints, he replied: "No matter, you have caught Marin's spirit. It is clear and concise: you define your words—mysticism for example." In the midst of it Dorothy Norman came in and Stieglitz started telling her about it.

I had many talks with Stieglitz either at his gallery or at dinner in the evening. He would tell stories and reminisce about his past. I recall a dinner party in 1930 with Stieglitz, O'Keeffe, John Collier, Wanda Gág, and Dorothy Brett. Brett had just come back from Taos and reported that Mabel Luhan had brought her memoirs up as far as the last fifteen years of her life. They were supposed to be very frank and she was planning to publish them twenty-five years hence. Stieglitz asked why she specified twenty-five years: it was possible that people might not consider the revelations so shocking then and wonder why she waited so long. Collier said it might be unfair to wait until the characters were dead since they would not be able to give their side of the story. Stieglitz said, even if the principals were dead, their heirs or children might be upset; if she was protecting people's feelings, she had not gone far enough. She should not postpone the memoirs indefinitely—which was absurd. Why not publish them now? (As a matter of fact, the first volume of her memoirs came out in 1933 and the fourth in 1937). Furthermore, asked Stieglitz, was Mabel really trying to put down facts objectively or was she trying to create a legend and justify her conduct? Brett answered that she had not seen the manuscript but she assumed that she was engaged in faithfully setting down her feelings, the ups and downs in relation to her husbands and lovers. The topic of Wanda's diary came up, and I pointed out how much more true the diary was over the memoir form because the facts and feelings were contemporaneous and not subject to later revision. Brett related that her father's recollections in diary form were sealed up, not to be published until sixty years after his death. Her father, Viscount Esher, was a power behind the throne during the reign of King Edward. Dorothy was a painter and eccentric who had grown up among the Bloomsbury group. Her appearance would not have attracted much attention except for a slight unconventionality in her dress and manner. She had a small round face and unruly hair. She was quite deaf and would thrust out an ear-trumpet when spoken to—which was disconcerting until one became accustomed to it. Underneath the singularity, however, there existed a quality of integrity, devotion, and sensitiveness that gained her the close friendship of Katherine Mansfield and D. H. Lawrence. I had many conversations with her about them and about Aldous Huxley, Middleton Murry, and others. She had come to America in 1924 with Frieda and D. H. Lawrence, and had remained in the Southwest permanently. In 1935 she brought out a book, *Lawrence and Brett,* another link in the Lawrence Legend. It is a curious work, due to her deafness, a predominantly visual account of people's behavior-—the external actions, which can be seen; not the overtones, which can only be heard. I exhibited some of her early paintings at the Weyhe Gallery. During her long sojourn in Taos her identification with the American Indians has grown. She has won their confidence and respect, with the result that her paintings of their ceremonial dances are striking, since there is a general prohibition against photographing and sketching during performances. Her paintings are impressive, rich in color, and without the saccharine sentimentality so often associated with the subject. She is a very active octogenarian.

I recall another dinner party, when I brought the Russian film director Sergei Eisenstein to meet Stieglitz. Ralph Flint and Georgia O'Keeffe also were present. Eisenstein recounted some of his frustrations with Hollywood. First they told him to work on Dreiser's *American Tragedy.* He drew up a scenario and went to the Adirondacks for local color. When he returned he was told that the project had been abandoned. The same thing happened with several other plays; there likewise was the imbroglio about his Mexican film. He had discovered a play, *Once in a Lifetime,* which he would like to take to Russia and produce there to save him the trouble of telling his story of Hollywood. He talked to O'Keeffe about painting and half-jokingly predicted that the cinema would swallow up all painting and music in the future. Painting had a sense of space but not of time; music had time but not space. The moving picture had a sense of time and a sense of space and therefore was more dynamic. Stieglitz told an amusing story about Montross and the show of modern paintings that was held in his gallery. Duchamp sent in a photograph of a house on which he had put a dot of red pigment. Montross came to Stieglitz and asked, "Did you see Duchamp's contribution; did you like it?" Stieglitz replied "Whether I like it or not is immaterial; I have seen it." Montross persisted, "But is it art?" "That is a nice question to ask me, a photographer," said Stieglitz, "to ask if a photograph is a work of art! Never mind; did you see the touch of color in the window?" "Yes," said Montross. "Well," was the reply, "that is where the art comes in."

On another occasion he talked about dealers; he was worried about what would happen to O'Keeffe, Marin, and Dove when he was gone. No one but himself knew which were the best Marins, for example, the ones that should not be sacrificed. Vollard had told him in 1907 that the clever thing to do was to hold back and never show the best paintings. One should work up a market by selling the second best. If people were to see the best they would want it, but they would not want to pay the proper price for it. He, Stieglitz, had made the great mistake of showing the best Marins. It may be said, however, that he did hold back the best of the Marins, Doves, O'Keeffes, and the best prints of his photographs: they formed the core of the Stieglitz Collection.

The Stieglitz Collection had a haphazard beginning. Stieglitz started to collect casually either to help an artist in need of encouragement or material aid, or to acquire a document for "The Record." As he once said, "I did not collect: I was collected." The idea of a record developed in his mind, and he began to collect with a purpose, namely, to show the evolution of certain artists in every phase by the choicest examples. He was in a position to do this because he had assumed the responsibility of guaranteeing the living expenses of the three artists in question. In return, he put certain of their most significant works into a reserve known as The Collection. In his choice he was guided by his own taste and insights, confirmed by the responses of other artists and friends. It was an ideal collection and, together with the sequence of his own development in photography, a remarkable and seldom-realized projection of creative achievement in art. It was ideal in many senses of the word, and particularly in the implied impossibility of its concrete perpetuation as an entity. Stieglitz thought a great deal about his collection but he could not decide how to insure its continuity. In this connection I recall a conversation I once had with Stieglitz about D. H. Lawrence. He was defending Frieda for her direct practical action in contrast to her husband's many vacillations: "Of course she destroyed some of his manuscripts; why did he give them to her? he knew she would destroy them." Stieglitz would not admit that his idea could not be realized without drastic modification. He therefore, by procrastination, turned the burden of decision over to O'Keeffe. In the summer of 1944, I showed practically the whole of the Stieglitz Collection at the Philadelphia Museum of Art. O'Keeffe had agreed to my proposal because it was an opportunity to view the ensemble in its entirety and thereby to help her make a decision as to its disposal. Stieglitz could not or would not come to see it, though he expressed approval of my printed catalogue. In 1946 Stieglitz died. I had hoped that the collection would stay in Philadelphia. We had offered to allocate several rooms as a sort of Stieglitz Center where significant portions would always be on exhibition, together with space for the storage of the remaining works of art and archival material. But in the end O'Keeffe decided to divide the collection into four parts in the following order of quantity and importance: the Metropolitan Museum of Art, the Institute of Chicago, the Philadelphia Museum of Art, and Fiske University in Tennessee.

Georgia O'Keeffe is a somewhat inscrutable character who has impressed some people as formidable. Her appearance and dress are unconventional, and her presence suggests resolute individuality and untold reserves of strength. As an artist, in addition to her essential feminity she has the ruthless drive for self-expression that is basic to all creators. When aroused or intently engaged she reveals a disconcerting directness of purpose. As one astonished person said: "she must have ice water in her veins." Yet, among other enigmatic traits, she has a kind of spiritual innocence, which sustains her on all occasions even when meeting the most sophisticated people (there were many such around Stieglitz!). It gives her self-assurance: she is not embarrassed at asking the most naive questions. She has a woman's innate practicality—no beating around the bush. There are indications that at times she is not averse to a bit of flattery. Ralph Flint once told me that she had asked him to escort her to a party at Elizabeth Arden's. She said she would stay only a few minutes, but she remained for two hours surrounded by a throng who gushed: "are you the famous artist?" And Stieglitz related the dramatic story of her first meeting with Francis Taylor. The renowned Director of the Metropolitan Museum of Art, with all his portly bearing, approached her saying, "Are you that great artist and genius among women, Georgia O'Keeffe? I have long wanted to meet you." And he bent down on his knee and kissed her hand. As she was telling the story to Stieglitz, he interrupted and said, "But you are not impressed by such a blatant piece of flattery?" "I realize that it was flattery," she replied, "but it was very pleasant to hear just the same." And then she went on with her story. Taylor spoke of his admiration of the artists of the Stieglitz circle and how negligent the museum had been in keeping up with creative developments. As a first step he felt that the museum should allocate ten to twenty thousand dollars for the purchase of Marin watercolors. To which O'Keeffe replied, "Which do you mean, ten thousand or twenty thousand?"

O'Keeffe on the whole had a wise and understanding point of view. I recall a luncheon with her when she discussed Stieglitz frankly. He was very dependent on people, she said. He was handsome and had been spoiled by his family in early life. If he felt he was not getting enough attention, he would get sick in order to attract notice and feed on emotions. Stieglitz's quirks would be hard to bear if he were not at other times so lovable, understanding, and magnetic, such an inspiration to creative endeavor. Perhaps his greatest contribution, she felt, might be his contacts with people, many of whom he did not even know. I asked if she had read my portrait of him. No, she had not, and she went on to say that the portrait of Stieglitz could not be written until after his death, because one could not until then say all the bad things about him that were necessary to the picture.

I shall not venture, in a foolish pose of omniscience, to assess the emotional constitution of Alfred Stieglitz. He was too complex, too ambivalent and protean in his psychological relationships with men and especially with women to warrant any pinpointing of his essential drive. One can regognize, however, a faintly recurring pattern of emotional affinities at various stages of his life without delving into all the intimate details. There seemed to be a touch of Svengali in him, a kind of urge to possess another's soul utterly. He could inspire enthusiasm and devotion to such a pitch that eventually the other person rebelled, and either went away or took up other pursuits. Whereupon he would complain sadly of betrayal.

He could be called a spellbinder, generally in the best sense, but occasionally with less edifying import, for there was a bit of the "ham" actor in him, as there was in a similar great character, Frank Lloyd Wright. He worked his spells by his provocative talk. Attempts have been made to set down his speech verbatim. They nearly always appear flat and banal because the timbre and vibrations of the spoken word are lost in the writing down. Nor were such transcripts always basically accurate even though literal. His stories often were not statements of fact but parables designed to point a moral or illuminate a state of feeling. Furthermore, his awareness of the attempt at transcription often brought out the histrionic feature in him: he sometimes strained for effect.

In his role of bringing art to the public through his three galleries, he had numerous friendly allies and understanding helpers. The founding and expansion of "291" would not have been possible without the assistance of Paul Haviland, J. B. Kerfoot, Katherine Rhoades, Agnes Ernst Meyer, Edward

Steichen, and Marius de Zayas. Among those who helped with the initiation of the Intimate Gallery were Mitchell Kennerly and Paul Strand. Likewise An American Place would not have been possible without Dorothy Norman. She is a highly gifted and many-sided woman. She came to Stieglitz as an eager young poet (he published her volume *Dualities*). She learned photography from him. Later she conducted a newspaper column, lived in India, and wrote books on the hero-myth and on Nehru. She founded and edited the publication *Twice-a-Year*, and assembled the text for the catalogue of Steichen's exhibition *The Family of Man*.

Alfred Stieglitz was a great photographer and a fascinating man. He operated both through his works and by his prophetic mission. He won the admiration of creative people in all walks of life, but also provoked disparagement and censure in many persons. In addition to his many stimulating contacts, he influenced my ideas on quality and individuality. I have perhaps best summed up my final impression of him in the paragraph I wrote for the *Memorial Portfolio*, which Dorothy Norman published in 1947.

These long talks with Stieglitz are perhaps my most cherished memory. They were always adventures of the mind and spirit, some discussion of current events, some evaluation of art or photography, of music or drama, some reminiscence of the past or flash of insight into character, some story or parable that grew naturally out of the discourse. Other people might drop in and then the ripples of talk would coincide or clash in a veritable counterpoint of psychological reactions. These contacts were sometimes exciting, sometimes serene, always illuminating, always emphasizing creative values. They revealed a man who was wise, understanding, and fascinatingly human—a character quite different from the mask and barrier that were superimposed by those who did not understand his language. I have often wished that such fertilizing experiences could have been preserved. With what careless yet engaging prodigality Stieglitz lavished his energies on a medium that by its nature was evanescent! Yet, when all is said and done, the effort was not entirely wasted: the effect still remains upon those who were fortunate to have participated in the experience. The pity of it is that now "The Record," as he called it, is complete; and that he lives not in the flesh but only in the memory.

15

William M. Ivins, Jr.

Among the many influences that shaped my taste and experience in art, and especially in prints, that of William M. Ivins has in certain respects been lasting and decisive. To be sure, when I encountered him, my tastes had already been formed. I was more of an admirer than a pupil. Nonetheless he was my mentor, so to speak, in matters pertaining to curatorship and the conduct of a print room.

I first knew him as an intelligent but modest collector at Keppel's print shop; he was practising law and I was an apprentice with the firm. We seemed to find each other congenial, and I used to see him from time to time outside the gallery. In 1916 he became the first curator of the newly formed Department of Prints at the Metropolitan Museum of Art. The war intervened and I left Keppel's; but I kept up my casual association with him. I have related elsewhere how I had dinner with him at his home on the night my daughter was born. I had been in charge of the Weyhe Gallery for several years when he sounded me out on the possibility of becoming his assistant in the print room. He asked if I had any independent income besides my salary from the Gallery. When I replied in the negative, he said, "Then, I will not have the effrontery to offer you a job at the museum, because the salary is so pitifully small that you could not live on it with a growing family." Thus ended my opportunity to work at the Metropolitan Museum of Art. The offer did plant some seed and arouse my latent ambition to become a museum curator. However tantalized I was at the time—and I admit I was a bit disappointed—I do not now regret missing the opportunity. Working under Ivins would have been difficult, for he was a complicated and overpowering personality. The experience would have shunted me onto different tracks, and warped my free development in other respects. I was still too young to be cloistered and subordinate. I am glad that I remained independent, and thus retained his friendship and respect. Ivins quarreled with many people but never seriously with me. As David Rosen, the noted conservator of paintings and a good friend of his, once said to me, "I never had a falling out with Billee because I never would let him."

During his thirty years' incumbency as curator, Ivins built up the print room from Harris B. Dick's legacy of British etchings into one of the great print collections of the world. He had not had any museum training when he was appointed. To be sure, he had been a print collector, and perhaps knew the art market and the dealers better than the academic art historians did. He also had a critical and logical mind, and could arrive at independent judgments while ploughing through "the literature." He had a conception of a print room collection far beyond the limits of the accepted classics in beautiful impressions, and he had a plan to extend its usefulness for a wider audience than the average print lover or museum visitor, for example, into the fields of ornament, architecture, and applied design. He did not stand in awe of taste; he created it. With his earthy sense of values, he was critical of the stuffy assumptions and scholastic verbiage of "the professors." He carried his learning lightly. He also had a canny sense of rarity on the market. He knew when a thing was rare, so exceptional that he might never have the opportunity again to acquire it. It is interesting that most of the print curators of the older generation—Ivins, Schniewind, Carrington, Rossiter, and myself—never had specific academic training (museum courses). They learned from their material.

Ivins, therefore, had unusual qualifications for building up a prominent and significant print collection. He was aided by two very important factors, ample funds and the lucky timing of his activities. Because the print room was recently established and consequently deserved favored treatment, he was able to count on more than a normal share of funds for purchase, and the Metropolitan funds were consdierable. This enlightened policy paid off, and the Department now has many priceless rarities as well as a broad coverage of the masterpieces of graphic art. Ivins started to buy heavily just after the First World War, when the American dollar counted for most through favorable exchange, and when many collectors and public institutions were forced to sell their possessions in the European market. Extraordinary things came to light that had been buried away and forgotten in monastic libraries and similar places. Ivins also knew what works he need not buy but could count on to get by gift or bequest, such as superb Rembrandts from Felix Warbrug or rare *Einblattdrücke* from J. C. Maguire.

When he was dealing with abstract problems, outlining a master plan for a comprehensive print collection, or theorizing on the functions of an ideal print room, Ivins was informed, proficient, and praiseworthy, but when he was dealing with people he wad far from admirable. He was moody and temperamental, and occasionally he was driven by some inner demon to insult people, deliberately and grossly. He had a brillian intellect and knew it. He could not easily endure stupidity, and had no compunction about telling people that they were fools or imbeciles. He also had a curious idea regarding the mainspring of conversation. He once told me that he no longer had immutable principles; but, he confided, he was able and willing, on the spur of the moment, to manufacture some that contradicted those of the person with whom he was arguing. This, he said, made for good conversation. He loved a tough debate, and, as a lawyer, he did not feel that he had to be right; he merely had to prove his case. Artist Henry Billings once recounted an incident when Ivins was invited to speak before a group of artists. Instead of talking to them simply, he read a paper full of classical allusions and scientific generalizations, which few understood. In the discussion later, the artists asked some searching questions. Ivins lost his temper, and there was a brawl. According to Billings, Ivins had a scholar's distrust of artists on the ground that they might sometime upset his classifications.

In his debates, Ivins seldom met anyone who could stand up to him intellectually, but I was present on one occasion in April of 1928 when he really met his match. I was living at that time with the Douglas Haskells on Columbia Heights, and we had Ivins and Orage over for dinner. The two fenced brilliantly the whole evening. I no longer remember all the particulars, but Orage, who was a skilled debater from his Fabian Society days, discoursed profoundly and effectively on Vaihinger's "as if" philosophy as a method for testing mystical intuitions. The next day I received a letter from Ivins.

> It's a dead, cooked, stewed, thing I am in the morning—but I had a grand time. The penalty or price is slight for the pleasure—for which so many thanks. Please thank Haskell for me—and as for that 'urricane of talk wot calls 'isself Orage, please present my sincerest compliments to him.

What made Ivins so temperamental? For one thing, there must have been a constant conflict between his intellect and his emotions. He had enthusiasms, infatuations almost, and would plunge headlong into a subject to saturate himself in it. It was a delight to see his smiling face, and hear his talk, almost in a stutter, as his thoughts raced too fast for his words. But after he had sucked the orange dry with an intemperate appetite—whether it was an idea, a person, or a work of art—he tossed it aside and had a terrible nauseous revulsion. His moods revolved around his stomach. Dyspepsia contributed substantially to his black or "down" days. He would cast off a subject by attacking it. His aversions were a record of his past loves. I put down in my journal an experience in 1934:

> Ivins came into the gallery in a nasty mood—wanted to be amused or excited: everything bored him. He picked out a few prints by Hayes Miller and Alec Brook for the museum. I showed him some etchings by Wickey. He said that landscapes bored him. I replied smilingly that I did not see how the artists could stop creating just because he was bored with landscape. He went on to say that all he was interested in now was illustration. Later he said he did not like propaganda. I said there was not much difference between propaganda and illustration. The Church had commissioned the old masters to make propaganda for Christian dogma. He said, No, what the old masters did was to illustrate ideas which were in everybody's mind. I replied that I did not believe in art for art's sake, and all art had a message, some kind of propaganda, in it. He disagreed, saying propaganda had nothing to do with art. For example, he continued, that is why he could not "see" Kollwitz's prints: hunger had nothing to do with art. It was my impression, I replied, that art had something to do with feeling and emotion, and I understood that hunger could be a rather intense feeling.

Likewise, on another occasion, he was feeling depressed. He knew nothing about the value of prints, what was art and what was not. He no longer wrote as a lover of prints but only as a dissecting surgeon. Then I introduced him to Gutman, who was starting to work in the editorial office of *Creative Art*. Ivins immediately became animated and began to give advice and ideas for articles, Winslow Homer's prints, Delacroix's Journals, Leonardo's Note Books, that marvelous chapter on taste in Veblen's *Theory of the Leisure Class,* one of the most brilliant essays, he said, ever written in this country, and so on. The change in mood was striking. Possibly all his moods were related to an inner drive: his ego needed constant reassurance. He had to make himself feel great by making other people feel small, or by attacking established ideas and reputations. Occasionally he might find a sympathetic and listening ear, where he could operate benevolently rather than caustically. He might perhaps have been a great teacher and played the role of master or guru to perfection. But I doubt if he could have maintained the part consistently: the black moods were too strong.

In his vehement intellectual life, Ivins somehow lacked

much aesthetic sensibility. Several artists have told me they doubted whether he ever experienced a real emotion before a work of art, and Mahonri Young went on to say that he considered him intrinsically to be a bookish or typographic man. I never hear him speak of music. When he was middle-aged, he learned to dance at Arthur Murray's, and he practiced the art with great enthusiasm. Several women who danced with him told me that the experience was grueling: he danced like a deaf drillmaster, one-two-three, one-two-three. Also, he was somewhat deficient in the gracious human touch. He might be generous with advice, but not with appreciation. When I was writing *Six Centuries of Fine Prints,* he was most helpful with photographs and friendly counsel. He never told me what he thought of it when it came out, but I heard later that he had recommended it to other people. One might almost say that Ivins never praised a man except behind his back, and never agreed with him face to face, if he could help it. He did make a rather penetrating, if not entirely commendatory observation about my second book, *The Artist in America,* to my face. He said that he for one would never attempt to make a work of art out of a piece of criticism: the critical and creative faculties were in separate categories. He sensed that I had tried to make it a work of art, for instance, by varying the style of the chapters to suit the different subjects. Only he and Kai Klitgaard had noticed the device.

I believe, however, that I saw more of the good side of his character than most people did. I was in a sense his protégé. For instance, when I was about to go on my first purchasing trip abroad for the Weyhe Gallery in 1923, he was lavish in giving me helpful pointers and advice. He enumerated sights to see, museum officials to visit, the most reliable dealers, the names of hotels and restaurants, and a thousand useful hints on foreign travel. Again, on an occasion when I had to make a speech, he discoursed eloquently on the theory and practice of public speaking, on the difference in style between reading a paper and purely oral delivery. He was most helpful. But the climax came when I was planning to go to Philadelphia as print curator. He enlightened me on all the practical details, the kind of mat board and where to get it and other materials, the technique of hinging, storage in print boxes, arrangement of the print room, cataloguing and the keeping of records, measures of security, and the like. Beyond the physical particulars, he expatiated on the function of a print room. Its chief reason for existence, he said, was to serve the public. The operation must always be subservient to the needs of the people who used it, the young art students, the collectors who came for advice or comparisons, the art historians or museum colleagues who came for study or identification, the commercial artists or craftsmen who wanted to adapt ornament and design. The curator and his assistants must at all times be patient, courteous, and helpful, even to the neglect of their own housekeeping duties. "The customer is always right." I might add in parenthesis that it was on this philanthropic program that his theory was sometimes at variance with his practice. I have heard wild tales that, when the mood was on him, he would sit on a table and argue for hours with visitors, telling them not to look at this but to look at that, and generally interfere with their program. He continued his advice to me on the conduct of the print curator:

> First of all, he said, *festina lenta.* Go to all the print rooms of the country, and take notes and classify. Ask all kinds of foolish questions, questions on how things are done. This is not for your edification, but to quote to trustees, etc. Next, learn everything you can about your director, his habits, his likes and dislikes. The same with colleagues and trustees. Do you know what a mortgage map is? Well, make something like that, with colored pencils of all wealthy Philadelphians—what riches they may have, who is related, who plays with whom, who hates whom, and the like. The last thing a print curator is concerned with is prints.

During the illness of the Director, Herbert Winlock, Ivins substituted as Assistant Director; and after the director's complete retirement in 1938, he served as Acting Director for two years until a new director was appointed. Ivins rather fancied himself in the executive role, and was disappointed when Francis Taylor, and not he, was nominated to the post. While he was Acting Director he said to me once at lunch that his colleagues did not like him as much as they used to. That was putting it mildly. The whole museum was in a tur-

moil. It is hard to believe to what depths of pettiness the relations between the embattled acting director and the exasp-
erated curators descended. Francis Taylor, when he assumed
charge, handled the situation with great tact, and created a
new position for him, that of Counselor to the Museum, one
that was eminently suited to his talents, for he could be most
useful and constructive in dealing with policy and impersonal
issues. He was totally unfit to be a director: he just could not
work harmoniously with people. It is a tragic waste when a
man aspires to an activity for which he is not qualified. Ivins
had two great achievements to his credit, two passports to
fame—the print collection at the Metropolitan and his writings.

Ivins first appeared in his full stride as a writer in the essays and reports published in the monthly *Bulletins* of the
Metropolitan Museum of Art. They were brilliant, provocative, and delightfully written. Ivins had a sense of style: his
was plainspoken, muscular, like Swift's, and brimming with
ideas. His ideas were not borrowed, but well-grounded in his
own common-sense philosophy. His erudition was considerable, though never pedantic. His pronouncements were challenging because they often cut across fashionable clichés. His
essays transcended the narrowly professional appeal of most
museum publications. By 1926 a sufficient number had appeared to warrant a reprint in book form, and Ivins set
about to make a selection. To aid him in his task, he asked
me what my choice would be. I submitted a list and was
happy to discover that the contents of *Prints and Books*
(Harvard University Press, 1926) included, with a few varia-
tions, practically all my nominations. It is amusing to note
that he did not give me an inscribed copy: he had one sent,
containing the printed form "with the publisher's compliments." Although the work is not a systematic history, it is
the most charming introduction to the world of prints and
books that I know of. Other books followed. *Notes on Prints*
was a compilation in book form of a series of labels to accompany an exhibition of prints at the museum. Ivins was a
pioneer in a new form of museum label, a kind of epigrammatic commentary on the historic or aesthetic significance of

a print or its creator. Mention should be made of two important exhibition catalogues or guides, *Italian Rennaissance Woodcuts,* 1917, and *The Arts of the Book,* 1924, both of them models of scholarship and erudition. In *How Prints Look,* he explored an unknown aspect of prints, namely, their enlargements in high magnification, to discover new insights into technique and the idiosyncrasy of the artist's hand. In *The Rationalization of Sight* and *Art and Geometry,* perhaps the most methodically developed of all his works, he showed his capability as a mathematical and philosophical thinker. He occupied himself with optics, perspective, and descriptive geometry to arrive at some startling and iconoclastic conclusions about Greek art. His last book, *Prints and Visual Communication,* 1953, written after his retirement, was to my mind a rather disappointing work. I wrote a review of it that appeared in the *Saturday Review,* August 1, 1953.

I turned in my review with some hesitation, since I felt that its somewhat critical tone might involve me in a polemic with Ivins. I had no direct communication from him, and Hyatt Mayor, who was enthusiastic about his book, was rather negatively noncommittal about my review. I never knew till a long time later whether Ivins had even seen it. In 1961, Prof. Theodore Sizer was going over his letters from Ivins with a view to giving them to the Yale University Library. One of them was not dated but had a reference to my review. Sizer wrote to ask if I could give a clue as to the date. This is what Ivins had written:

> Such a wonderful review in the Saturday Review—poor old C.Z.—do you remember, there was an early German engraver of the same initials, who made even Jesus cross-eyed.

In my review of his book I criticized Ivins for not grasping the full significance of the influence of photography upon printmaking. He was so intent upon building up the importance of photomechanical methods as the medium of the future (the impersonal translation of the object or the image into the print) that he ignored the creative potentialities still inherent in the traditional printmaking media. Incidentally,

Tubby Sizer, to whom I had sent a copy of my review, wrote me that he considered my critique eminently fair.

In 1955 I sent Ivins a catalogue of an exhibition of medical prints that I had written. He acknowledged it as follows:

Many thanks for the catalogue of medical things. You were right in thinking that it would amuse me. It seems so long since I attempted one—even so long since I have read one! Pretty soon I'll have forgotten the language just as I've already forgotten most of the stuff. How it does fly!

I answered:

Your letter intrigues me. Granted that works of art, and particularly the jargon of discussing them, have at the moment little interest for you, I cannot conceive of a mind as keen as yours just vegetating. There surely must be some absorbing activity, some area of speculation or research that drives away ennui. [My interest stemmed from curiosity not censoriousness.]

To which he replied, bristling:

I don't suffer from lack of a subject but from the insistence of too many. If accédie ever gets me in its toil, I'll be the most surprised man in the world. Don't forget that I was bred to the law—Have you ever heard of a good lawyer or doctor or priest that died of boredom? The reason is that everywhere one of them looks, he sees a problem that's full of charm and interest—and, frequently, of great importance. They die poor but happy.
So far from worrying about myself, I'm inclined to wonder about you—that clings to a subject like a life-belt. Why don't you let go of it and go swimming, and diving and surf riding? Remember that the "life guard" at the beach don't wear no life belt. This may sound silly—but I never said a truer word.

Late in 1959, I wrote him to ask if he would contribute an article to the Year Book of the Print Council of America, which I was assembling. I even suggested a title, "The Qualifications of a Print Curator."

He replied:

Many thanks for yours of the 8th. I appreciate it but the answer is No. I'm very uncomfortable and haven't seen a "fine print" this long since. However I'll hand you a suggestion, if you can find the time to follow it up. Get an article on "Nonrepresentational Art and the Old Masters of Ornament." It might stir up a little interest in some forgotten but very wonderful artists. Good luck.

On June 15, 1961, William M. Ivins died after a long illness. In recent years his fame has suffered a strange mutation. He has been adopted as a minor prophet in the pantheon of Marshall Macluhan. I wonder if Ivins would have relished his apotheosis.

16

Arthur B. Davies

My *first encounter with Arthur B. Davies* was in Weyhe's bookstore. He seemed to take a fancy to me, and it was a fortunate
coup, for he was an aloof and mysterious figure in the art
world. He had a great name and an eager following: he sold
everything he made. I learned that he was interested in making prints again; he had made some etchings and drypoints
about five years before, which had been shown with the New
York Society of Etchers at the Montross Gallery in November
1916. As a matter of fact, I had compiled the catalogue of
the exhibition and written an introduction for it. Davies was
now interested in lithography. I introduced him to George
Miller, who supplied him with stones and zinc plates, with
lithographic crayons and tusche, and then did the printing.
Davies was launched on an exciting lithographic adventure.
It was his custom to immerse himself completely in a
medium and produce prodigally. He was a born experi-
menter and adept in technical manipulation. He experimented with crayon and washes and even with color

209

printing. And I offered him a sympathetic outlet for his prints through the Gallery. We sold a great many during the early years. I aroused his interest in etching again; he got out his old plates and printed them. He added new work to some, always experimenting. He played around with aquatint, producing some of his best work. He liked poetic titles and I supplied quite a number. Apparently, in his manner of working, the impulse for the print came from feeling, and the meaning and title were supplied later. He was always interested in what I would read into a new print. I took some notes on the states and especially the dates of the prints. I tried to make more notes and questioned him about them, but he was impatient of such details. He could not or would not remember when and how he made them. This was true of his paintings also: relatively few were dated.

I was one of the few who were allowed to visit his studio. The studio was a secluded place. He had an unlisted telephone; only a few of his intimate friends knew the number—Miss Lillie Bliss was the only person I knew who had it. He would say "come tomorrow at three o'clock," and I was instructed to ring, wait one minute, and then ring again. Only after such a ritual was I admitted. He had a large apartment in a nondescript building on East 57th Street. It was sparsely furnished. The rear room, facing the north, probably was his painting room—I do not remember seeing it—but the large front area contained an etching press and various works of art, a couple of exquisite Louis XV armchairs, small Greek bronzes, and Cycladic stone statuettes on the mantelpiece, Romanesque enamels, Persian miniatures, Coptic and other Oriental textiles, modern paintings and drawings, art books galore. In a corner was a platform or low table piled helter-skelter with his own drawings and prints. I never saw him at work, nor shared in the pleasant camaraderie of the studio, as I had when I helped Rockwell Kent or Emil Ganso with their printing. I saw only what Davies wanted me to see. He probably was aloof and secretive by nature, especially when engaged in creative work—no extraneous influence. I learned later that there might have been an additional reason for this obsessive privacy of his studio. I was told that for many years he had had an intimate relationship with a dancer. The fact that he also had a wife might have shocked the rich ladies who were his best customers. I am sure that his wife was aware of the situation and acquiesced in it. She was a country doctor in Rockland Lake, New York, where she lived with their two children. She was an admirable character and much beloved by the community. She would occasionally visit the gallery to see his exhibitions, and he also spent considerable time at their farm in the country.

Due no doubt to his Welsh heritage, there was a poetic, romantic, almost mystic strain in his character. He was a "feeling" type, not at all intellectual, almost feminine in his sensibility. He would sometimes be carried away by a notion or thesis. For instance, he held firmly to a theory of Greek art, namely, that in all genuine works the figure was portrayed in the act of inhalation. This, he claimed, gave the body its lift, its spiritual quality. Again, Betty Hare once told me that a woman astrologer, whom Davies never saw, directed his life, telling him what to do each year. He seemed very positive and somewhat unpredictable in his beliefs. Although we were on good terms, I never presumed too much. I had seen him bristle at salesmen and dealers who were aiming to exploit. As a successful artist he was fair game. In general, he was canny and did not expose himself knowingly to uncongenial company. With artists, at least with some artists, he was sympathetic and generous in support of artists' causes. Kent has testified to his prompt and substantial help with the early show of the Independent Artists (not the No Jury Show). He also contributed to *The Masses* at a time when it required courage to do so. He befriended the sculptor John Flannagan and let him stay on his farm for almost a year.

He had a tender and almost sentimental regard for children and motherhood, which was especially evident in his earliest work. But for all his aesthetic sensibility, there was also a more rugged side to his nature. He was quite a baseball fan. He told me interesting stories about his early adventures as a surveyor in the Southwest. He also had flashes of earthy humor—such as his story of visiting an art exhibition with Maurice Prendergast, who was quite deaf.

Davies innocently remarked, "That's a nice nude." Prendergast answered "What did you say?" This was repeated several times, each time in a louder voice, and still Prendergast could not understand. Finally Davies, feeling very silly, shouted out once more, while the whole gallery turned to look at the two of them. Davies vowed he would never discuss a nude with a deaf man again. I also remember with what relish he told the story of H. H. Benedict's marrying his nurse when he was in his seventies and having a baby the next year: "She was the spit and image of her father, and he no thing of beauty!"

In the early years, Davies's painting dealer was Macbeth, a man of charm and integrity; in the last years the dealer was Frederick N. Price, a man of somewhat different caliber. I never understood how Davies, sensitive as he was to overtones, could have trusted him for long. But he did, and furthermore he allowed Price to undermine his good relations with Weyhe's. Price took over the sale of the prints as well as the paintings. He made the bid for it by publishing an elaborate and pretentious catalogue raisonné of the prints. I am not being prejudiced or envious when I say that it was one of the most useless catalogues ever made. It was slapped together without any order or sense—nothing but a hodgepodge arranged neither chronologically nor logically by subject matter, nor alphabetically by title. There were mistakes in dating, in edition numbers, and in other information on almost every page. It was no contribution to scholarship, and, in Price's introduction, contained some of the lushest examples of purple prose every perpetrated.

Davies's early paintings had idyllic charm. Upon his native romantic symbolism, he grafted at the time of the Armory Show a kind of cubist or lozenge-shaped prismatic pattern—actually a not very convincing combination. The felicities of figure painting, really his greatest gift, were lost in a welter of camouflage. His painting had no bones or guts. Nor did his later landscapes seem other than surface painting. To my mind his strongest contribution was in his prints and drawings. He was a beautiful draftsman and a proficient and imaginative printmaker. The best of his prints have a vitality that is lacking in most of the paintings.

17

At the Stettheimers'

In the 1930s I occasionally was invited to parties at the Stettheimers' at 182 West 58th Street. Curiously, the invitation came from Ettie the writer and not from Florine the artist. I did not have much direct contact with the artist; she was reserved and involved in her own concerns. Of the three sisters, Carrie was the most narcissistic and Ettie the most outgoing and aggressive. Ettie had a kind of feline and smolderingly sensuous quality. She wrote novels under the pseudonym of Henri Waste. I never read them but they were supposed to be very very frank. I was a bit afraid of her. All three sisters represented the ultimate in sophistication.

The Stettheimer apartment was amazing, to say the least. Their ménage—in the same class as the Cone sisters' place in Baltimore and Gertrude Stein's in Paris—was the nearest approach to a "salon" in New York, a milieu where wit and smartness and taste were reckoned of prime importance. The three sisters and their mother—I never knew what happened to Mr. Stettheimer—had ample means and lived a completely self-centered and self-indulgent life. They gave the appearance of being on a perpetual holiday. Whatever there may have been of heartbreak in their private lives was carefully concealed from a casual visitor such as I was. Which was to their credit. With my more proletarian sympathies, I felt slightly alien in their environment, though I had to admit that they had turned their life into a work of art, and that others with more money and more opportunity squandered their substance and created nothing. It was a feminine work of art that they had created, for they lived in a completely feminine world. Their Victorian boudoir in pink was perfect of its kind, the last word in Victorian femininity. And the Republican Room, with its red, white, and blue ribbons, the portraits of Washington, Lincoln, and Hoover, the speaker's chair and table with the glass and water pitcher—all combined to create a charming bit of Americana. The Doll House—Carrie's *magnum opus*—had a place of honor in a room all to itself. The other sisters had their own claim to fame, but Carrie will be remembered by a toy house. It was indeed an exquisite creation. Marcel Duchamp, Picabia, Gleizes, Archipenko, and other artists made miniature paintings to adorn its walls, and Lachaise and Zorach made miniature sculpture. The furniture and furnishings were dainty and elegant and perfectly in scale. Did she find some fulfillment for the needs of her life within its walls? did she let her fancy play with it or was it all for show? Did any one of the sisters ever sleep in that pink boudoir—a Princess of Romance for a night—and ruffle the static perfection of its decor? I never knew. But I did feel a grudging admiration for a dedication to perfection so absolute, even if so decadent. No doubt other such domiciles may exist in some odd corner of England or France, together with a Proust to describe them, but in America it was a rare and curious phenomenon.

The Stettheimer apartment was a perfect setting for Florine's paintings. They were the apotheosis of feminine sophistication. It is only in modern times that women have been able to function freely as artists, and not many have managed, as yet, to paint basically as women. Käthe Kollwitz and Georgia O'Keeffe each did in their different ways, and likewise Florine Stettheimer. Florine's pictures could have been painted only by a woman. In their emphasis on dress and feminine frills and detail, they appeared restricted to one woman's point of view, and still further circumscribed into the sphere of a woman of leisure. In her set portraits of men, Carl Van Vechten, Henry McBride, Alfred Stieglitz, or Marcel Duchamp, for example, the subjects appeared to me to be completely emasculated. I do not believe that she tried to be malicious: she just saw men as sexless or perhaps feminized. She made Marcel look like a popinjay. Perhaps he was—in some minor aspect of his personality—but he had other masculine traits, which tended to blot out that impression. Similarly, no one else would have depicted Stieglitz as a mollycoddle. I doubt whether her motivation was ever censorious, even in the so-called Cathedrals Series, which seemed to be made for satire. In the *Cathedrals of Art, Cathedrals of Fifth Avenue,* and the rest of them, she gathered together many pertinent details and incidents, and, with feminine relish, arranged them into neat pictorial catalogues. The heat, the bite, the painterly emotion did not extend beyond the act of assembling. It was as if the artist marshaled and deployed her details like toy soldiers in a parlor game: it was not war but playing at war. A fantastic milieu was projected in Florine's oeuvre, a solipsist's purview, a precious, narcissistic, sheltered, and asthenic world! It had a kind of irrational fascination for me, all the more because of my totally different outlook.

There was, however, one phase of her art for which I had unqualiifed enthusiasm: her designs for the opera *Four Saints in Three Acts.* But in this instance, one might say that her phantasy—the decor and costumes—was translated into flesh and blood. A group of ultra-sophisticates, Gertrude Stein, Virgil Thomson, Florine Stettheimer, Maurice Grosser, and Frederick Ashton, united to create a modern masterpiece in the Baroque spirit, not a pastiche of historical style, but the Baroque of never-never land, the super-truth of nostalgic imagination. However strange it might have seemed to a seventeenth-century man, for us it was a flawless equivalent.

I was not one of the elect who saw the first performance at Hartford, but I saw it several times in New York shortly thereafter. I wrote in my notes in March 1934:

> Visually the opera was a constant delight, a kind of "moving picture" that always unfolded to new beauties without making any sense. The costumes and settings, designed by Florine Stettheimer with cellophane at a cost of only five hundred dollars, were utterly charming. Virgil Thomson's music was witty and amusing. I believe he could set the telephone book to music and make it sound interesting. But it was the Negro cast who really gave the production its flair. They performed beautifully: they sang well, looked handsome, and entered into the conception with just the right spirit. There were moments of spiritual ecstasy and moments of both subtle and rollicking burlesque. It was a happy idea of Virgil Thomson's to use an all-Negro cast.

The parties at the Stettheimers were elegant and distinguished affairs. Delicious food was served but no liquor. Their parties were truly *conversazioni,* social gatherings where art and literature were discussed, though generally on a superficial level. Gossip was the order of the day. Let the following account, taken from my journal of March 14, 1930, be a sample of a typical Stettheimer entertainment:

> To a party at the Stettheimers in honor of Stieglitz. I saw the three sisters, of course, and Stieglitz and O'Keeffe. There was a huge crowd. Many unfamiliar people, but many I knew: Marsden Hartley, Carl Van Vechten, Paul and Becky Strand, Orage, Louise Goepfert, Philip Moeller, Anna Strunsky, Louis Kalonyme, Henry McBride, Carl Sprinchorn, Thelma Wood, Lee and Helen Simonson, Lloyd Morris, Blanche Knopf, Edna Kenton, Aaron Copland, Muriel Draper. Gossiped with McBride, as I always do. He told about Matisse's recent visit here on his way to the South Seas. He stayed here only about four or five days on the twenty-fourth floor of the Ritz Tower. He was crazy about New York and he did not hesitate to spend money. It was the first time he had been away from his connections in about ten years. All his friends were surprised that he took the Tahiti trip alone. *Vous allez seul?* they asked. They suspected a *petite amie.*
>
> Talked with McBride and Hartley about Lawrence and *Lady Chatterley's Lover.* I was shocked at the indecent attitude they revealed. Henry also recounted what Mabel Dodge had said about Lawrence—that he was always impelled to wipe out whatever impression he made on people by recreating the opposite impression. His relations with Mabel were a series of catastrophic op-

positions. He also related the tale of the dinner and benefit which Middleton Murry had staged on Lawrence's return to England. Murry made a speech so eloquent and emotional that Lawrence broke down and cried. Next morning Lawrence, feeling that he had been taken in by Murry's emotionalism, wrote him a letter which has kept them enemies ever since.

18

Fiske Kimball

The name of Fiske Kimball will always be associated with the growth of the Philadelphia Museum of Art at its present location. He had little to do with the building itself; the key name associated with the edifice was Eli Kirk Price. When he came to Philadelphia as Director, he found that a big empty shell was being erected on the site of the old reservoir at Fairmount. He made a living museum out of it. He finished practically all of the interior and filled it with art treasures. He transformed a provincial museum—first located in a building left over from the Centennial Exposition in 1876 with holdings consisting largely of decorative arts after the model of the Victoria and Albert Museum in London—into a major museum of international renown, one of the six leading museums of this country. He can be accounted the chief architect of this far-reaching enterprise. The biography of Kimball by George and Mary Roberts is appropriately entitled *Triumph on Fairmount.*

His achievement is all the more remarkable when one considers the cultural climate of Philadelphia that he found on his arrival. This city had once been the artistic and intellectual capital of the country, but it had lapsed into provincial smugness. The press was aggressively "lowbrow" (in the slang of the day), and either ignored the museum or sneered at its aspirations. Only when a fountain broke or an art object was stolen was the event considered noteworthy. There was resentment among many citizens at the excessive cost of the huge structure on Fairmount: it was a white elephant, and hollow at that, for there was not much art to put into it.

One very small ultraconservative section of "society"—I never encountered more than half-a-dozen examples of such extreme DAR psychology—had a rather provincial view of a museum's function. This view was seldom blatantly expressed; rather, it was implied in their tacit assumptions. They considered the Museum their private domain, designed solely to house the objects their ancestors owned: family portraits, furniture, silver, ceramics, costumes, and the like. They wished to retain control of its policy without assuming any of the costs and burdens of maintenance. Their attitude was snobbish, exclusive, usually anti-Semitic, but happily seldom encountered. In spite of the generous and dedicated support of a few families, such as the McIlhennys, the Stokeses, the Elkins, the Ingersolls, the McFaddens, some of the Wideners, and others, the Museum did not have a broad enough base among the public at large to inspire interest and participation.

After his arrival in 1925, Kimball had only about four boom years in which to solicit funds and collections, and to purchase objects of art, before the stock market crashed in 1929. The important Foulc Collection of Renaissance decorative arts, for instance, was purchased in 1929 just one day before the debacle. The financial obligations assumed by the Museum for its purchase hung like a millstone around its neck for many years. During the Depression, building operations throughout the country were to a great extent suspended. Not so with Kimball and the Museum. He was able to continue with his program by a brilliant maneuver unheard of in Philadelphia, where Franklin D. Roosevelt was always called "that man in the White House." He enlisted Federal relief measures to complete the interior of the Museum, that is to say, he offered, as matching funds, works of art (architectural ensembles and the furnishings of period rooms) in return for the labor costs of installing them. As a relief operation it was a success, for it benefited everyone concerned. It helped workers (carpenters, masons, electricians, laborers, and the like) to earn a living wage and thus carry them through the depression, and it enabled the Museum to install its treasures without a staggering outlay of money. That the Museum continued to develop and expand during the Depression—in spite of a brief curtailment of services because the city could not pay for guards—is due largely to Kimball's foresight and planning. He had laid out a master design, a coherent and rational plan for the distribution and arrangement of the Museum's holdings, that made an art lover's visit both pleasant for the feet and pleasurable to the eyes. Unfortunately, the design of the building imposed some retracing of steps for a total purview. The second floor was designed for the general visitor and offered an epitome of art history in choice examples, together with an impressive array of architectural ensembles and period rooms for which the Museum has become famous, such as the Chinese Palace Hall, the Indian Temple, the Romanesque Cloister, the English and French rooms of the eighteenth century, Pennsylvania Dutch and other American period rooms. On the first floor were assembled the systematic collections of interest to the specialist in paintings, prints, furniture, costume, silver, ceramics, and glass. The administrative offices, library, restaurant, auditorium, and department of education were placed on the ground floor. The Philadelphia Museum is one of the few that did have a logical plan. Such was the background of the Museum when I came on the scene.

When I took up my duties at the Museum as Curator of Prints and Drawings at the beginning of 1941, much of the groundwork of the master plan had been carried out, although Kimball continued to finish and furnish to the very end. I had been invited to join the Museum staff as a result of pressure by Lessing J. Rosenwald upon the trustees to establish an active print department. Previously the print room and its token print collection had been marking time under a more or less volunteer curator who was often absent. It was my task to give the job a professional touch. Not that I could be called a professional curator: I had never taken art courses in college and had never worked in a museum before. Fiske was taking a certain gamble in hiring me. That the hazards had crossed his mind is revealed by an incident that took place about a year after I had started to work. He called me to his office and told me that I had won over the trustees and all the people who count in Philadelphia. They all liked me. Even John Jenks (Vice-President of the Museum)—as unlike me, according to Fiske, as anyone could be—seemed to be favorably inclined. He wanted me to know that I had clinched my place in the Museum and that I would be taken care of in any emergency.

Fiske Kimball had a commanding, almost formidable, physical presence, a height of over six feet, with ample girth, created, as he used to say, by his wife Marie's good cooking. There was a touch of gaucherie in the movement of his bulk: he often reminded one of a bull in a china shop. His most formidable feature, however, was his cannonball head with its roundness emphasized by the shortness of his haircut. From it emanated persuasive ideas and an undeviating purpose. He was a titan of directed energy. The direction came from his sense of dedication to the Museum. That institution was his creation, his lifework. I recall his saying to Henri (Marceau, Associate Director) and me: "I have no hobbies. You, Henri, have your fishing and you, Carl, have your garden. But I have no such relaxations: the Museum is my life." In the single-minded and sometimes ruthless pursuit of his goal, Fiske reminded me of a character in Antoine de Saint-Exupéry's novella *Night Flight*. He was Rivière, the airport chief who held his pilots inexorably to the performance of their obligation, namely, to get the mail through. He sacrificed all considerations of decency and humanity to his stringent sense of duty and the fulfillment of his chosen task.

As Rivière reflected: "To make oneself beloved one need only to show pity. I show little pity, or I hide it. To be sure it would be fine to create friendships and human kindness around me. But I am the servant of events, and to make others serve them, too, I must temper my men like steel." Kimball was not entirely Rivière: he did show some human kindness. At least he did toward me and I know of several instances toward others. On numerous occasions he complimented me on a job well done or on my skill in diplomacy. To be sure, flattery is cheap, as Emanuel Benson of the staff, had occasion to say about Kimball. But I considered it not flattery but guidance: he advised me, a newcomer, about people and the background of the Philadelphia scene, he set me on the right track and showed me what pitfalls to avoid. I have no cause for complaint, although I am quite sure that if I had not been such a willing and perceptive instrument, I would have felt the cold steel of his will.

Recently in conversation with Lessing Rosenwald I mentioned that I intended to do a portrait of Kimball. He ventured the waggish comment, "Fiske was not completely photogenic." I laughed and said "Oh, I'll put in the warts and all!" It is true that people have had unfortunate experiences with him, and therefore have viewed his actions and motives in a bad light. Miss Edna Donnell, who had once collaborated with Kimball on a research project, burst out: "Oh yes, Dr. Kimball has a heart of gold—gold plate!" There can be no question but that Kimball used people without compunction. But it must be kept in mind that he did it for a cause and not for personal aggrandizement. If he used me, it was for an aim which I also believed in, and therefore I was a willing partner in the enterprise. Less savory was his cynical attitude toward gratitude. I remember being shocked when he said that since Frederick Keppel of the Carnegie Corporation had retired it was not necessary to be nice to him anymore. He often quoted a modification of La Rochefoucauld's maxim: "Gratitude is the lively sense of future benefits to come." Another of his less ingratiating traits was his clumsy technique at flattering a prospective donor or a VIP. The adulation was laid on so crudely that it hardly seemed possible for the recipient to be unaware of its speciousness. Kimball had none of Marceau's innate tact and benevolence. Fiske apparently was unable to bring his feelings into play and had to operate with his intelligence, which betrayed him. He had his share of intellectual arrogance and did not suffer fools easily. He showed no pity for those who were slow on the uptake, and members of the staff sometimes emerged from his office with tears in their eyes. Apoligies and long-winded explanations enraged him; he felt that uninterrupted locution was his exclusive privilege. Staff meetings and lunches generally consisted of monologues on a high level, enlivened by anecdotes and analogies from statecraft. In company, he apparently felt that he had a social obligation to "entertain." Because he did it well, he tended to monopolize attention, forgetting that others might also want to make a contribution. With his peers and on his best behavior, Fiske had an attractive quality of mind and a fluent mastery of his erudition. He was a practiced speaker by reason of his long experience as a college teacher. (He claimed that preachers and professors had the best training for public speaking.)

It was an exciting experience to work with Fiske Kimball. He was indeed a slave driver. Yet he never asked one to do something he was not prepared to do himself. And he did not interfere with his curators once he was convinced of their competence. Furthermore, if one could sell him an idea, it would be almost equivalent to getting it accomplished, for he would try to get the money for it and defend it before the trustees. Incidentally, I found that the best way to put over an idea was to submit a memorandum beforehand. He appreciated concise and schematic presentations—but seldom got them. In this way I could get my facts across before he started questioning. In his relations with his curators he was never devious; you could rely on his word. He never would sell you down the river behind your back or use you as a scapegoat to get himself out of a mess. The staff at the Museum was small; indeed, Fiske used to boast that we had the smallest staff of any major museum in the country. Under his direction we accomplished wonders—on a shoe-string. We established an esprit de corps. On occasion when there was an opening or a crisis, we would pitch in and aid the one who needed help. There was little bickering or internecine politics among the staff: all resentments and petty contentions were focused on the Director—again the stern father image of Rivière comes to mind. Indeed, some members of the staff used to call him Papa. Kimball made quick and firm decisions. They might have been wrong—no one is infallible—but generally were right, as revealed by hindsight. There was, however, a special virtue in the quickness and firmness. The person who can not make up his mind, who procrastinates interminably and then makes a wrong decision, is totally unfit to be a director. Fiske had other traits of the good executive. He always answered his mail promptly and was accessible to his staff. By instinct and training he was able to delegate responsibility and yet maintain control.

The Museum has always, but especially in the early days, been hampered by lack of operating funds. Kimball, with his many connections in the scholarly world, had gathered together an able staff. He was a judge of character and competence. But he did not always have the money to retain them, and some, for instance Joseph Downs, Calvin Hathaway, Francis Henry Taylor, Horace Jayne, and Lawrence Roberts, left perforce to advance elsewhere. For several departments Kimball had to rely on what amounted to voluntary help. There is some significance in the fact that those particular departments had chiefs (Kimball and Marceau) as well as curators. As a general rule Fiske preferred curators, who, like career diplomats, made museum work their exclusive occupation, over those who gave their services gratuitously or almost so. This was not necessarily because the volunteers were incompetent—they often were well qualified by taste, training, and experience—but because as members of the socially elite class they were exposed to a conflict of interest through a responsible job at a museum. Life in "the social set" is a demanding career in itself. Its members must devote their time and energy to a daily round of entertaining and being entertained, to concern for personal well-being and adornment, to attendance at the opera or charitable ball, not to mention the obligation to be seen at the correct season in the fashionable resorts of Europe or the Caribbean. I am not implying that such people are reprehensible: they live a life of pleasurable pursuits and of cultivated leisure that many people envy. They can be, as I well know, amusing and charming in company and can offer delectable hospitality. From a detached viewpoint, however, it is obvious that by reason of their absorption in their own vocation, they could not give the Museum the dedicated service that Kimball demanded.

In addition to absenteeism and similar matters, Kimball had to contend with problems connected with the power structure of the Museum. One was the dominance for a period of John Story Jenks as Vice-President and Chairman of the powerful Committee on Museum. He was a businessman with conservative leanings, who had managed to acquire great influence in Museum affairs without special qualifications for the post. His inclinations were toward solvency, living within income, and never toward expansion. We used to call him "The Undertaker." As Fiske once said, Jenks was capable of entertaining only one idea at a time, and it was the Director's task on the day when the Committee met, to lunch with him and coach him on the relevant idea. It was extraordinary how patient Fiske could be, how much he could subordinate his personal feelings and preferences to the achievement of his long-range goal. Jenks seemed to have little sense of humor. Fiske recounted the story of taking him around my exhibition of Humorous Prints and Drawings. Not a smile or chuckle appeared on Jenks's face. In desperation Fiske said "Here is something really funny" as he paused before a sequence of drawings by Alfred Frueh poking fun at the rivalry between two dairy firms. At the Borden Company's barns, the well-trained cows, when they saw an airplane writing the word *Sheffield* in the sky, instinctively bunched together to form the word *Bordens* on the ground. Jenks could not recognize the jeu d'esprit; he looked at it in business terms: "Yes, yes, I know Mr. Milton, chairman of the board of the Borden Co., a fine man. The company must have commissioned the drawing."

R. Sturgis Ingersoll succeeded John Jenks as Chairman of

the Committee on Museum and later succeeded J. Stogdell Stokes as President of the Museum. It was the beginning of a fruitful association between Kimball and Ingersoll. With his brilliant mind, his gusto for experience, and his passion for art (he was an enthusiastic collector), Sturgis brought a more vibrant sense of life into the staid halls of the Museum. Fiske had no need to coach him on ideas, for he was brimming over with aesthetic reactions and plans. Nonetheless, Fiske showed the same deference toward him that he had toward Jenks and probably toward others in authority before I came to the Museum or was in a position to observe. No doubt it was a basic element in his personality, but I never ceased wondering how Kimball could be so domineering to his inferiors and so humble and respectful to his superiors in rank. I recall a lunch where Sturgis was host to Kimball, Marceau, and me at the Philadelphia Club in February 1951. Sturgis broached the idea of a Festival of the Arts as an extension of the Jubilee of 1950. Fiske took on the assignment as a loyal minister should, never questioning the validity of the project, but committing the staff and the whole Museum to the task at hand: "We three are the inner circle, we will bend to the wheel." Fiske could easily have fitted into a monarchical form of society. Indeed, by choice of studies and partly by innate prefence, Fiske seems to have identified himself closely with Louis XIV and his era. One of the great moments of his life was, I am sure, the intimate candlelight dinner party, *souper aux chandelles,* in celebration of the installation of the Louis XIV Room in May of 1954. A select group of fourteen people dined on dishes chosen by Marie Kimball and served on authentic accessories (Sèvres china, French glass, and the like) to the sound of a trio playing the music of Lully.

It is small wonder, in view of his admiration for French eighteenth-century life, that his tastes were on the formal side. He dressed conservatively and well. He had become acutely conscious of the conventions imposed by Philadelphia society. I recall that he cautioned me about going without a hat. Hoddy Jayne of the Oriental Department, he said, was the only person in Philadelphia who was allowed to go bareheaded in polite circles. Dinners at his house on Lemon

Hill were always formal. In the depths of winter the event could be a trial for the guests, especially for the women in décolleté gowns, since the big elliptical drawing room was heated only by two tiny fireplaces. I never understood how Marie, even with her fur stole, could endure the penetrating cold. I once had a discussion with Fiske on the amenities of modern heating. I wondered why the inheritors of the Roman Empire had not kept up the Roman tradition of central heating. Fiske argued that *comfort modern* was not really different from the custom in *l'ancien régime*. It was merely a question of replacing a huge retinue of servants by a system of gadgets and appliances. Nevertheless, the dinners at Lemon Hill were always an event, for Marie was a marvelous cook as well as a gracious hostess.

She was friendly and considerate to me, and especially to my wife, Laura, as newcomers to Philadelphia. As the Director's wife she played an exemplary role. She never played museum politics or interfered in museum affairs. She did help her husband in writing and research, in addition to being a charming hostess. Fiske was devoted to her and affectionately called her "Puss." They certainly were an unusual pair: she petite and feminine, he a big bull of a man. He must have been strongly sexed, but he remained ardently monogamous. I once made some reference to a joke, current at the time of the First World War, that had as the punch line, "and give my compliments to the Duke." Fiske said, "Do you know, that used to be my nickname in the old days." At any rate, Marie was the only person who could manage Fiske and keep him within bounds. Incidentally, as a motorist he was a demon driver. He would charge through red lights, cut sharp corners, and speed at eighty miles an hour. There used to be a St. Christopher medal at the Museum that was lent to the staff member who was slated to ride with him.

On the scholarly side, Kimball was well qualified for a museum post. He had a substantial background of art history to give his policies a consistent direction. He wrote a number of books that are a real contribution to scholarship. He was trained as an architect and had practiced his profession—an asset for one who was building up a museum. He was know-

ledgeable not only in the decorative arts so dear to Philadelphia taste but also in painting and sculpture of the past and
present. He was fully aware of the avant-garde of his day. At
the beginning he concentrated, and rightly so, on decorative
arts and period rooms. He had a big museum to fill and they
gave it a unique character. He was a pioneer in the incorporation of historical architectural elements into the structure
of the edifice and in the arrangement of significant art objects in an appropriate period setting. But he did not entirely
neglect paintings. Even if he did not have abundant aesthetic
reactions—he was more a scholar than an artist—at least he
had the knowledge to determine what was important, and
some connoisseurship to know what was right. The list of his
achievements is impressive. In the decorative arts there were
the rehabilitation and furnishing of the Park Houses as subsidiary musuems, also the contents of the period rooms (notably the Elinor Elkins Rice Drawing Room and the Lans-
downe Drawimg Room), the Wistar Harvey furniture and
fund, and numerous other classes of decorative arts. Fiske's
courage in buying for a high price the Randolph wing chairs
is noteworthy. In sculpture there was the acquisition of the
bronze Diana by St. Gaudens, the Clodion and Pajou sculptures from the Stotesbury collection, not to mention exceptional pieces in the Foulc (Renaissance marbles and bronzes)
and Barnard collections. Among the famous paintings acquired under Fiske's directorship were Cézanne's *Big Bathers*
and *Mont Saint Victoire,* Charles Willson Peale's *Staircase
Group,* Poussin's *Triumph of Neptune and Amphitrite* from the
Hermitage collection, and Rubens's *Prometheus.* (Incidentally,
it was Henry P. McIlhenny who alerted the Museum to the
worth and availability of the Rubens painting.) In Oriental
art may be cited the Williams carpets, the Crozier porcelain
and crystal, the Caspary-Gow porcelain, the Jayne, Rockefeller, and Archbold Japanese prints, and the Kramrisch Indian
sculpture; in prints and drawings, the Collins manuscripts,
the great collection of Watteau prints given by Lessing J.
Rosenwald, the complete collection of Lautrec posters given
by Sturgis Ingersoll, the eighteenth-century prints given by
E. A. Ballard, Mrs. Hawkes, and Dr. Rosenbach, and the

Staunton Peck prints and fund. The really big collections acquired during Kimball's tenure were of course the Eakins paintings given by his widow, the George Gray Barnard medieval collection (acquired by Barnard after he had sold his first collection to John D. Rockefeller for a huge sum to form the nucleus of The Cloisters in New York), and finally the Lisa Elkins, the Gallatin, and the Arensberg collections. Nor should the negotiations (in which Henri Marceau participated) leading to the provisional transfer of the great John G. Johnson collection to the Museum be overlooked. In the acquisition of all these notable works, Fiske showed himself to be an able and persuasive negotiator for gift or purchase: he always came up with a decisive idea or gesture that clinched the deal. For instance, Kimball's purchase of a painting *The Wrestlers* by Thomas Eakins for $400 from the Sesquicentennial Exposition in 1926 was a decisive, though by no means the only, factor that induced Mrs. Eakins to give the big collection of her husband's paintings and sketches to the Museum in 1929-1930. Incidentally, Kimball's gesture was not premeditated but prompted by his own pleasure; nevertheless it was effective, because he was the only person who bought a picture at the show and Mrs. Eakins was duly impressed. Kimball's initiative in telephoning Gallatin on the day he heard that his collection was to be evicted from its cramped quarters in New York University, and his courage in contracting to show it complete—another museum offered to show only a dozen pictures—won him the collection. At that time (1943) Miró, Arp, Mondrian, Léger, and Picasso were not accepted as they were thirty years later. In the case of the Arensberg collection, where the competition was keen, Kimball's strategy in dealing with Walter Arensberg (who never could make up his mind) was to bring along Marie, who made friends with his wife, Louise Arensberg. It was she who made up Walter's mind. Of course, Fiske also had one ace in his hand that tended to eliminate some competitors for the prize: thanks to Eli Kirk Price, he had the space available to show the collection in its completeness. In the quest for the Chester Dale collection, Kimball came on the scene late. Nonetheless, his daring in promising to exhibit a contoversial painting, *La Visite* by Toulouse Lautrec, aroused the collector's interest—even though he was already committed to Washington and Chicago—and gained his approval for a loan of modern paintings to Philadelphia. Kimball's success here, however, was only temporary. After ten years the loan was withdrawn, but so was the far greater and presumably more permanent loan to Chicago, both in the interest of the National Gallery in Washington. Kimball's hopes also were disappointed when after a long and pleasant cultivation of the Robinsons, Edward G. and his wife Gladys agreed to disagree. The California law on joint holdings forced a liquidation of the estate and Onassis snapped up the distinguished collection of paintings.

Fiske thus did not succeed every time in the competetive game of netting art collections. Perhaps the biggest fish to get away was the Joseph Widener Collection. It was not for want of effort, for Kimball employed all his resources of persuasion and diplomacy. He was hopeful to the end, but the cards were stacked against him. He could not revise past history. There were many factors involved, no one of which could be considered decisive. Philadelphia society had given P. A. B. Widener and his son Joseph the cold shoulder (Joseph, for instance, had been blackballed by the Philadelphia Club). The Mayor of the city, J. Hampton Moore, in conversation with Widener is supposed to have said "Who cares about art anyway." It was a fact that the Philadelphia Museum of Art almost went broke during the Depression, and might do so again, whereas the National Gallery in Washington was backed by the credit and prestige of the whole nation. It also has been said that Kimball's hands were tied because the Vice-President insisted on negotiating with Widener—he could do it, he said, because he sat next to him at board meetings. Kimball had worked out an ingenious plan to display the paintings and other objects, but was never able to show it to Widener. If he had, he might have persuaded Widener. Speculation in might-have-beens, however, is endless and unprofitable.

I acted as the liaison for a bid to acquire the whole of the Stieglitz collection (it was shown at the Museum in 1944).

And again the odds were against us: it turned out that the huge collection was not destined to be kept intact, and Philadelphia came off third in the division. I, was of course disappointed to learn that Lessing Rosenwald's superb collection of prints and drawings was destined for the National Gallery before I came upon the scene. Nonetheless, Lessing became and still is a good friend of the Museum, and especially of the Print Department. By contrast, my quest for the Eldridge Johnson collection ended up in complete frustration. When I arrived I learned about this fabulous collection with its many rarities—Dürer and Rembrandt prints, complete in many states, also Schongauers and eighteenth-century color prints. I was never able to get to the proper authorities to state my case. After Johnson's death, the collection was sold at auction. Johnson's son later told Stodgell Stokes that it would have been more advantageous for the estate to have given the prints to the Museum on account of the high inheritance taxes.

There have been various accounts of Dr. Barnes's feud with the Philadelphia Museum of Art. I witnessed an amusing incident in the Doctor's campaign against Fiske Kimball. It was during the Matisse exhibition of 1948, when the Museum arranged a course of lectures on various aspects of Matisse's art. One of them was to be given by Prof. David Robb, the art historian at the University of Pennsylvania. Barnes exerted so much pressure on the university authorities that Robb at the last moment felt unable to give his lecture. It was too late to cancel the lecture and so Kimball took his place. Barnes came with his retinue determined to heckle the speaker and break up the meeting if possible. The lecture started mildly enough: Kimball explained that he was substituting unexpectedly and therefore was lecturing off the cuff. He continued with a few generalities about Matisse and his life, and then the first volley of the Barnes campaign was launched. One of Barnes's men got up and asked a few questions. He was Abraham Chanin, a former student at the Barnes Foundation and at the time a staff lecturer at the Museum of Modern Art. Fiske answered his questions and then with great presence of mind said to him: "You seem to know a great deal about Matisse; won't you come up here and tell the audience about Matisse's style and derivations." Chanin was flattered and complied. Fiske, stalling for time, kept him talking and then suggested that Chanin should analyze some of the key pictures—in other words, give a gallery talk. He was discoursing on a painting owned by the Museum of Modern Art when Dr. Barnes, playing the innocent, said out loud: "That man speaks very well about art; I wonder who he is." I was standing about eight feet away from him and said: "You know perfectly well who that man is." "Oh," said he, "so you are in the know!" and came toward me with hand outstretched to shake my hand. But I turned on my heel and left him dangling. The rest of the lecture passed off without incident. Fiske's quick wit had spoiled Dr. Barnes's strategy and prevented the meeting from ending in a brawl. The same kind of direct and unexpected action was in evidence once when Dr. Barnes's cohorts were picketing the Museum. Kimball came out and walked back and forth with the picket line, talking to the leader and trying to find out if he had any grievance of his own. Henri Marceau recalls that when he telephoned Kimball to tell him of Barnes's death and how he had run through a red light and was clipped by a truck, Fiske's instant comment was "how characteristic."

The climax of Kimball's career came in 1950 with the Jubilee Celebration of the Museum's Seventy-fifth Anniversary and in 1951 with his receiving the Bok Philadelphia Award. The first in a way was an intramural satisfaction, an acknowledgment of what he had done for the Museum; the second was in recognition of what he had done for his adopted city. The Jubilee was an exciting and triumphant year. An extensive campaign for gifts was inaugurated. The installation of a group of paintings given by the Kress Foundation was to my mind the only false note in the otherwise joyous and successful celebration. Fiske had so ardently wanted to have a donation of Kress paintings as a crowning triumph for the Jubilee. He forced the issue when the Foundation was not prepared to make the gesture, with the result that some paintings of dubious value were included only because they were available. About a year later, Ingersoll and Kimball went to Guy Emerson of the Samuel H. Kress Foundation and asked if they might return a portion of the group in exchange for other paintings. Emerson did not consider this feasible and asked for the return of the whole group "without prejudice." In 1959, through Marceau's tactful negotiations, the Kress Foundation finally presented to the Museum the great series of tapestries originally executed for the Barberini Palace in Rome. The thirteen large tapestries designed by Peter Paul Rubens and Pietro da Cortona and depicting episodes in the life of Constantine, now grace the second floor of the Great Hall. For the Jubilee two major loan exhibitions of paintings and drawings were assembled by Henri Marceau and me. In addition to the Museum dinner for the lenders, Sturgis Ingersoll and his wife, Marian, gave a special dinner in honor of Henri and me in one of the Sutton Scarsdale memorial halls. I look back on it as the most pleasurable dinner party in my museum experience. It was a gay and happy party: the setting was elegant, the food delicious, and the drinks were plentiful—champagne from beginning to end. We all woke up the next morning feeling unreal. Sturgis confessed that he had asked the newspaper vendor at the hotel for a copy of the *Philadelphia Ledger*—a newspaper that had been out of existance for a great many years.

The Philadelphia Award was a personal triumph for Fiske. The city had changed much during the thirty-odd years he had lived there, and some of the changes were due to Fiske. There was a new look in the city and its people: gone were the old lethargy and smugness, together with the *Chinese Wall.* More people loved and respected the Museum now, and the press was more cooperative. The Museum had opened wider horizons in many avenues, not only by introducing the design of today (Joseph Downs put on a show, *Design for the Machine,* in 1932, which antedated a similar exhibition at the Museum of Modern Art by two years) but also by bringing to the city the masterpieces of the past on a worldwide scale (the Salt Mine Pictures of Germany and the treasures of the Vienna Museum). He introduced the works of the innovators close to the future, the Matisses, the Picassos, and the rest of them. In the midst of all the elation, however, Fiske could still look at the future soberly. He considered the Jubilee more or less as the end of an era. In the early part of his career he had relied on private collections and big fortunes to attain his purpose. Now he foresaw that the returns from that source were apt to diminish. In the future he thought he would have to rely more and more on the city fathers for support, and their only criterion was an attendance figure. Yet he was more resolute than ever to insist on high aesthetic standards. He would not give in to the lowest common denominator.

The formal opening for the installation of the Arensberg Collection occurred on October 15, 1954. A few days before, George Widener had given a private dinner for the appropriate dignitaries in the art world. Marcel Duchamp and his wife, the d'Harnoncourts, the Ritchies, the Sweeneys, the Finleys, Nelson Rockefeller, Mayor Clark, as well as numerous members of the Museum family, were present. Walter and Louise Arensberg had not lived to see the installation of their collection, but Walter's brother from Pittsburgh was there. There were speeches, and the visiting dignitaries were properly appreciative. It was one more triumph for Fiske. But on the night of the private opening for Museum members, a hurricane was raging. Laura and I dodged falling trees to get to town, and then arrived at the Museum in company with Adrian and Sophie Siegel and the Mitchells. We got there at a quarter to nine and counted only a dozen arrivals. Marie was sitting forlornly on a stone bench in the Johnson octagon, Fiske was prowling around the galleries. As the storm abated a few more people drifted in. The New York contingent on the six o'clock train was marooned outside North Philadelphia and did not arrive at the Museum until half past ten. Those who had taken the seven o'clock train never got to Philadelphia until past midnight, when the Museum was closed. All in all, 184 hardy souls managed to get to the opening. Such was the modest beginning of the crowds that poured into the Arensberg Wing thereafter.

On May 19, 1943, I had lunch with Fiske at the Museum.

In the course of desultory conversation he made a statement so startling that I made a note of it in my journal. I do not remember what led up to it, but this is what he said: "If I last eight years more as Director I will be doing well." I was to learn later how prophetic the statement was. Late in 1951 Henri Marceau mentioned to me that he sometimes came upon Fiske sitting in his office in moods of deep depression. But he snapped out of them and did not act queerly otherwise. At the beginning of 1954, however, there was no doubt of what was happening. Fiske was suffering from a manic-depressive psychosis, and it was progressively getting worse. On January 22 Henri felt that he ought to go to Sturgis and tell him about Fiske's queer actions. He was not, he said, trying to engineer a palace revolution, but he was worried about Kimball and what was happening at the Museum. Sturgis, however, was reluctant to take drastic action for the time being. As long as Kimball confined his vagaries to the Museum staff, we could be understanding and tolerant, but when he dredged up sexual fantasies from his subconscious and insulted people outside the fold, the situation became more serious. Marie had become ill with a heart condition and could no longer control his behavior. Fortunately, no decisive outburst took place and soon summer and vacation time arrived. In the autumn Fiske returned to the Museum in a more relaxed frame of mind, and seemed reasonably sane for the Arensberg opening. Alas, the bad spells returned early in December when Marie became seriously ill. On January 21, Ingersoll had no recourse but to ask Kimball to his office and accept his resignation.

There is little point in dwelling on the tragic details of the next few months. Fiske's friends John Canaday, Franklin Watkins, and Erling Pederson joined us in trying to persuade him to submit to treatment—without avail. Marie's funeral at Lemon Hill on March 5th was a nightmare, with Fiske in a high state of euphoria. On April 15 he sailed for Europe, and on August 14, 1955, word came of his death and blessed release. The sad story of the "Gotterdämmerung" is told in detail in the Roberts book.

During the whole episode, Sturgis Ingersoll conducted

himself in a wise and humane manner in spite of the insults that Kimball heaped upon him. He was constantly in touch with us and commended us all for our loyalty and forbearance. Indeed all of the staff, with one notable exception, remained loyal under great provocation.

The man who carried the heaviest load during Fiske's decline and fall was Henri Marceau. As Associate Director he had worked closely with Fiske for many years. He now had a double burden: in addition to his own duties he had to run the Museum in spite of Fiske and undo the mischief he caused. One can have nothing but admiration for the quiet and efficient way he did his job, just as one must respect and cherish him for his self-effacing loyalty. In many ways he was the opposite of Kimball: where the one was blustering and ruthless, the other was gentle and understanding. One believed in authority, the other in decency and cooperation. My own instincts are for Henri and cooperation, but regretfully I must concede that most people require the whip. Marceau was appointed Director to succeed Kimball. It was a fitting choice and a welcome change. There were ruffled feelings to soothe and wounds to heal after the disastrous years.

Marceau's record as Director, however, must not be considered as a palliative appendage to Kimball's regime, but should be judged on the basis of his own tangible achievements. On that score it ranks high. Henri was a consolidator and builder, not a freebooting raider. Like Fiske, he was an architect by training. He completed a considerable part of the Museum Master Plan. He was on good terms with City Hall and was able to obtain, through diplomacy and expert knowledge, the necessary allocations for the capital building program. With these funds he finished and installed the Far Eastern Wing (comprising the Japanese Temple, Tea House and Garden, Chinese Temple Hall, and Scholar's Study) and the Renaissance Hall on the second floor; and the Decorative Arts Wing (Rush Sculpture Court, Pennsylvania Dutch galleries, Philadelphia Silver, etc.) and the Fashion Wing on the first floor. He also built the Van Pelt Auditorium and finished the ceiling and walls of the Great Hall. He made friends easily, but what is even better, he kept their friendship. He contributed ably to the negotiations leading to the transfer of the Pennsylvania Academy collection of foreign prints and drawings to the Museum. And it is doubtful if the John G. Johnson collection would ever have been housed in the Museum without Marceau's active collaboration. Through his sensitive and courteous cultivation of potential donors he retained or obtained for the Museum the collections of Titus Geesey, Louis Stern, Mr. & Mrs. Caroll Tyson, S. S. and Vera White, and Carl Otto von Kienbusch, even though some of them were not installed by the time of his retirement. The soft approach in solicitation can be as effective as the hard sell—witness Aesop's fable concerning the efficacy of the sun and the wind! Henri was an excellent administrator and had cordial and equitable relations with his staff. In his chosen field—paintings were his specialty—he had a connoisseur's eye and a scholar's judgment. His long association with David Rosen—one of the great conservators of our time—gave him the knowledge and discrimination to decide when and how much to restore a painting in question. He also assembled at the Museum three huge shows of contemporary sculpture in conjunction with the Fairmount Park Art Association.

My association with Fiske Kimball during fifteen years was an exciting and rewarding experience. The harrowing end seems but a minor and irrelevant part of the man. I prefer to remember him in his prime, working and fighting with un-flagging determination. I remember breaking the news to Fiske that Francis Taylor had resigned from the Metropoli-tan Museum of Art and was going back to Worcester. Fiske's instant reaction was "confession of failure." This is more re-vealing of Kimball's attitude than of Taylor's, for it was, in my opinion, a courageous and sensible act on Taylor's part: he knew when he had had enough. If Fiske had had as much sense, he might have retired before he broke down in har-ness with Wagnerian overtones. Kimball and Taylor both were picturesque characters. In a moment of fancy I once speculated on the avatars of some of my friends. Coomaras-wamy in Boston was a Brahmin among Brahmins, Ivins a Jonathan Swift bred to the law. I could see Kimball as a scholar-courtier during *le Grand Siècle,* perhaps as an energetic *Directeur des Bâtiments* at the Court of Louis XIV, and I saw Taylor in a toga as a "wisecracking" Roman Senator or member of the College of Augurs. Fiske and Francis had numerous things in common. They both had gusto and a Rabelaisian sense of humor, which shocked many people. (William Ivins used to leave the room when Francis started to tell a story.) Both had a touch of the grotesque—that is the word used by Juliana Force—in physical appearance. Both were scholars and men of affairs. Both could be swashbuckling buccaneers and raid each other's preserves of donors and funds without compunction. Yet each had a sensitive and tender side. The generous and responsive side of Francis Taylor's nature is revealed in a tribute he paid to Fiske——perhaps the most beautiful tribute anyone could pay to him. It appears in the inscription he wrote in the presentation copy of his book *The Taste of Angels,* 1948:

To Fiske Kimball
    To whom I am only now realizing how much I owe.

19

Henry Allen Moe

My idea of Henry Allen Moe, before I met him, was that of a remote, almost Godlike presence, dispensing stipends to deserving artists and scholars. It turned out, when we became better acquainted, that he is a humane and delightful human being. My first contact with him was when I received a Guggenheim Fellowship in 1939 (for a study of American printmaking). He was gracious and understanding, and could not have been more helpful in providing advice and numerous letters of introduction. He made me feel that he was genuinely concerned with my problems and was prepared to back me up on whatever I wanted to do. Other Fellows have told me that they had the same experience. I was much impressed by the idea behind the philanthropy and was interested in finding out how it had started. The benefaction was established by Senator and Mrs. Simon Guggenheim in memory of their son, John Simon Guggenheim, after his untimely death in 1922. The bereaved parents, concerned with founding a suitable memorial for their lost son, sought advice from Henry Moe, who, as a brilliant Rhodes Scholar, had recently returned from Oxford with a degree in jurisprudence. In the dialogue between him and them, the idea of a philanthropic memorial took shape: "to promote the advancement and diffusion of knowledge and understanding, and the appreciation of beauty by aiding—without distinction on account of race, color, or creed—scholars, scientists, and artists of either sex in the prosecution of their labors." Henry had a vision not only of the goal but also of the means of achieving it. He had no model to follow because the Foundation was a pioneer venture into the field of giving aid to individuals in the broad spectrum of the arts and sciences. It is easy to give away money indiscriminately or in large masses; it is much more difficult to make sure than an individual will use the money to the best advantage. There is no certain way, but Henry's method produced a high average of results. First of all, the recipient Fellow was always treated with decency and respect; he was put on his honor and not required to give any accounting of what he did. The touchstone of selection was to screen the applicant for technical competence by a jury of his peers, and then to have the achievement potentials in the various arts, sciences, and humanities balanced and coordinated by a dedicated and highly qualified super-committee. Here Moe's uncanny judgment of character served him in good stead. He was able to select the proper persons for his juries and committees of selection, and also to inspire in them a devotion to high ideals. Such were the ways and means he set up when the John Simon Guggenheim Memorial Foundation was incorporated in 1925 with capital furnished by Senator Guggenheim, and with Henry Moe serving as Secretary-General or Director.

After I had completed my Guggenheim Fellowship in 1939 and 1940, I still maintained occasional contacts with the Foundation. In 1942, for example, I wrote a letter on Foundation policy in wartime in response to a form letter sent to all Fellows. It apparently impressed Moe, and he sent me an appreciative letter. Most of the time I wrote confidential appraisals of artists who had asked me to sponsor their applications. Not many of the printmakers whom I considered worthy ever seemed to get a Fellowship: my words evidently carried little weight. I began to think about the problem, and speculate whether there was a flaw in Henry's system. Finally, toward the end of 1944, I mustered up courage to write Moe a letter expressing my reservations about the personnel of the art jury. One point was a specific comment: there had always been painters and sculptors on the jury but never a printmaker. In view of the current upsurge in American graphic art, this omission implied neglecting a strong and active segment of American creative endeavor. The second point was a general plea for younger blood on the jury. The composition of the jury had remained the same for many years; all of them were over sixty. I knew them all; they were decent and fair-minded people, but with the best of will in the world they were bound to acquire an unconscious bias as they grew older. The times were changing and new trends were coming to the fore, which could not be judged by old standards. I suggested that the Foundation was losing its flexibility in at least one field and thus overlooking sizable potentials. Henry Moe's answer was as characteristic of him as it was unexpected by me. He invited me to be a member of the artists' jury for the year 1945. Moe told me long afterwards that he had already considered the possibility of my joining the jury and had even talked it over with Beal, Burchfield, and Young. My letter had merely precipitated the action. His method with juries was pragmatic and experimental: if one jury did not work, he would try another. He started out originally with a jury consisting of an artist (Fraser), a museum director (Harshe), an architect (Emerson), and an art critic (Cortissoz), and even an art dealer (David Keppel). Gradually it became clear to him that nonartists did not understand artists' problems. More artists were put on: Gari Melchers, Rockwell Kent, Gifford Beal, and Eugene Speicher. James Earle Fraser continued to stay on.

Thus it came about that on one March morning in 1945 I arrived at the Polo Storage Warehouse near 125th Street in New York City along with the other jurors: two painters, Gifford Beal and Charles Burchfield; two sculptors, James Earle Fraser and Mahonri Young. Mahonri I knew very well, and I was fond of him; we used to have fun together in Paris (as I have told elsewhere), but I did not always see eye to eye with him in judgments of art. Fraser was the only one whom I had not known personally, and I took to him at once. Except for a certain rigidity in sculptoral matters, I found him surprisingly open-minded. Often he would be the only one who was sympathetic to my plea for a fresh look at things. I doubt whether I affected the selection of awards to any extent that year. I did not try to throw my weight around, for I am not an aggressive debater. I sought rather to gain the jury's respect for me as a person who could talk their language and look at things with as much insight and sensitivity as they did—in short, to be accepted as one of them. I was able to make my reactions to specific works of art comprehensible to them, and also to encourage discussion of various trends on occasion. For instance, they did not seem to know what surrealism was all about, and at lunch together I had a long argument with Mahonri about William Hayter and his work. I knew I was on probation; I wanted to make good in order that I might later be able to speak for artist minorities and unrepresented areas of endeavor. In due course Henry reported to me the favorable reaction of the jury: I was in. I therefore was invited for the following year and for many years thereafter.

It might be illuminating to recount the typical procedure of a Guggenheim Fellowship art jury. The sessions were usually held in a storage warehouse (for instance, Manhattan Storage Co., Lincoln Storage Co., and Santini Brothers). For a month before, paintings, drawings, prints, and photographs would be received and placed in bins or shelves for easy access. A special room was outfitted with an exhibition wall and a battery of chairs for the jurors and for Henry Moe and his recording staff. Extra heating arrangements had to be made because the room was usually cold in March; we always wore extra sweaters and sometimes overcoats. On the first morning, the jurors separated into groups for the preliminary round of viewing. Every entry was looked at by least one or possibly two jurors. The object of the preliminary examination was to reduce the number of applications to manageable

proportions. Since anybody, even art students, Sunday painters, and incompetents in general—it was a revelation to see
what passes for art throughout the country!—were free to
apply it was obvious that a lot of work could be eliminated
without further ado. The two sculpture jurors withdrew to a
trestle table piled with photographs of sculpture and studied
them. Actual sculptures were not submitted, but jurors in the
later sessions might ask for examples and the Foundation
would endeavor to supply them. In any case, the jurors were
trained to judge sculpture from photographs. I would withdraw to another trestle table and look over batches of prints.
I set aside those which I felt had no chance whatsoever, and
reserved a sizable group for consideration by the whole jury.
The painting jurors had the toughest job: they had to plough
through all the paintings, many of them huge and unwieldy.
They would sit patiently while the installation crew set up the
pictures on or by the exhibition wall, a long and tedious process. By lunch time, the print and sculpture jurors would
have finished their stint and would be watching the painters
at their task of winnowing. After lunch we might continue to
watch the painters, thereby getting acquainted with the material submitted. After they were finished, Henry Moe might
call for a review of the print or sculpture entries by the entire jury. It was Henry's idea that the whole jury should pass
on works in all media. He reasoned that the excellence of an
applicant's achievement should be apparent to practitioners
in other disciplines and not only to specialists in one
medium. Such a regimen built up a greater esprit de corps
and also provided a slight check on specialized ivory-tower
judgments, but it certainly was more time consuming. During
the first round of examination by the full jury, one affirma-
tive vote sufficed to hold the applicant's entry for further
consideration. Nonetheless, quite a number of pictures were
weeded out on the first full round, since we had to start
somewhere. There might be five hundred painting entries
(out of a total of four times that number), each one of which
consisted of from five to ten large paintings or double the
number of smaller ones. There often were discussions of
specific works: if a juror felt strongly pro or con, he had to

justify his position by argument. On the second and subsequent rounds, two or three votes were necessary to keep the entry in. The final reckoning came on the last day. The very few unanimous choices were secure, but then there was a battle royal over the doubtful list. A juror might withdraw his choice in the face of overwhelming opposition. Another juror might be won over by convincing arguments. In the interest of elimination the jury might be confronted again and again by an either-or choice. It was at this stage that Henry Moe, with his marvelous psychological insight, was most in control. He had watched the reactions of each juror carefully during the sessions. He noted the intensity of their convictions and the cogency of their reasons. Horse trading was unheard of, for the jury was not awarding prizes but investing in talent. Moe would never tell the jury how many Fellowships they could award. He was not interested in the tally of votes. He looked beyond the mechanisms of expediency toward intuitions of quality and convictions of excellence. The jury might be hopelessly deadlocked and still wrangling over relative claims when Henry would call for attention and say, "Gentlemen, I believe I can recommend to the committee the following," and he would enumerate the selections in order, beginning with the unanimous choices at the top and ending with the doubtful and controversial ones at the bottom. He asked if we agreed, and we did with grateful relief. He sensed when we had reached rock bottom in our opinions. Henry's handling of the final situation was his subtle way of compensating in favor of minority opinion, so often steamrollered by majority votes. If an individual belief was so great that it could keep an entry in against overwhelming opposition until the very end, it deserved some recognition. In Henry's eyes the contribution of each one on the jury was equally valid. To return to the narrative, sometimes Henry might say: "I am not sure that the budget will carry all of your recommendations; I will present them all to the committee, but those at the bottom of the list are in danger of rejection." It must be remembered that our jury always acted only in an advisory capacity: it made recommendations to the committee of selection, which in turn decided how much money could be spent on art as against other categories.

When the number of applications for Fellowships grew larger, Henry increased our term of service from two to three days per year. The first two days were spent going over the entries and weeding out all but the most promising work. Then we returned for one morning in the following week for our moment of truth. Henry figured that in this way we would have a week to think over what we really wanted to fight for. After the final decision was made, we all went to a good restaurant for a jolly luncheon. Once it happened that the wives of two jurors, Ida Watkins and Laura Zigrosser, were present and were invited to come along. Thereafter the custom became general and the wives of all the jurors were invited to the final luncheon. I recall the gatherings at the Spanish restaurant, Fornos, as the most pleasurable of our luncheon experiences.

Beginning in 1958 Moe instituted the pleasant custom of giving a dinner for the jury at the Century Club on the evening before the day they started to work. The dinner always was sumptuous, truly a meal for gourmets, with delectable food and wine. The get-together served to introduce a new juror to his co-workers, and in general set a tone of good fellowship and serious endeavor, thus building an esprit de corps. Both Henry and his assistant, Jim Mathias, were imbued with joie de vivre with regard to the amenities. Henry had the rare faculty of distinguishing between and recalling various taste and flavors. He was an ideal connoisseur of wine, and with good reason was chairman of the wine committee at the Century Club. Some of the jurors liked good food and drink, Mahonri Young, Lewis Iselin, Franklin Watkins, and myself. I still remember out shocked surprise when Gener Speicher ordered ham and eggs at Fornos Restaurant while we feasted on *moules marinieres* or *calamares en su tinto*. The Foundation took us to the best restaurants, and in fact treated us as VIPs in every way.

The composition of the jury varied considerably during my participation. Usually it consisted of a pair of painters and a pair of sculptors together with me, who represented printmaking by myself until 1963, when Misch Kohn became my associate. For two years (1958-1959) there were only three members, Watkins, Maldarelli, and I; our responsibilities were proportionately greater. Among those who served on the jury during my tenure were eight painters, Gifford Beal, Charles Burchfield, Franklin Watkins, Louis Bouché, Edward Hopper, Eugene Speicher, Arthur Osver, Robert Motherwell; six sculptors, Mahonri Young, James Earle Fraser, Oronzio Maldarelli, Lewis Iselin, Ezio Martinelli, Theodore Roszak; and two printmakers, Misch Kohn and Mauricio Lasansky. Some of them could be designated as regulars, others as temporary replacements for absent regulars. At lunch or dinner, and during the intervals when the crew was taking away one batch of paintings and bringing in another, we would chat or reminisce. There was a tone of courtesy and good fellowship, a sense of cooperation among equals working for a common cause. It occasionally happened that an elderly regular, or perhaps a temporary replacement for a regular, lost sight of the main objective and slowed up the orderly procedure. He might launch into tedious reminiscence or let his mind stray toward personal concerns, such as how the artist under review had handled a technical painting problem with which the juror himself had also wrestled. Such lapses, however, were rare. The jurors felt their responsibility and were genuinely concerned to select the most worthy applicants. It is interesting that during most of the time I was a member, the general outlook of the jury was visual and nondocumentary. The members relied entirely on the work they saw before them for their judgments. They hardly ever looked at the sponsoring letters or other data in the Foundation dossier. They occasionally asked for the artist's age, but had little interest in the artist's life and personality. There were, of course, inherent differences in the reactions of the individual jurors: some were quick in their judgments, others were laboriously slow. After all, they were being asked to switch from their habitual subjective-creative approach to an objective-critical appraisal. Those painters who also were teachers fared better because of their more objective involvement in their students' work. Not being an artist, I had no problem: I was used to making value judgments. But the problem was more aggravating for the creative artist. Franklin Watkins told me that after such a surfeit of pictures each year he would suffer indigestion, as it were, and might not be able to paint for a week or more.

Of all the members of the jury, the one to whom I felt closest was Franklin Watkins. To be sure, I knew him better and had seen more of him in Philadelphia, in Rome, and on the New Jersey shore at Avalon, where we went surf-fishing. But the tie was cemented by our mutual respect. Watty once said to me that Andrew Ritchie and I were the only museum men he knew who had the artist's basic point of view. And he was always exclaiming, "How do you know so much." I in turn had great admiration for Watty as a man and as an artist. In my opinion he was an ideal juror: he was sensitive to creative potentiality and open-minded toward work outside of his personal style. He felt great responsibility regarding his choices and would worry whether he had made the right selection. In his judgment of Fellowship potential, he (as did I) looked beyond the basic standards of technical competence toward what use the Fellow might make of his skills. We confined our search to the solid middle ground equally remote from the two extremes of an exclusive quest for the new and a stuffy contentment with the old. We both agreed that the extreme dernier cri is often the first to grow stale and become dated. Watty also worried about the deteriorating quality of art teaching, summed up as the blind leading the blind, or about incompetents, successful by publicity and promotion, teaching incompetence to others. He was a keen observer, which made him a good teacher. For instance, when he was introducing me to the fine art of casting in surf-fishing and I was having difficulty with the conventional way of casting, he suddenly said to me "Are you left-handed?" And indeed I am in certain respects; although I write with my right hand, I throw and bat left-handed. When I switched to a left-handed stance my performance was much better. Watty was an agreeable and all-around companion: we—and our wives—have had many pleasant times together. His conversation had rare charm. His responses to life and art did not stem from habit or routine but from nerves exposed and tinging. He had an ingrained creative approach.

My relations with my fellow jurors in the print field were

also based on long acquaintance and mutual esteem. I know Misch Kohn better, because I have seen more of him. I value his continuing friendship, as I do that of Mauricio Lasansky. I regret that my contacts with Arthur Osver were cut off when he left the jury. I somehow responded more readily to the sculpture jurors than to the painting jurors, possibly because printmaking has a closer bond with sculpture than with painting. Oronzio Maldarelli, with his warm Italian nature and lack of pretense, was comfortable to work with. I clicked at once with Lewis Iselin. I enjoyed his boon companionship and respected his aesthetic and critical intelligence. Ezio Martinelli was an old friend: I had known him as a printmaker and sculptor from his Philadelphia days. He was the only one who toasted my departure on my last day at the Guggenheim. Although I met Theodore Roszak only during the 1965 session, I was impressed by his charming personality. He always seemed to be smiling and accessible. He made one feel that he was genuinely interested in what one said. He also spoke with authority about sculpture and gave reasons for his judgments. With only one juror were my relations slightly frigid, namely, with Robert Motherwell. No doubt the dislike was mutual, and I have no doubt that he can treat a member of a jury as an equal. As far as I am concerned, however, an esprit de corps that had endured for twenty years was shattered.

Toward the end of my tenure as a juror I began to feel embarrassed at serving for so long a period. After all, I had joined the jury under the slogan of "more young blood," and my blood was not getting younger. I suggested to Henry that I retire, but he would not hear of it. In 1963, however, after the jury had met for the year, he himself retired, and Gordon N. Ray took his place. In 1965 Osver and Watkins retired; I also renewed my plea for retirement and it was accepted by Gordon, although he asked me to stay on for another year to break in my successor, Mauricio Lasansky. In my final year, 1966, Gordon Ray was getting into gear and beginning to effect innovations. It was inevitable that he would have to take new measures to keep in step with progress. It was natural, therefore, that he would seek new counsel and in general change procedures to meet changed conditions. And so ended one phase in the history of the Guggenheim Fellowships and my connection with it.

The John Simon Guggenheim Memorial Foundation was by no means Henry Moe's only interest: he was active in numerous art and philanthropic organizations, including the American Academy of Rome, the Museum of Modern Art, the Clark Foundation, the Ditson Fund (musicians), and the Tiffany Foundation (artists). He has been for many years President of the American Philosophical Society, and, as presidential appointee in 1965-1966, Chairman of the National Endowment for the Humanities. Yet somehow he has never seemed to me to be the typical bureaucrat or foundation executive. He is too human and too identified with the individual and his creative potentials to be concerned solely with details of impersonal corporate management. To take an example from the annals of the Guggenheim Fellowships, in the season of 1959 the Foundation staff had assembled the obviously unacceptable paintings in one location to save time in carting them back and forth to the exhibition space. When Watkins, Maldarelli, and I (there were only three of us that year) were assembled, Moe explained that he had done this only as an accommodation: any one of us was free to check over the material and pull out anything for submission to the whole jury. Watty dutifully went over the whole lot, and found some work by an unknown artist, James Joseph Hoffman, intriguing enough to warrant having it brought out for the rest of us to see. Moe explained that this man's work had been set aside not for aesthetic but for technical reasons. It turned out that Hoffman was suffering from incurable cancer and was honest enough to say that he had been given only a year to live. All he wanted was a chance to work uninterruptedly for a brief spell without having to think of earning his living. Moe had decided that his case was not in the province of the Guggenheim Foundation, which had long-range benefits in mind. Oronzio and I agreed with Watty that his work, thought not a major contribution, had considerable potential. We had a long discussion; our hearts went out to the artist in his plight and we wondered what we could do about it. Moe finally spoke up: "Gentlemen, if you see merit in this man's work, I will talk to my committee and try to arrange a special grant for him." A few weeks after our sessions were over, I received a note from Henry that the grant to Hoffman had been arranged. In reply I wrote how good it made me feel that a great and distinguished organization such as the J. S. Guggenheim Memorial Foundation had sufficient compassion to let a tiny fragment of the creative spirit have a final fling. Such a gesture of true fellowship or human fellow feeling reminded me of a passage in Tristram Shandy:

> A-well-a-day! — do what we can for him, said Trim, maintaining his point,—the poor soul will die—*He shall not die, by G—*, cried my uncle Toby.
> The Accusing Spirit, which flew up to Heaven's chancery with the oath, blushed as he gave it in;—and the Recording Angel, as he wrote it down, dropped a tear upon the word, and blotted it out forever.

The next year, I asked Moe what had happened to Hoffman. "He died within the year," said Henry, "but he died happy." Henry showed a similar consideration with regard to another human problem. A certain sculptor's work had been approved by the two sculpture jurors and was still in the running toward the end of the judging, when Moe offered the following comment: "The bestowal of a Guggenheim Fellowhsip carries with it a double distinction, a mark of honor and a cash award. This man has a private income. I see no reason why he should be deprived of the honor because he does not need the cash, provided—and this is very important—that his work merits the award. So judge the work strictly on its merits." The man got the Fellowship, and many years later even served on the jury of selection.

In addition to his many public and corporate activities, Henry Moe has been friend and counselor to countless persons—just how many, only Henry knows. I can give one example from personal experience. Around 1952 the trustees of the Guggenheim Museum, dissatisfied with the incumbent director, Hilla von Rebay, were looking for a trustee knowledgeable in museum affairs to advise them on the conduct of the museum and the choice of a new director. Harry F. Guggenheim, chairman of the board asked his friend Henry Moe (whom he admired greatly and in whom he had great confidence, as he told me later) to suggest a possible candidate. Henry suggested me. And thus I was appointed a trustee of the museum. During the interval between Rebay's resignation and the appointment of James Johnson Sweeney as director, I practically ran the museum with the aid of the business administrator, Clinton Hunt. I remained a trustee during the incumbency of J. J. Sweeney and Thomas Messer, and during the building of the present museum, designed by Frank Lloyd Wright. My experiences as a trustee however, can best be told elsewhere.

In 1966 The American Philosophical Society commissioned Franklin Watkins to paint a portrait of its president, Henry Allen Moe. When it was completed, Henry wanted me to see it and had the oil painting sent to the Philadelphia Museum of Art. The letter I wrote to Moe thereafter, tells something of Moe and Watty, and I quote it here as another facet of the unique quality of Henry Allen Moe:

> I had a strange vision at the Art Museum yesterday! I saw Henry Allen Moe resplendent in his scarlet Doctor's robe. No question about it—the man was Henry!
> Joking aside it is a masterly portrait. There is much of Watty and much of you in it—which is as it should be. On the artistic side, it is rich in color and dynamic in composition. There are many details and passages beautifully painted: the ear, the hand, the hair, the swirl in the folds of the robe. By the manipulation of tactile values and structural tensions, and the device of combining the profile and the three-quarter view of the face, Watty manages to suggest a living presence, the illusion of breath and movement in a human being.
> The artist, we are agreed, has painted a work of art. But has he made a good portrait? How much of you is in it? I would say that there is a great deal, but not all of you in it. But since the expression of a "total you" is impossible, everyone is entitled to decide what traits of character are the most important and typical. Watty has chosen—and it is his privilege as an artist—to stress one aspect of your personality, and it is a lofty and laudable aspect. He shows you as a Recording Angel, as a Judge sitting in judgment (not on men but on eternal values), as a far-

sighted planner, building for the future. We see the architect of the concept of the Guggenheim Memorial Foundation and the courageously independent thinker of the Cosmos Club lecture.

But I also see in you another side—your benevolence and your love of humanity, your sympathy with and understanding of creativity in all its forms. I have seen that determined set of your mouth relax into the smile of warm-hearted friendliness. Watty has emphasized the superhuman at the expense of the human qualities. I am sure that Watty recognizes your compassionate side, but he could not express it without destroying the unity of his portrait.

I for one hope that you will long continue to gaze so fiercely into the future. And I congratulate both of you for having produced a distinguished portrait and a great work of art.

20

René d'Harnoncourt:
A Tribute

The art world and the many friends of René d'Harnoncourt were shocked by his accidental and utterly needless death at the hands of a drunken driver in 1968. His passing has left a void in my roster of cherished friends.

I first met him in Mexico, and we liked each other instantly. I have written of my Mexican adventures elsewhere and shall limit the present brief tribute mostly to American reminiscences. He looked me up when he first came to New York—it was in August of 1930 and there were not many people around. I saw him almost continuously for a week before he started on his travels around the country to arrange for the eight showings of his big exhibition, *Mexican Arts*. He was on the go for a month and during that time he spent fifteen nights in Pullman sleepers, quite an ordeal for a man of his height. But during the week he spent in New York, I was privileged to introduce him to the customs and mores of

Yankeeland, and show him the sights and landmarks of the metropolis. It was fun to watch his response to the ludicrous nuances of American life. He relished such preposterous extravagances as the Paramount and the Roxy theaters that "cost a million dollars and every nickel of it showed." For him, who had lived for many years in a single homogenous society, it was exciting to discover the world in miniature, the miscellany of many cultures that constitutes New York. For me the experience was amusing: I took delight in his delight.

René had come to the United States to accompany and lecture on the exibition that he had organized at the suggestion of Ambassador Morrow. It had had its initial showing in Mexico City earlier in the year and it was the most comprehensive display of Mexican arts and crafts, past and present, ever held anywhere. It was a personal triumph for him. Owing to his knowledge and experience, it was easy for him to assemble the objects of applied art; for years he had been traveling all over the country gathering just such material. But collecting the modern paintings was a more difficult matter. It required all his tact and diplomacy to persuade the artists to join in one single exhibition. The artistic life of Mexico was intense and factional. There were animosities that prompted statements such as "If that man's work is in, I will not allow mine to be shown." But René's mediation prevailed, and for the first time in history all the painters showed under one roof. When it was all over, he said he felt qualified to undertake any diplomatic mission, no matter how complex. Incidentally, René recalled how he had taken the British Ambassador around the exhibition. The envoy was a disconcertingly taciturn man. He answered all questions in monosyllables and never ventured a comment of his own throughout the tour—with one exception. When he came to a drawing by Rivera, a study for his mural *Continence* in the Ministry of Health Building, depicting a voluptuous nude holding a snake twined around her body, the Ambassador paused and said "I would like to be that snake."

After his long stint with the Mexican Arts show, René decided to stay in this country and become a citizen. Eventually he found a job with the Indian Arts and Crafts Board of the Department of the Interior, finally becoming Commissioner. He was well qualified for the post by reason of his wide acquaintance with folk art and his sympathy for the individual craftsman. He told, for instance, of a problem the bureau had with the Navajo silver workers. They had been in the habit of getting their metal from silver dollars, which they pounded out to the requisite thinness. Some efficiency expert in the bureau decided that the preliminary beating out was a waste of time, and illegal to boot, and therefore arranged to supply the Indians with thin sheets of silver. The Indians showed a stubborn resistance to the innovation and refused to work with the ready-made sheets. René was dispatched to find out why. He discovered that the Navajo craftsman devoted the time allotted to the preliminary beating, to thinking about the design he was going to make. The shortcut upset the whole process of invention. René often told stories—he was a good *raconteur*—that revealed more than a whole treatise could.

René undertook some cultural missions to South America for the Coordinator of Inter-American Affairs. His mastery of Spanish and familiarity with Latin-American psychology made him an engaging ambassador of good will. The same could not be said of all our envoys in the field. René related an incident he had witnessed in Buenos Aires. A young assistant at the embassy ventured to make a speech with little knowledge of the language. He started out bravely: "I am embarrassed at my lack of Spanish. . . ," translating the word embarrassed as *embarazado*—which in slang means to be pregnant! One can imagine the fun the Argentinians had with that story.

René once gave a talk on folk art and enumerated its two main enemies: the Tourist and the Purist. The tourist looked for things that were strange and exotic (he often had weird likes and deplorable tastes). Because the tourist was ignorant of the craftsman's pride in his work, he could be singularly insensitive in his demands. René cited the story of the American tourist who bought a chair and bargained for a wholesale price on a dozen chairs just like it. He was outraged when the craftsman asked a higher price *pro rata* for a dozen than for a single piece. He could not understand that the craftsman might feel that it was more effort and more boring to make a dozen chairs exactly alike than to make a dozen as they came from his hand. The purist, on the other hand, wanted to keep things unchanged, never resolving the question of how a craftsman could be creative if he merely copied his grandfather. Outside influence sometimes vitalized a craft. René told the story of how he invented, out of his Austrian heritage, the Painted Pig in the illustrations of a Mexican story by Elizabeth Morrow, and was startled to find that it was transformed, as it were, into Mexican folk art.

René and I once participated in a symposium on Posada and Mexico at the Chicago Art Institute. I read a paper on Posada as a graphic artist and Walter Pach delivered some ponderous platitudes on Mexican art. But René put on a good show in describing the people of Posada's Mexico. He spoke without notes; he dramatized and told stories. He appealed to the emotions and made people laugh. He got more response from the audience than we did. Yet he did not project all of Posada's Mexico: he played safe and said nothing about oppression and revolution, except for a reference at the very end. Nonetheless, as Katherine Kuh remarked, only those who knew Mexico could really appreciate the quality of his dramatization. Many of the subtler and clever and charming parts of his projection must have gone over the heads of the audience. It was beautifully done, with playful irony, comic bits, and genuine *vacillada*. This, one might say, was the keynote of his own *Weltanschauung*. He looked at life as a charming spectacle and saw only those things which were amusing and charming. He was like a true Austrian, for whom a situation might be alarming but not serious. He never challenged, he entertained—and people liked him for it. It is curious that with his aristocratic background he should understand so well and be sympathetic with—yet always with the slightly superior attitude of finding it amusing—the little man, the *petit bourgeois*, the *Indio* with his burden, the plight of the lone individual. I have wondered whether this sensitive and understanding side could have come from his having at one time known the pinch of poverty. In any case, he was a man blessed by good fortune. He seemed always to get what he wanted out of life. He was the archetype of the diplomat, suave, entertaining, detached, and always in control. He found his true vocation when he became the Director of the Museum of Modern Art, a job that required a superabundance of diplomacy to run successfully. He was also a master of the art of display. He could install a show with dramatic flair to please the eye and stimulate the mind.

In recent years I saw little of him. We both had more than our share of commitments and we lived in different cities. When we met, however, we always proceeded with the same relationship as before. I did have a chat with him before his retirement at the opening of the new Study Center of the Museum of Modern Art. He looked forward to finishing a book and other projects and especially to enjoying his garden in Key West. Then came death and the end of all his plans. It was tragic to be cut off in his prime—and yet, one remembers the adage, "Those whom the Gods love, die young."

PART III

Period Pieces

21

The Masses

The monthly magazine The Masses was both a symbol and a symptom of the times. It began as a rather innocuous publication in 1911, but at the beginning of 1913 it was taken over by a group of artists and writers and issued as a cooperative enterprise. The magazine was in the spirit and tradition of *Assiette au Beurre, Gil Blas, Simplicissimus, Fliegende Blatter, Der Wahre Jacob, L'Asino;* and there was need for a similar manifestation here. The program was advertised on the masthead.

A Revolutionary and not a Reform Magazine; a magazine with a sense of humor and no respect for the respectable; frank, arrogant, impertinent, searching for true causes; a magazine directed against rigidity and dogma wherever it is found, printing what is too naked or true for a money-making press; a magazine whose final policy is to do as it pleases and conciliate nobody, not even its readers.

Among the roster of its editor-owners were, for literature, Max Eastman, Eugene Wood, John Reed, Mary Heaton Vorse, Louis Untermeyer, and William English Walling; for art, John Sloan, Art Young, Maurice Becker, George Bellows, Cornelia Barns, and Stuart Davis.

It was, therefore, an illustrated magazine, and carried out its mission both by word and by picture. In the years before and after the First World War, indeed one might say during the whole decade 1910-1920, there was great social tension and unrest. Capitalism, having become rich with few restraints and regulations, fought ruthlessly to maintain the status quo, and justice and the press were far from being impartial. Labor was the underdog then; it is hard to realize, nowadays, that workers bled and died to establish so reasonable and commonplace an institution as the eight-hour day. On the labor front, there was the same crusading spirit that today animates the struggle for racial equality. The labor organizers and other spokesmen for the workers in their inarticulate aspiration for better working conditions, were beaten, railroaded to jail, or murdered; and the masses themselves, when goaded by desperation to strike, were crushed down by brute force or cowed by starvation. Many of the intelligentsia were concerned over this acute social crisis, and their thoughts and feelings were in a sense stimulated and focused by a handsome young poet and philosophy teacher named Max Eastman. Other periodicals of revolutionary import were being issued at the time, but they were written for the more professional reader. Eastman's monthly feature in *The Masses,* under the title *Knowledge and Revolution,* surveyed the field without recourse to a purely class-conscious vocabulary, and was addressed toward a literate audience of intelligence and good will. Eastman had an air of reasonableness and a persuasive flair. He affirmed that socialism was a scientific problem, "the great experiment." His point of view was revolutionary but not doctrinaire, and embraced a wide range of sympathies from crucial strikes (Patterson textile workers, Colorado miners), the plight of leaders such as Tannenbaum, Mooney, Haywood, Debs, John Lawson, and others, to the struggle for women's suffrage and Negro rights. The viewpoint of Eastman, John Reed, William English Walling, Amos Pinchot, and the other editors was basicly radical and not just liberal or reformist, and it had sufficient bite to it to involve the magazine in a libel suit by the Associated Press, and attempts at censorship and suppression by the postal authorities and the district attorney's office. An able group of political cartoonists led by John Sloan, Art Young, Maurice Becker, and later, Boardman Robinson and Robert Minor, effectively reinforced the printed word by their cartoons and caricatures.

The contretemps with the Associated Press was occasioned by a cartoon of Art Young's entitled "Poisoned at the Source," in the July 1913 issue, showing a man, labeled Associated Press, pouring a bottle of lies into a big well, labeled News. The AP started proceedings, not in a civil suit for damages, but for criminal libel. Later the AP, with the active cooperation of the U.S. District Attorney, dismissed the first suit and instituted a second, this time for personal libel against Frank B. Noyes, President of the Associated Press, the strategy being that thus any facts showing that the AP actually had poisoned the news, would not be admissible as evidence. In characteristic fashion, the magazine in its February 1916 number announced the dismissal of the second suit, not by an editorial but by a cartoon of Art Young's depicting the AP as a fat bejeweled lady on a walk. Behind her on the sidewalk was a tiny rolled document. The legend read, "Madam you dropped something." Then—and it was such tactics that endeared the magazine to its readers—a double page spread by Art Young appeared in the April issue, repeating the original offending drawing in almost every detail except that the personification of the AP was now a shining white angel who was pouring out a white liquid labeled Truth. In the corner were kneeling figures of Max Eastman and Art Young weeping tears of mock repentance. The cartoon was entitled "April Fool." the humor of *The Masses* was irrepressible and their ridicule could be devastating. I recall, for instance, a drawing by Cornelia Barns with the legend, "No, this isn't another picture of an outcast woman; it is W. J. Burns in disguise on Fourteenth Street." Burns was head of a much-hated private detective agency.

On one crucial issue, *The Masses* was unequivocally opposed, namely, to America's participation in the war. Long before, its editors had excoriated, by word and picture, militarism, profiteering by the munitions and other industries, and the ghastly horrors of war itself. When the crisis came, most of the editors except William English Walling stuck by their principles. Their uncompromising stand was a great comfort and inspiration to all those who shared their pacifist beliefs. Early in July of 1917, the August issue of *The Masses* was declared unmailable by the U.S. Post Office. The attorney for the magazine filed a bill in equity to the federal court to enjoin the postmaster from excluding the magazine from the mails. On July 21 the motion for injunction was argued before Judge Learned Hand, who granted the injunction. Judge Hand, in an extended decision, sustained *The Masses'* contentions at all points: the construction placed by the postal authorities on the Espionage Act was shown to be invalid. On July 26, the very same day that Judge Hand signed the formal order in New York, U.S. Circuit Judge C. M. Hough in Windsor, Vermont, several hundred miles away, signed an order staying execution of Judge Hand's order—a most unusual though perfectly legal procedure. The August issue therefore was effectively banned from the mails for many months, until the several appeals could be heard. Whereupon the Postal Department in Washington revoked the second-class mailing privileges of the magazine because the August issue had not gone through the mails, and by reason of such irregularity *The Masses* had ceased to be a "newspaper or periodical within the meaning of the law." I cite this example of "the law's delay, the insolence of office," not so much to dredge up discreditable legal machinations from the past, as to suggest the savage and irrational temper of wartime America. The editors of *The Masses* replied to the challenge by suspending publication and starting a new magazine under the name of *The Liberator* in January 1918. A few months later four editors were indicted and tried for conspiracy to obstruct recruiting under the provisions of the Espionage Act on the basis of material contained in the August, September, and October issues of *The Masses* of 1917. The trial ended with a hung jury. The second trial, held late in the same year, after the war was over, also resulted in a split jury (eight to four for the defendents). In that epoch of hysteria, a mistrial was equivalent to acquittal.

If *The Masses* had been only a political or socialist periodical it would not have had the following that it did. True to its announced program, it covered a much wider front. If it was ture that capitalism was too bloated, it was also true that the arts were too genteel and saccharine. Both were in need of a dressing down. Thus, as a travesty on the "pretty girl" magazine covers by Gibson, Christy, or Harrison Fisher, *The Masses* offered Stuart Davis's cover design of two working girls (or were they prostitutes?) with a caption "Gee, Mag, think of us bein' on a Magazine Cover!" Not only was it an admirable drawing; it also was sane and amusing propaganda.

John Sloan was the dominant influence among the artists. As a socialist of long standing, he had the requisite political experience or background. For a considerable period he served as chief art editor, just as his wife, Anna, served as business manager at the beginning. They both were good organizers, and were in the thick of many movements. His early training as a newspaper illustrator served him in good stead: there was much reporting to be done in the magazine on the pictorial as well as on the editorial level. Therefore his work in *The Masses* was often in the nature of reporting with a revolutionary slant, such as in the drawings of the "Constabulary in the Philadelphia Trolley Car Strike" of 1910, or the dramatic confrontation of Frank Tannenbaum and the unemployed at the church door, or *Direct Action* or *Political Action* (based on his experience as a watcher at the polls). Such drawings might be considered in a broad sense as political cartoons, but they actually were documentary cartoons. They protrayed a situation, not an idea. His canvas was too broad and cluttered with corroborative details and characters to make its point purely as a cartoon. He was more in the tradition of Hogarth than of Daumier.

John Sloan, however, was an artist as well as a reporter, a realist in that vein of naturalism which had its parallel in the novels of Theodore Dreiser, Frank Norris, or Stephen Crane. In a conversation I had with him some years before his

death, he denied that his art was in any sense literary or social in its implications. I was surprised by the vehemence of
his assertion, for it disclosed a certain defensive attitude regarding his realistic art. At any rate, it revealed that in his
mind there was a clear-cut distinction between pure art and
propaganda reporting—a quite defensible position. It is interesting to note that his series of etchings (pure art) from
1905 to 1911—now considered among the finest graphic
achievements of the period and including such masterpieces
as *Turning out the Light, Woman's Page,* and *Night
Windows*—were offered at two dollars apiece with a subscription to *The Masses.* Sloan told me later that there were no
takers at the time. The magazine was on the firing line and
few examples of disinterested observation appeared in it. In
general, Sloan contributed, and induced others to contribute,
propaganda pictures, dramatic compositions with a cutting
edge or purposive social comment, such as the famous
Women's Night Court scene or *The Unemployed* (box holders at
the opera).

The only reference in *The Masses,* as far as I know, to the
Armory Show of 1913 and the modern art movement from
France, was Sloan's good-natured burlesque of cubism in the
drawing and poem beginning "There was a cubist man and
he walked a cubist mile." Sloan and his school were bursting
with things to say, and were not to be distracted by exploring
novel modes of expression. Sloan always had a kind of pun-
ning sense of humor, occasionally verging on the banal; examples can be found in the titles of some of his etchings, and
in such magazine drawings as *The Orango Tango* or *The Common Caws* (crows or vultures feeding on a dead body). But I
still remember the collaboration, in the December 1914 issue,
between Sloan (in a marvelous drawing) and Howard
Brubaker (in a poker dialogue) to produce one of the classic
comments on the European war under the title, "At the End
of the War." St. Peter, looking out of his golden window says,
"I've got a full house!"; and the Devil from below replies,
"You lose. I've got four kings!"

George Bellows was a frequent contributor to *The Masses,*
even if his reactions were more emotional than politically

oriented (witness his melodramatic renderings of German atrocity stories during the war). He had a certain boyish enthusiasm that was very American in its response to sports and the American Scene. Some of his best early drawings appeared in the magazine: *Business Man's Class, Splinter Beach, At Petipas', Boxers, Solitude, Benediction in Georgia, Why don't they go to the Country for a Vacation?* (slum scene), and a wicked caricature of Anthony Comstock under the caption *Exposed at Last*. Bellows once told me that even in his serious drawing he had constantly to hold himself back from exaggeration, and that some quirk in him always made him strain to the limit of caricature. In his satiric drawings, therefore, he was in his natural element.

Satire also came spontaneously to Cornelia Barns. As a draughtsman she had a witty and incisive line and a deft sense of characterization. Her comments usually had a feminine slant, and she could nonchalantly but effectively puncture the silly pretensions of certain masculine types, as in *Lords of Creation, United We Stand* (cigar store types), *Voters, Was this the Face that Launched a Thousand Ships?*, and *Do you Prefer Brains or Brawn?*. She showed a sympathetic feeling for little children in *Mommer! The Merry-go-Round!* or *Spring* (little girl trying on a new hat), and for teenagers in *Dream Dresses*. The plight of the popcorn vendor, under the caption "And all the pennies are going to buy War Extras!", carries a message that is nonetheless valid for being subtle and indirect. Her drawing, "My dear, I'll be economically independent if I have to borrow every cent!" became a classic in feminist circles. She made some delightful covers, *Circus* (bareback riders) and *Dancing School* (organ grinder and dancing children). She had a genuine sense of style. She has become a somewhat neglected artist, but she belongs, along with Peggy Bacon, Mabel Dwight, and Caroline Durieux, in that rare group of artists with a derisive pencil who make merry as women and not as men.

In contrast to Cornelia Barns's waggish sallies, Stuart Davies's comments were heavy-handed and brutal—one might almost say that they were typically masculine. Even in his early, socially conscious phase, Davis displayed the forceful drive and the uncompromising statement so characteristic of his later and more abstract work. In his life as in his art, he was gruff and plainspoken. But he had a terrific power. In his cover designs he showed a strong poster sense—derived perhaps from a study of Steinlen and Lautrec—an ability to arrange bold masses and lettering effectively for eye-catching appeal. Characteristic of his social commentary are such drawings as "That's right, girls, on Sunday the Cross—on weekdays the *double cross*", or "Philosophy in the depths; Gee, but women are lucky—born with a job." I also remember his back-cover color design *Spring,* with a figure obviously a self portrait. But the drawing that haunts me most is entitled *Return of the Soldier*. It shows a Negro boy in uniform fingering the keys of a piano.

Glenn Coleman, the dedicated chronicler of Greenwich Village scenes, contributed numerous drawings. Many were studies in local color or documentaries of everyday life, such as *The Sawdust Trail, The Jefferson Market and Jail,* or the picture of *The Masses'* office on Greenwich Avenue under the caption "Mid Pleasures and Palaces—." The magazine could sometimes poke fun at its own labor union beliefs, as in Coleman's *Class-consciousness:* "You wasn't in the breadline las' night—Nah, they don't use the union label." Occasionally his drawings carried a more barbed comment, such as in the marvelous back-cover design, showing a music hall interior and a singer, dressed as an Indian girl, who is singing a ditty, "Oh give me back my place again—T'row Lincoln off de cent!" The reference, of course, is to the change of design on the penny from an Indian head to the head of Lincoln. In its tawdry vulgarity it somehow epitomizes a milieu or an epoch.

Art Young was a star contributor. He was the chief political cartoonist of the magazine, indeed he is one of the great American cartoonists of the century. He had much in common with Thomas Nast—the same crusading zeal, and, in his drawing, the same hard, factual, and rather insensitive line. Due to his early newspaper training, he could always be understood by the masses, and he never shied away from the obvious. Because he was adept at portraiture—he had a quick eye for character, and could sketch in the salient features and achieve a speaking likeness—he was thereby a forceful caricaturist, for he knew what lineaments to emphasize or distort. He had the expert cartoonist's knack of creating types—the capitalist, the politician, the militarist, the kept press, and the like—that could serve as widely comprehensible symbols. Through his long service as a pictorial reporter on more conservative periodicals—for six years he was Washington correspondent for *The Metropolitan* magazine—he had a wide acquaintance with politicians and public figures. It was great fun to hear him impersonate a Southern senator offering his flowery tribute to American Womanhood in the halls of Congress on Mother's Day. He loved the political scene: it was his life and *métier*. But he also had a conscience and great sympathy for the workers in their attempt to obtain a fair share of the products of their labor. He was really a part of that wave of grass-roots individualism and idealism exemplified by such diverse personalities as Robert La Follette, Eugene Debs, Charles Lindbergh, Sr., Clarence Darrow, or Lincoln Steffens. He sacrificed many lucrative jobs to crusade for the workers. He was a gallant and lovable character, and funny in the bargain. He used to send out a Christmas card every year to his friends. Usually it was a self-portrait with a droll by-line, but once it was a check for one million dollars and no sense in asbestos currency drawn on the Hell National Bank. His self-portraits were utterly delightful. I remember one in the guise of a dog, where he looks out pathetically from behind a muzzle labeled Espionage Law; the caption read "For the Safety of the Public." In company with many other cartoonists, he had aspirations to be recognized as an "art artist" and make "pure" pictures with no topical interest. He built himself a little art gallery on his country place at Bethel, Connecticut. In it hung, among other things, the original drawings for his series *Trees at Night,* with their fantastic and ghostly shapes. They were his favorites, and they also were quite popular when reproduced in the Saturday Evening Post. I always found them a bit obvious. His less pretentious sketches from life, such as *Nut Sunday* or *Man and Beast* seemed to me more aesthetically satisfying. The end papers of his book *Art Young: His Life and*

Times, show him sitting at his drawing board and looking at the wall, where he has scribbled the names of his friends. It is a distinguished list. I am proud to be included among the roster.

Boardman Robinson was more of an artist than a propagandist. He did, however, draw some stunning cartoons, such as the return of the exiles in *Siberia 1917, Europe 1916* (donkey lured on by the carrot of victory dangled by Death), or *Labor and the Peace Conference.* The *Siberia,* in particular, is a masterpiece in which the exultation, the high hope, and the new-found freedom are admirably suggested in the heroic figure of the prisoner returning from exile. Admirable also, though in a more sardonic vein, is the drawing of the brash soldier dragging Christ with a rope, entitled *Billy Sunday* (recruiting officer): "I got him! He's plumb dippy about going to war!" I well remember the first drawing by Robinson to appear in *The Masses,* namely, *What a Peach of a Day!,* where a man is sitting by his office desk and looking out of the window, while Pan is lurking in the shadows and playing his pipes. It was a superb drawing which needed no explanation, although the editors did insert some feeble and irrelevant comment in the attempt to give the idea a class-conscious slant. All these drawings and others of his—just as in the case of Daumier and Kollwitz, for example—transcend an ephemeral or partisan interest. They are social comment but also works of art. They are rendered with a vivid sense of form; the figures are solid and convincing in their reality. The role of Boardman Robinson as an artist and teacher has not yet been gauged at its true worth. He was a notable draughtsman, and his work will hold its place, I trust, in the final appraisal of American art in the twentieth century. He was a rare human being, too—warm, generous, and honorable in character.

There was a younger generation of cartoonists and caricaturists—Robert Minor, Clive Weed, Cesare, Gropper, Frueh, Marsh, and Dehn, for example—whose first work, I believe, appeared in the magazine. I remember specially several by Bob Minor, *The Perfect Soldier* (all brawn and no head), and two caricatures of Anthony Comstock, *O Wicked*

Flesh! (Comstock slashing at a gigantic female nude) and the court scene "Your Honor, this woman gave birth to a naked child." By a curious coincidence, Gropper's early sketches were very similar in style to the drawings made later by James Thurber (for example, *You're a Liar!* in *The Liberator*).

Many well-known artists appeared in *The Masses* without making drawings specifically for the purpose. Their presentations, in their own individual styles, were more in the nature of gestures of sympathy or support. Of such contributions the most numerous were by Arthur B. Davies and Maurice Sterne, but Jo Davidson, Mahonri Young, John Storrs, Albert Sterner, A. Walkowitz, and Ilonka Karasz appeared sporadically. It is interesting to note that of John Sloan's Philadelphia associates of the "ashcan school," only Glackens contributed a single drawing (early in 1913); neither Luks nor Shinn made a contribution. It is possible that they were not in sympathy with the social aim of *The Masses*. Robert Henri, always more of a painter than a draughtsman, was more radically inclined, but he offered only two rather minor sketches. It should be mentioned that several artists, such as Eugene Higgins, Charles A. Winter, and his wife, Alice Beach Winter, whose styles were not in the realistic manner of the rest of the magazine, were nonetheless staunch supporters.

The text of the *The Masses* was as exciting as the illustrations. In addition to the regular features, and, in a sense supplementing them, were numerous special articles by such figures as Helen Keller, Elsie Clews Parsons, Mabel Dodge, Bertrand Russell, Lincoln Steffens, and Hutchins Hapgood. There were short stories and plays by Sherwood Anderson, James Hopper, Mary Heaton Vorse, Miles Mallison, and Susan Glaspell. There were poems by Carl Sandberg, Louis Untermeyer, James Oppenheim, Amy Lowell, Harry Kemp, Gelett Burgess, Vachel Lindsay, Arturo Giovannitti, Witter Bynner, and a host of others. Book reviews, written mostly by Floyd Dell, who became managing editor in 1914, kept the readers *au courant* in significant contemporary literature, especially foreign—Shaw, Wells, Gorky, Rolland, and the like.

In those early years a new number of *The Masses* was an

event, something to look forward to once a month. I had more than an impersonal interest in the contents; they often included drawings or letterpress by my friends, chiefly among artists such as John Sloan, George Bellows, Boardman Robinson, Art Young, Stuart Davis, Adolf Dehn, and Bill Gropper. I even submitted an occasional satiric paragraph or book review, and one full-page article entitled *Contacts.* But I was not a regular contributor. My writing was in the nature of social satire which, as Floyd Dell ruefully admitted, was subordinate to political propaganda in the magazine. Besides, during part of the period I was editing a magazine of my own, *The Modern School.*

As I look back on *The Masses,* the dominating personalities were Max Eastman, John Sloan, Art Young, Louis Untermeyer, and Floyd Dell. In *The Liberator,* which succeeded it, the romantic John Reed was a strong influence, for the magazine was devoted largely to describing and interpreting the Russian Revolution. But the guiding spirit over both magazines was Max Eastman. It was he who, with his many connections, raised most of the money to keep the periodical going. His combination of rational philosophic intelligence and poetic sensitivity to beauty gave it a unique flavor. And the magnetism of his personality welded the group of individualistic writers and artists into a functioning whole. He was the most eloquent and convincing defender in *The Masses'* trial for conspiracy. He later became disillusioned with the outcome of the revolutionary movement in the Soviet Union and attacked it bitterly. Many of us also were disillusioned by Stalin's tactics, but we were unpleasantly surprised by Eastman's using for purposes of attack channels of communication that had been anathema to him in his youth. Nonetheless, he was an impressive if somewhat controversial figure in American life and letters. I can not say that I knew him well—I was on the fringes of the movement. But from time to time I used to see him and his radiantly earthy Russian wife, Eliena Krilenkov (who always wanted to make a painting of me as St. Sebastian, but never did) at The Meeting Place, at parties at the Gannett's, and at Croton, when I was visiting Boardman Robinson.

In many ways *The Masses* was the characteristic journal of Greenwich Village. Many types congregated there: artists, poets and other writers, teachers, social workers, labor agitators, feminists, and free spirits who wanted to live their own lives. The Village has been aptly characterized by three words, *sandals, candles, scandals,* and the phrase does suggest its bohemian and unconventional atmosphere. It could also be epitomized as Mabel Dodge's *Salon* on Lower Fifth Avenue *and* the Women's Night Court, The Brevoort Hotel *and* Romany Marie's cabaret, Greenwich Settlement House *and* Josephine Bell's Washington Square Book Shop. The times were bad; there were poverty and exploitation everywhere. One could not help being emotionally involved, but one also laughed and danced and made love, even free love. There was ferment in the air—stirrings not only of political revolt but also of social and cultural revolt. All this was reflected in the pages of the magazine. It was iconoclastic, and set out to puncture the pious hypocrisies and double standards of conventional morality. It had a field day with the hell-spouting revivalist, Billy Sunday, and with Anthony Comstock, the self-constituted censor of obscenity. It was resolutely concerned with prostitution as a social problem. It advocated birth control, women's suffrage, and other feminist causes. It was against militarism, munitions manufacturers, and war. Howard Brubaker, with his witty paragraphs, and Col. C. E. S. Wood, with his *Heavenly Discourses,* were the sharpshooters with shafts of ridicule in the great battle against stupidity and humbug. Thus *The Masses* was one of the authentic mouthpieces of the era from 1910 to 1920.

22

On the Fringes of Art

Once upon a time there was an artist named Howard Kretz-Coluzzi. This simple statement is tantamount to an act of faith, since there is not much tangible and convincing evidence of his reality as an artist. He seemed to have a compulsion toward cross purposes and oblivion as far as his art was concerned—another kind of *auto da fe*. He was born in 1877 and had professional training at the National Academy of Design. I have heard vague tales of mad pranks at art school, of adding satiric touches to canvases by an unpopular monitor of the class. He was invited to exhibit at the Armory Show of 1913, and I was sufficiently impressed (even before I had met him) to make some comment about his watercolors in my catalogue: "Howard Coluzzi, distinctive watercolor technique, use of brown and white masses." I classified him in a group with A. P. Ryder, Arthur B. Davies, Agnes Pelton, and Van Deering Perrine. I learned later that Arthur B. Davies had encouraged him and bought his watercolors.

I first met him around 1918 at the Sunwise Turn Bookshop. He was stocky and powerfully built, with gray-blue eyes and light hair. He was then about forty years old, and legends had already gathered around his name, recounted to me chiefly by the violinist Alexander Bloch (later to become conductor of the Florida Symphony) and Henry Alsberg (who later became director of the Writers' Project in Washington). They told tales of an artist-hermit who lived in abandoned lumber camps in the Adirondack Mountains and was immersed in a fantasy world of American Indian myth. He would write and illustrate Indian legends on odd scraps of paper with complete indifference to their ultimate survival. Once he delivered to the Alsberg household a freshly killed chicken wrapped up in a piece of paper with exquisite drawings on it.

His physical strength and endurance were phenomenal. If he wanted to go to a particular place in the mountains, he would take a beeline toward it, ignoring roads or trails. If a mountain intervened, he would go straight up and down it, or if a lake was in the way, he would swim straight across it, as an animal would. He once traveled from the Adirondacks to New York City for ten cents—and I am not sure that it cost that much. He told about it only because Allie Bloch had complained that it cost so much to travel up to Saranac. Howard said, "I came down for ten cents! I hopped a freight in the mountains and rode to Albany. There I boarded the Hudson River night boat to New York. They collect the tickets only when you get off. Just before dawn, when it was still dark and the boat was about opposite Yonkers, I jumped off quietly and swam to shore, and made my way to the city."

There is also a legend that he jumped off the Brooklyn Bridge. It happened after the death of his father, when he was living very much under the sway of his mother. He felt, he has said, that if he could do something "impossible," it would give him "power" to extricate himself from her domination. He brooded over the challenge of Steve Brodie. Finally it became an obsession that he had to meet. He jumped off with his arms tightly clasped around his shins. I have heard two versions of the plunge. One was that he swam ashore unaided, the other that he was rescued by a police boat. Incidentally, the name Kretz-Coluzzi refers both to his father's and to his mother's name. I had always supposed that Coluzzi was his father's name, but according to his death certificate, his father was called Kretz and his mother Coluzzi.

When I first became acquainted with him, he was teaching art to children at Margaret Naumburg's "Children's School." I do not know how much art he taught them, but he had a way with children. He stimulated them to observe pantomime and characteristic gesture, and he inspired them to act out elaborate dramas: "Now you be a chicken, and you be the fox." He was a great mimic himself. One of his hilarious stunts was to impersonate a cross-eyed man imitating a robin. He was not without guile in maneuvers to mock and hoax. At a party he pretended to be impressed by the device of musical notation: "Isn't it wonderful that those little black marks mean so much!" It turned out that he used to play operatic scores on the piano by the hour.

He received a commission to paint a mural in a house in New York. He did not ask for money: he stipulated merely that staple food and chocolate be left in the room, for he intended to work undisturbed during the night. The arrangement continued for some time. The owners would see a wonderful and exciting composition develop on the wall. Just when it was almost completed, it would be erased and a new composition begun. They endured the tantalizing confusion as long as they could, but they finally had to terminate the arrangement without getting the decoration.

Coluzzi had an air of mystery. He was elusive and evasive, a legendary figure. No one knew how or where he lived. The rarity of his works and his complete indifference to them enhanced their preciousness. Only genius could possibly be so careless, so superior to the vulgar satisfactions of accomplishment. To acquire a reputation on the basis of scanty achievement is indeed an easy way to gain distinction! I managed to purchase two of his drawings through the bookshop, and I considered myself lucky to have obtained such rare and estimable works. Not that they cost very much, for Coluzzi was not at all grasping in money matters. They were charming and imaginative illustrations of folk tale or myth, the fruit of a romantic identification with Indian legend. They were less saccharine than other of the artist's drawings I had seen. As I look at them now—they are in the Philadelphia Museum of Art—they do not appear to be earthshaking, yet they are still delightful and far above average in technical skill and imaginative power. There is one other drawing by him in the Philadelphia Museum of Art, given by Alexander Bloch. These three drawings are the only early drawings I have been able to locate anywhere.

Around 1924 Coluzzi left New York and settled in the Southwest. I never saw him again. The Blochs have recounted how they once met Witter Bynner at a party. Allie Bloch had occasion to tell an anecdote about Coluzzi. Bynner exclaimed, "Why, that man works for me as a gardner at my place in Santa Fe. I had no idea that he was an artist!" It seems rather strange that Bynner did not know who Coluzzi was in view of the fact that Coluzzi made a decorative illustration for a poem by Bynner, *Chariots,* which was published as a broadsheet by the Sunwise Turn around 1918! This is but one of the anomalies that somehow turn up in connection with Howard. I remember, for instance, seeing an exceptionally fine watercolor of his in the window of the Ferargil Gallery on a Sunday afternoon. It depicted an Indian standing by a horse against a forest background, and was one of the few completely finished works by him I had ever encountered. It had been in the collection of Arthur B. Davies. Later, when I asked to see it, the gallery owner assured me that he never had a picture of my description from the estate of Arthur B. Davies. Of course, Fred Price was notorious for his conveniently bad memory, but he was so positive and vehement on the subject that I began to wonder if I was suffering from hallucinations. Another finished watercolor of a fawn leaping in the woods, belonging to a friend of Henry Alsberg, was stolen while being moved from one apartment to another and was never found again.

I lost track of Coluzzi, and knew little of his subsequent life in Santa Fe until recently, when I asked several friends (E. Boyd among others) to bring me up to date on the final chapters. The reports were varied and often conflicting. In general, they indicated that his Southwest phase was a sad decline from his earlier high promise. It was not so easy to be a man of mystery in Santa Fe as it was in New York, especially without a steady income. Everything is wide open in the Southwest, and the descent into indigence was obvious. Coluzzi lapsed into an unkempt and hand-to-mouth existence. A few charitable souls, whom he had impressed with his genius, could excuse his lack of cleanliness as a personal eccentricity, but most of the white elite did look askance. Of course the Indians and Mexicans were not so squeamish about dirt, but on the other hand, they were not wealthy patrons.

Apparently Coluzzi did not long remain in the anonymity of Witter Bynner's garden. Indeed, he proclaimed far and wide that he was an artist, and traded on it. He soon acquired the knack of painting in fresco, and executed many decorative murals on the walls of grocery stores, restaurants, and cafés in barter for food. They were generally tailored to the taste and comprehension of his patrons, and thus were geared to the lowest common denominator. Most of the frescoes have since disappeared—which is understandable in a country where buildings are ephemeral and plastering is a common and widely practiced art. He also took up wood carving and fashioned both masks in the Japanese style and portraits of local gentry. He had a hard time getting along until he received a small legacy from a relative in New England in the late 1930s. He bought an adobe house and camped out in it for the rest of his life.

One of his diversions was to hang around the La Fonda (hotel) and engage the attention of a tourist with a hard luck story. Often he would be staked to a meal, and would consume literally every item that was allowed on the menu. At the end of the repast, he would sigh and say, "I could eat that dinner all over again." The incredulous tourist would wager that he could not, and he always lost his bet. The artist could easily play the role of a panhandler.

He was always ready to expound his philosophy of art to a sympathetic listener. One of them has testified to the magnetism of his discourse: "His face was lit with inspiration and his thoughts covered the globe and the universe and all time." Yet somehow, the samples of his noble thoughts that were set down in cold type seem rather banal. To an interviewer on the *New Mexico Magazine* he said: "If you ask me what I consider myself to be in art, I would say that I am the Arrowsmith of Art. He, you remember, had hundreds of test tubes which he used to find one bacillus, eliminating others one by one until he found the one he sought. So have I many test tubes, although they do not look like Arrowsmith's. Mine are crates, piled ceiling high, full of sketches."

He still kept up his custom of tramping over the mountains (although they were much higher than the Adirondacks) without regard for comfort or fatigue. He might be out for several days without a bedroll or any equipment, sleeping on the ground or in some culvert. He would go to Indian dances and occasionally visit the pueblos. He got along well enough with the Indians, but he did not really understand the pueblo tribes. His portrayal of them was apt to be superficial and a little on the sweet side. The reality of community living in the Southwest was very different from his early romantic visions of "Noble Redskins."

In 1942 Coluzzi died of blood poisoning induced by the scratch of a cat. He who had such great promise as an artist ended up as a "morning glory," a "four-flusher." Henry Alsberg once analyzed the cause of his failure: "He was a case of genius blocked from rich production by some hidden psychosis. I suspect that his father, who died before I met Howard and who terrorized the boy, and later his mother, who was a dominating old bitch, both ruined him. There was some sexual anomaly. As long as I knew Howard, he was a virgin, literally; I suspect that he died one. Yet the thought of sex obsessed him. He was a weird bird, but the most entertaining individual I have ever bummed around with. If one only had time to write a book about him!"

Henry Alsberg knew Coluzzi better than did I, who had met him not more than a dozen times. I can merely add a few reflections to his estimate, based upon my own experience and other sources. Whatever may have been the cause of his trauma, it would appear that he never grew into maturity. He remained undisciplined and could not maintain interest in any direction for long. His attention span, like a child's, seemed to be of brief duration. Thus his preliminary sketches were superb, but they remained stillborn. Alsberg recounts, "He would give you a painting study, and then later ask to have it back on the plea that he would finish it. But if he got his hands on it again, it would disappear for good."

In the final analysis one wonders whether the creation of art was really his prime motivation. Could he have been a psychopathic personality so wrapped up in his own fantasies that art became a means and not an end? How else can one explain his indifference to his own productions and his destructive lack of respect for them? (Vulgarization of art is one form of destruction). He also was literally a spellbinder —there are many such in all walks of life—who can endow his productions with a magic that evaporates in his absence. His absorption in fantasy and in the roles he chose to play tended to divorce him from reality and often involved him in actual deceit. The "crates of sketches piled celing high," for instance, about which he spoke, existed only in his imagination. They were authentic for him in his role as Arrowsmith, but they had no physical reality. His propensity for mockery and deception, manifest at an early age, later became ingrained. It is indeed depressing to contemplate the ironic discrepancy between his infantile dream of a primitive Eden and the sordid realities of his end. He was sick with one of the common ailments of modern civilization, psychic disturbance and arrested development. It warped his personality and made him a sorry misfit in our society.

Such is the story of my "Quest for Corvo," my search for the identity of Howard Kretz-Coluzzi. I am reminded by contrast of another character whom I knew around the same time. Tom Purdy was part Indian, part Negro. One might call him a primitive who had adjusted sufficiently to modern society to live in it and yet to preserve some measure of freedom. He did not have a conscious attitude toward the encroachments of civilization; he merely had some saving grace by which he survived where other primitives, genuine or make-believe, failed. He never succumbed to the inferiority complex, also a disease of civilization. No doubt he was a mute, inglorious Milton, but it did not bother him a bit. It was around 1918, when I moved to the area between Mamaroneck and White Plains in New York State, that I first caught sight of Tom Purdy with his knapsack and staff, striding along the road like a prophet of old. He was straight and tall as a well-formed tree. He had an animal-like face, a swarthy complexion, and a scraggly grayish beard. After my first encounter, I had many glimpses of him sitting motionless on a stone fence at dusk, or fishing in the stream at night beside a tiny fire made in the Indian fashion, or sprawling lazily by the door of his cabin. At that time there was a surprisingly large amount of wild land in the vicinity so near New York—taking into account the extensive Saxon Woods and hundreds of acres of fallow land—and he knew the area like a book. He was a trapper and fisherman; in their season he procured fish, rabbit, and woodchuck. He gathered wild strawberries and blackberries. He eked out a living by weaving baskets and doing odd jobs. Sometimes he would leave his shack for days, carrying a few necessaries in his knapsack, and putting up wherever the mood struck him. He sauntered through life as he sauntered across the hills—a rare achievement in our high-power age.

Tom's sister, Rosanna Purdy, lived with him at the little house and kept it as neat and tidy as a bird's nest. Wood was piled up here and there, and there were flowers everywhere. She had the acquisitive nature of a magpie, and had gathered various objects that she reckoned might be useful some day, such as automobile tires, old bottles, tin cans, and the like, all neatly sorted and stacked. She was less outgoing than her brother, and more suspicious of strangers. She had something of the shyness and furtiveness of a wild animal. She had the habit of sinking into the bushes and freezing into immobility to avoid being seen. She also used to bend over and rest her hands on her knees, sometimes for half an hour at a stretch, and this gave her a weird and eerie presence. She was usually clad in a crazy quilt of patches.

Tom and his sister did not get along together. They would

quarrel and not talk for weeks. A story is told of him that thows light upon the difference in response between primitive and civilized man. It seems that Tom began to miss things that he kept in a special cupboard of his own. He suspected Rosanna. Instead of buying a lock and key—as most of us would have done—he worked out the following plan. He gathered some willow branches, the springiest he could find, and arranged them in the cupboard in such a way that they would snap out unexpectedly when the door was opened. Not long thereafter Rosanna was seen with some welts on her face, and nothing ever disappeared from the cupboard again. Rosanna in her way was proud of her brother, though she often concealed it under a scolding manner. It was she who usually insisted that he play the fiddle before strangers. He seldom complied, nor was he at his best under such circumstances. But I surprised him several times playing the fiddle while sitting on a stump by his shack. He did not tuck his instrument under his chin but pointed it at his chest as the Southern mountaineers do. His playing was an improvisation, somewhat like the song of a bird or the drone of a cicada. His fingers were still nimble in spite of his sixty-odd years. I have been told that in the old days he was much in demand as a fiddler for square dances, and that actually he was the best sqaure dance caller around the countryside.

Tom Purdy had another accomplishment, wood carving. Whenever he found a fantastic root or a likely piece of wood for a staff or cane, he picked it up and carved on it. He let his imagination play over the conformation of the wood, and sometimes mulled over the problem for weeks at a time. He called it "seein' what's in the wood." He must have carved quantities of them entirely for his own amusement. It was not until Bill von Schlegell, Heinz Warneke, and I came along that he ever sold any canes. The head or top of the cane would consist of an animal or a face. The treatment, either realistic or stylized, was always based on observation of nature. Some of the carvings had a slight resemblance to African sculpture, though it is doubtful whether he had ever seen a primitive mask or idol. His motivation apparently was unconscious. When asked what he meant by a particular piece, he would reply, "Oh, it's just a fancy." Heinz Warneke recalls that he once came upon Tom whittling in front of the cabin. Tom called to Heinz, saying "I hear that you do some whittlin' yourself and sell it. Now how much do you charge for it by the inch?" While Heinz was pondering on what to answer, he went on: "Now, I charge twenty-five cents an inch. Do you think that is too much? Can you sell your whittlins for that price an inch?" It was the beginning of a cordial understanding between them—two whittlers talking about their craft.

It was difficult to get Tom Purdy to do anything he did not want to do. His sense of independence was strong. He could be clever in repartee and slide out of a tight place by his wit. He put off a group of six of us for over an hour by one fantastic and amusing excuse after another, while we were trying to persuade him to play the violin. It must have been an amusing spectacle, as I recall; the six of us were standing watching Tom, who was comfortably seated on an inverted pail, hacking at an obstinate cedar stump. He asked him why he was chopping the wood—he had to have kindling for his breakfast. In vain we asked him why he had to chop that particular chunk of wood; we offered to chop a whole pile of kindling for him. Standing on one foot or another, we watched him hack at that stump for an hour and we did not hear him play.

Tom sometimes came out with an expressive phrase. I remember once that we discussed canvas tents and the fact that they leaked wherever one touched them with the hand. He challenged us to give the reason for this to him unknown fact. None of us could give an adequate explanation, and so he replied with a chuckle "It sounds like a *say so* to me." Later on that same day we got talking about going to church in connection with radio broadcasting. Tom let his imagination play over the possibilities of religious broadcasting. He had heard a radio once, or at least Rosanna had, for she piped up and told us about it. "Pretty soon," Tom speculated, "nobody will have to go to church anymore, everybody can stay home and listen to the sermon, and best of all there won't be any collection." When we told him that such things were already happening, he was astonished and said "It sounds like another *say so* to me." His *say so* and *hear say* neatly described the things one habitually accepts without challenge. At another time we were discussing why animals had a keener sense of smell than humans. Tom thought it was because animals "tasted the smell."

On one momentous occasion there was great excitement at the Purdy place. The house burned down! Tom, I was told (for I was not present), rushed into the house and brought out his fiddle, a basket containing provisions, and a coat. The firemen arrived in short order, accompanied by the whole countryside, but practically nothing could be rescued. During the whole time Tom made no effort to join in the excitement. He sat on the stone wall and played his fiddle. Such was the passing of the Purdy homestead! I often wished that I could have seen the interior of that cabin. One wonders what it might have contained. Rosanna, for instance, had once alluded to a bushel basket of pipes carved by her brother.

Rosanna, when I saw her after the fire, complained that she had lost everything she had in the world, and enumerated them as follows: a barrel of flour, thirty pounds of sugar, eight lamps, four lanterns, all her best dresses, a lot of sheets and pillow cases, and a library of books. When I discussed the affair with the Warnekes, I intimated that Rosanna must have been indulging in a bit of wishful fantasy in the catalogue of her possessions. Jessie Warneke said she was sure that it was not a fabrication at all and related an incident that happened some time before. An old lady lived alone in a little house nearby. Nobody knew much about her. Finally she died and her son arrived to dispose of her effects. Among them were many clothes of the Gay Nineties era—she evidently had been a lady of fashion who went to Saratoga for the races and the like. While the son was sorting out things, Jessie's three young children, Dick, Delight, and Priscilla hung around the house, and so did Rosanna. It was obvious that he was going to leave quite a few things behind, and sure enough, just before he drove off, he said to the little group, "You can have anything you want out of the stuff in there, and welcome to it." There was a wild scramble, the children searching for costumes for themselves and Rosanna out to grab anything she could lay her hands on. The dresses, when Jessie saw what the children brought back, were quite special, and must have cost hundreds of dollars even in the old days—dresses with whalebone fittings inside and ruffles of fine black lace outside, and stockings of heavy pure silk in brilliant colors, red, orange, and peacock blue, embellished with hand-embroidered clocking in contrasting colors. What tales those clothes could have told! Rosanna probably secured a number of dresses as well as an armful of bedclothes and musty old books, for which the children had no use. Rosanna must have felt great satisfaction over the windfall, and perhaps a bit of her heart's desire was thereby fulfilled.

We went on to discuss how it happened that there were white and black Purdys in the neighborhood. It seems that Tom told Heinz that his name was Purdy because his parents had been slaves of the "white Purdys." (This was plausible, because Tom was born before the Civil War.) According to Jessie, Tom and Rosanna did not own their cabin but were allowed by the Purdys to occupy it during their lifetime. The surviving member of the white Purdy clan was Charles Purdy, Old Man Purdy, who had inherited all their holdings through no merit of his own except possibly that of longevity and a dull-witted sense of possession. He lived in a squalid fashion not much above the primitive level of the black Purdys. I know, for he was my landlord. It was small wonder that there was so much wild and fallow land roundabout. Purdy's only son, a wild and undisciplined boy, killed himself racing in a car over the quiet country roads.

To return to the chronicle of Tom Purdy. When I saw him after the fire I told him how sorry I was to hear about his misfortune. He did not complain, in fact I suspect he was relieved at not having so many things to take care of. Unlike his sister, he was not acquisitive. His only comment was: "All this excitement and losin' everything, just sort of makes me lazy." When I asked him where he was going to sleep he replied that that was easy: he would stretch a piece of tin from that tree crotch to that post, put some hay underneath and he would have his home and his bed. Rosanna, who overheard this, interrupted in a querulous voice, "Don't you go usin' my post, that's for my grape arbor, and don't you go choppin' my wood for kindlin' either." Tom just shrugged his shoulders and smiled lazily. Shortly thereafter Rosanna was taken to the poorhouse and languished there until she died. Tom, I was told, stayed around for a spell and afterwards disappeared. I had moved away from the region and never found out what happened to him.

I am glad to have known a man like Tom Purdy. I did not know him well, and I question whether any civilized person could know him well. I am glad to have met him because he was the last living link with a primitive Indian past—an environment of nature and animal instincts, a world of concrete images and elemental facts, where a *say so* did not exist. Tom lived bravely by the only values he knew. Perhaps the only people who ever made him feel that they respected those values were two artists, Bill von Schlegel and Heinz Warneke, and myself. Thoreau would have approved of Tom Purdy, even though the neighbors roundabout called him Crazy Tom.

23

Mail Order à la Mode

Mass distribution of books, records, and pictures is becoming more and more prevalent, and the techniques of mass appeal and management more and more organized on an efficient mechanical level. Not being in the habit of getting my culture in regular monthly doses, I am not very sympathetic to this approach, but once in 1954 I did succumb to an enticing advertisement about the American Recording Society. It had launched a recording program of Two Hundred Years of American Music, which had been "started with a grant from the Alice M. Ditson Fund of Columbia University." Under such respectable sponsorship, the enterprise seemed most worthy of support. The prosepect of getting acquainted, by repeated hearings, with the works of our leading contemporary American composers appealed to me. In due course I was enrolled as a subscriber. The recordings were good. I felt very much a part of the organization. When I sent my check I would include a personal note. Once, for example, I suggested that the Society print a list of previous recordings:

since I had not joined at the beginning, there might be some records I would be willing to buy. Again, when notices of worthless and irrelevent books advertised in the cheapest kind of sales talk were included along with the announcement of forthcoming record releases, I was properly indignant and asked if the Ditson Fund was aware of this debasement of their list. There also were some complaints about accounting methods. None of my letters was ever answered. I did not realize the full significance of this fact until later.

A month and a half before I went to Europe, I wrote a letter along with my check, asking that my subscription be temporarily suspended. When I returned after four months, I found that my instructions had been ignored. Among my pile of mail were two records, also several polite, oh so polite, dunning letters, forms 25 and 40. Number 25 read in part:

> Unfortunately, we are forced to abide by the policy our firm of auditors has imposed, limiting credit for each of our many thousands of subscribers to a fixed amount. We are most anxious to release this month's recording to you. All we ask is that you attend to the enclosed bill. If the amount is a little more than you can conveniently pay at this time, we'll be glad to credit your account with a partial payment.

Form 40 was quite cute in handwritten facsimile:

> Dear Subscriber
> It's really only a *small* bill—probably you just overlooked it.
> Won't you please TODAY use the enclosed envelope for your remittance and save us both the continued bother.
> Thank you very much.

I wrote at once and refused to take any responsibility for the unauthorized shipments. Some instinct prompted me to send the letter by registered mail. I soon received a typewritten reply signed by Alan Sloane, apologizing for having ignored my instructions and offering me two alternatives: either to return the records at his expense or to remit for one record and receive the other as a bonus to which I would be entitled. Whereupon I wrote him as follows: "A member of my family had inadvertently unpacked the records, and it will be too much trouble to pack them up for mailing again. I am therefore sending you a check for one record, which I understand will settle my account. I still wish to terminate my subscription."

For a short time I was left in peace, but then to my great astonishment I received a bill for one record, forms 25 and 40 included. Form letter 43 followed:

Dear Friend

It's a very rewarding job to sit here and direct the shipment of records to lovers of fine music all over the land.

But as in most things, I must take the bitter with the sweet, and there comes a time I have to discuss money.

We have sent you several reminders and I have been hoping to receive your payment any day.

This is not the usual letter, but I am trying to prove to my superiors that more faith in fellow men and less bills and business will result in a membership to which more of the right people will want to belong.

Enclosed is a bill, overdue for quite some time. Just attach it to your check or money order and return it to me—now.

Thanks

Sincerely yours,
Joyce Rutherford

I had ignored these communications in the belief that slowly but certainly the Society's accountants would catch up with the error. But then I received a letter from my old friend Alan Sloane, who should have known better since he had promised to settle my account and terminate my membership if I paid for one record. To be sure, it was not from him in person, but from his form—form 44. According to it, I was back in the fold as a subscriber:

Dear Subscriber

Last week our firm of independent accountants completed their annual audit of all American Recording Society's accounts.

Here is a statement of your account as taken by the auditors, showing money owed to you by us if you are a prepaid subscriber, or money due us from you. Won't you check it against your records? If it is correct and you are indebted to us, please rush your payment at once. Otherwise, notify us of any error so we can make any last minute adjustments before the report is finalized.

I was bewildered by the discrepancy between the facts and the Society's slick representations, and felt helpless in the face of an error that was assuming gigantic proportions.

While I was debating what technique to employ in meeting the situation, I received form letter 44A:

Dear Member:

Will you help me win an argument I'm having with our Credit Manager?

He says you have not paid for merchandise in the amount shown on the enclosed statement and he wants to place your account with the MAIL ORDER CREDIT REPORTING ASSOCI-ATION for collection.

I disagree with him, because I am convinced you have merely overlooked his bills or have a good reason for ignoring them. I have prevailed upon him to delay sending your account to the MAIL ORDER CREDIT REPORTING ASSOCIATION for a few more days.

The Credit Manager wins—if I do not hear from you. I win—if your payment, or reason for disregarding our bills, reaches me within ten days.

The enclosed envelope, marked for my personal attention, can put you and me on the winning side.

Let's show the Credit Manager *he's* wrong.

Very Sincerely yours
John H. Cassidy
Executive Manager

Here was a chance to talk to the Executive Manager himself and tell him what I thought of his management. I wrote immediately the following, in the envelope that had been enclosed for the purpose:

Dear Sir

I am answering your recent communication with wrath in my heart. I have never encountered an organization that had more slipshod accounting methods than yours. Your appalling inefficiency is matched only by the insulting coyness of your dialogues with your Credit Manager. Fiddlesticks!

I suppose I shall have to go through all the agonizing details once again. (There follows a complete factual account from the beginning.)

I thought that the matter was ended, but now I receive letters threatening to impair my credit rating. I resent very much the time it has taken to dig into old records and compose this letter. Will you please tell me what else I must do to head off any further harassment from your organization?

Very truly,
Carl Zigrosser

There was no reply, even though my letter had been sent

to his personal attention, as requested. Then form letter 45 appeared:

Dear Friend
Your name has been sent to us by the American Recording Society to be included in our files.

Having wide experience with the time payment method of selling, we know that in many cases misunderstandings arise through non-receipt of mail or other causes that destroy the pleasant relations which both the company and the customer would ordinarily be anxious to maintain. Our member assures us that courteous efforts have been made urging you to bring your account up to date, but that they have apparently been ignored by you.

If a misunderstanding does exist, won't you kindly get in touch with the American Recording Society and clear up the matter without delay?

We strongly urge you to give this important matter your immediate attention by writing to our member at once.

Very truly yours
Matthew Corrigan

Mail Order Credit Reporting Association

To him I replied as follows:

Dear Mr. Corrigan
After having sent several letters into the void of the American Recording Society—without benefit of reply—I welcome a new correspondent, in the hope that I may strike a human and responsive chord despite the ominous stereotype of a form letter.

In your letter you say "Our member assures us that courteous efforts have been made urging you to bring your account up to date, but that they have apparently been ignored by you." I can assure you that their "courteous efforts" have not gone so far as to reply to my letters or acknowledge that they have made a mistake.

I enclose a copy of my letter of January 31, 1955, which states my case. To date I have received no reply. Can you suggest any way I can be relieved of these dunning letters for something which I positively do not owe?

Very truly
Carl Zigrosser

In the course of my correspondence with the American Recording Society I often speculated about the people who worked there. What did they do with the letters that came to them? Didn't they even take a little peek before they threw them into the waste basket? I had employed a variety of epistolary styles from the hortatory and cooperative to the deliberately insulting, and not one of them produced the slightest reaction. No doubt I could have made sure of getting answers if I had registered all my letters. But that, I felt, would not be cricket. I wanted to see if I could get a human reaction through regular channels—an exercise in frustration, as it turned out. The one "live" letter I received in answer to my registered one, seemed human enough; and I would judge that the person who wrote it was reasonably well-meaning and intelligent. But the personalities vaguely associated with the form letters baffled me. They offered nothing more tangible than a cliché, and I wondered if those shadowy figures who spent their lives manipulating the repertory of forms ever became flesh and blood when they emerged from work. Were they cynical or dedicated in their attitude, or did they just do a routine job? Or perhaps they did not exist at all, and were merely the creations of one master mind, a dramatic novelist, but a mediocre one, whose characters never came to life.

Pursuing this question of reality and nonreality, I became almost convinced that the Society was in fact nothing but a vast and intricate automaton, functioning without benefit of human personnel. This monster consumed checks and money orders, and every month disgorged a record. It could not understand any communication except money. Personal letters and all matters not pertaining to its usual routine were shunted into some waste receptacle. There was, indeed, only one human being in attendance, to answer registered letters. If the machine did not receive its monthly stipend, or if a prospect of a gain was recorded (however mistakenly) to which according to its uncomprehending memory it was entitled, then the wheels moved and the levers clicked to produce a series of printed form letters in mechanical sequence, regardless of the appropriateness of the situation. These letters, in spite of their seeming reasonableness and their cunning play upon human feelings, were in reality inhuman, the hollow pretense of a mechanized humanity. They lacked even the touch of a human hand. Their very premises had no reality. It was a terrifying picture. Was this a glimpse and foretaste of our future society?

I must report that two weeks after my letter to the Mail Order Credit Reporting Association, I did hit the jackpot after all. A letter came from the American Recording Society. It was form 4, and began as follows:

Dear Friend
    The items checked below will show the current status of your account according to our records.

There was a check mark against the item, "Your account is in balance," and—wonder of wonders—following that, the words "and cancelled," written by hand in ink. The letter ended thus:

May we take this opportunity to express our appreciation for your continued interest in the American Recording Society.
Very truly yours
Alan Sloane

When all is said and done, however, my jackpot was really only a hollow victory. The organization never explicitly acknowledged that it had made a mistake in dunning me for something I did not owe. There was no form letter to meet such a contingency. My triumph over the machine consisted merely in getting out of its clutches.

24

The Beginnings of
the Print Council of America

During the summer of 1954 a number of print curators, collectors, dealers, printmakers, and art critics assembled in New York to discuss the possibility of establishing a National Print Council to further the interests of prints and print collecting. I do not know upon whose initiative the group first met, since I was in Europe at the time. I attended the second meeting in mid-September and it was obvious then that the potential members were separating into two factions with divergent aims. It began to dawn upon the museum curators (who outnumbered the commericial element) that such a Society could easily be turned into some sort of Print-of-the Month Club, for example, and that their role would merely be window dressing to add prestige and respectability to a commercial enterprise. Shortly thereafter I met with several other curators (Hyatt Mayor, Una Johnson, and Bill Lieberman), equally concerned to see what could be done about the situation. On the way to New York by train I jotted down a few notes to outline the strategy to be employed:

> If we are to do anything about controlling the situation, we must know what we want to do and plan beforehand. Betty Mongan [whom I had consulted previously] suggests that we call for a new deal and start electing the council all over again. Whether this is possible depends upon whether anything has been done about incorporation. Several ways out of the impasse. One: use the authority of President and Vice-President (not yet elected, but necessary under any charter); decide on a slate and take the initiative. Two: add more names to present council, making it in essence an honorary list of sponsors; vest authority in a new and small executive committee. This body should determine policy and activities. The executive director, a paid employee, should be responsible to it, and merely carry out its wishes. Decide upon a slate and then move to have nominations closed. Argument for such a committee would be that present group is too unwieldy and not always available. Tactics: if any proposal comes up that is unacceptable, some one gets up and says that it is impossible to get his trustees to approve it. Call for a vote and the other curators should back him up.

The third meeting of the National Print Council was scheduled to take place at Alverthorpe Gallery in Jenkintown on November 18, 1954. I had conferred with Lessing Rosenwald and Betty Mongan beforehand, and we agreed on a certain line of action. The meeting did take place and the following were present: Betty Mongan, Una Johnson, Martha Dickinson, Doris Meltzer, Margaret Lowengrund, Adelyn Breeskin, Braziller, Haas, Marshall, Friedman, Gusten, Reese, von Groschwitz, Lieberman, Spruance, and Rosenwald. After Lessing had welcomed the group to Alverthorpe, I got up, saying that I spoke for a number of curators, and pointed out that we were the largest single group present (with potentialities of even greater numbers), that we wanted to increase and enhance the appreciation of graphic art in this country—as did everybody else—but we wanted to do it in our own way. We were not against dealers or commercial enterprise, and certainly not against artists, but we felt that we were in a better position to advance their interests and our cause if we operated above the battle, that is to say, without suspicion of ulterior motives. I outlined a skeleton organization, namely, an execuitve committee of curators, scholars, and social-minded collectors for the shaping of policy, and advisory committees representing the interests of artists, dealers, and art schools. When I finished, my move was seconded with considerable applause. Discussion continued and I was called upon to elaborate. Irvin Haas demonstrated his good sportsmanship by saying that since a bombshell had been put under his agenda, he yielded his chairmanship (upon my nomination) to Lessing Rosenwald. No one spoke against my plan. Lessing and I, however, tried to keep the discussion outside the range of personalities, and spoke in broadly objective terms. We adjourned for lunch, and it was pleasant and delicious. Edith Rosenwald was a gracious hostess. Everybody looked at books and pictures—Alverthorpe is fabulous—and Lessing gave everyone a copy of his book on the *Fior di Virtu* (Florentine woodcuts) as a keepsake. After the party was over, Ben Spruance, Bill Lieberman, Betty Mongan, and I went to Betty's apartment for a drink.

Although there were no meetings of the Council during 1955, the idea of a curators' council was by no means abandoned. We did some hard thinking about its functions and purpose, and eventually we did some organizational groundwork in drawing up a certificate of incorporation and in drafting the bylaws. They were executed by Joshua Binion Cahn, who has continued to act as legal advisor for the Council to the present day. The seven charter members who signed the documents were Adelyn Breeskin, Gustav von Groschwitz, Una Johnson, William Lieberman, Elizabeth Mongan, Lessing J. Rosenwald, and Carl Zigrosser. It became increasingly evident to me that the Council would not be successful unless it had an energetic executive secretary. The curators who acted as directors were to involved and busy to do anything but outline policy. It had been suggested that some retired curator could be found to implement their directives. I doubted whether anyone old enough to retire would be capable of doing the job, provided that a suitable curator were even available. A creative, dynamic approach was essential for such a task. I believed that the only man around who had such qualities was Theo J. H. Gusten. He had successfully built up a society for the distribution of artist prints on a noncommercial basis, and therefore knew his way around the New York art world. He had sound ideas and lots of common sense; he was a shrewd judge of character and a hard worker. I became acquainted with him through his International Graphic Art Society. He had enlisted the aid of a number of leading print curators to evaluate the technical competence or aesthetic merit of the prints he had commissioned from artists, before distributing them to members of his society. I found him an amiable and pleasant person to work with. Some artists have told me that he had been a bit gruff and dictatorial in his dealings with them. It appeared to me that this was only a minor fault compared to the many advantages he offered. He was willing to take the job when I sounded him out. I therefore proposed him to Lessing as the executive secretary. Looking back on what has happened, I believe that it was a good choice. Indeed, I would go so far as to say that without Rosenwald as President and Gusten as Secretary, the Print Council would never have gotten off the ground and functioned for as long as it has. I also recall that Betty Mongan was a tireless and resourceful ally in all the negotiations leading to the formation of the Council.

In 1956 further discussions were held by key members, preliminary to a meeting of the Council in Cincinnati on May 27. It was not an important meeting, because only three or four curators were present beside Lessing and myself. But it was necessary in order to ratify certain steps leading up to the crucial meeting at Alverthorpe in Jenkintown on September 21-22. This date marks the official beginning of the organization under its new name, the Print Council of America (previously called National Print Council). On the first day the attendance was limited to those eligible to be directors, and consisted of Una Johnson, William Lieberman, Lessing J. Rosenwald, Carl Schniewind, Jakob Rosenberg, Paul J. Sachs, Karl Kup, Alice Parker, A. W. Heintzelman, Henry P. Rossiter, Louis Stern, Robert M. Walker, A. Hyatt Mayor, Gustav von Groschwitz, Betty Mongan, Adelyn Breeskin, and Carl Zigrosser. Leona Prasse was there to represent Henry Sayles Francis, and Joshua Binion Cahn and Theo Gusten were present by invitation. The agenda consisted principally of the election of the full board of directors by the seven charter members, the election of the titular officers, and the ratification of the bylaws. The full board of directors was comprised of the above list of eligibles, with the addition of seven others not present: Henry Sayles Francis, Bartlett Hayes, Jr., Harold Joachim, Grace McCann Morley, John S. Newberry, John Rewald, and James Thrall Soby. The titular officers were Lessing J. Rosenwald, President; Carl Zigrosser, Vice-President; Hudson D. Walker, Treasurer; and Adelyn Breeskin, Secretary. Theo Gusten was elected Executive Secretary. We adjourned for cocktails and dinner, happy that the Print Council was launched at last.

On the next day the group was expanded to include a sampling of artists, dealers, and other persons interested in prints, namely, Albert Reese, Doris Meltzer, Bertha Wiles, Vernon Bobbitt, Martha Dickinson, Grace Mayer, Kneeland McNulty, Bertha von Moxchzisker, Felice Stampfle, and Benton Spruance. The general meeting was devoted to the question of how the Council could be of service to the print world, the artist, the dealer, and the collector; and to a consideration of specific proposals, such as the organization of simultaneous exhibitions for a selected group of American prints with a single catalogue for showings at some twenty-five museums—all in the interest of contemporary American printmakers; publication of a periodical along the lines of the old *Print Collectors Quarterly,* to publish check lists of prints by important artists and articles on old and modern masters and various aspects of collecting; and finally, dissemination of technical information on the care of prints, and other similar projects.

Lessing Rosenwald did an excellent job as chairman. Always urbane, he was intelligent, thorough, and fair in his exposition of the issues. He was on complete control all the time. He was the ideal chairman and host. He made all feel that they were participating, he always said No graciously, he kept the discussion constantly in motion, and he knew how to shunt it to another issue when the talking became sticky. He was enthusiastic about the usefulness of the Council (his wife, Edith, told me she had never seen him so enthusiastic about any undertaking before), and his enthusiasm was infectious, for we all were happy and sanguine. We met our colleagues in the print and museum world, and we learned to know them better in a relaxed and convivial atmosphere. This stimulating factor in itself was one of the fringe benefits of the Print Council: the opportunity to meet annually and discuss matters of mutual interest against a background of pleasant sociability.

Such was the genesis of the Print Council. This is not the occasion for a detailed assessment of its achievements. Some of the projects suggested at the first meeting did materialize, others did not. For instance, two series of multiple exhibitions of contemporary American prints were launched under teh sponsorship of the Council in 1959 and 1962. The aim to provide information on the proper handling of graphic art was realized by the publication of *A Guide to the Collecting and Care of Original Prints* in 1965, under Council auspices, and of *Guidelines for Museum Curators in the Lending of Prints,* written recently by Eleanor Sayre. Owing to the difficulty of getting funds for the publication of periodicals, the revival of the old *Print Collectors Quarterly* never came to pass, but some of the material that had been solicited for the purpose was eventually published, under the *aegis* of the Print Council as *Prints: Thirteen Essays,* 1962. A project not announced at the beginning later occupied the Council for several years, namely, the problem of fraud in the sale of prints. The Council, having accumulated considerable data, brought the issue into the open and publicized it. In the long run, however, members of the Council felt that their role was primarily educational and not disciplinary. They had neither the inclination nor the authority to act as policemen. A recent undertaking, the compilation of a huge index of oeuvre catalogues of individual printmakers, will undoubtedly become an important contribution to scholarship. These are a few of the accomplishments of the Print Council outside of its social function. Its members have met annually in such places as Washington, Jenkintown, Pa., New York City, Boston, and Middletown, Conn. In 1971, for their fifteenth anniversary, they met in Los Angeles and San Francisco. The Council now has much wider participation by curators than when it began: the number of present and past directors has grown to fifty-eight. It has demonstrated its usefulness. As I look back on the Print Council and its achievements, one figure stands out most clearly above the rest, Lessing J. Rosenwald. He was truly its founder and leader. He supported the Council in many ways, and worked tirelessly in its behalf. In 1969, he retired from the presidency largely because of increasing deafness. At the meeting in Washington during that year, the curators gave him a volume made up of their personal tributes to him. I quote from mine:

> It is difficult to compress my feelings of friendship for Lessing and my experience of well over a quarter of a century into a few sentences. The special quality of Lessing J. Rosenwald could, however, be summarized as variations on the theme, *Humanity*. He is *human* and has foibles and faults as all of us have. He is *humane*, that is to say he is kindly, sympathetic, and understanding. He is a *humanist* in his devotion to art, literature and the *humanities*. He is a *humanitarian* in his unassuming generosity and his wide range of philanthropies. Such is my personal tribute to the man. As far as his contribution to The Print Council of America is concerned, the record is unequivocal: it would never have come into existence without him.

25

Commencement Address

(delivered at The Pennsylvania Academy of Fine Arts,
May 1964)

When I was young, and on the receiving end of such festive occasions as this, I never dreamed that some day I would be standing up here on the platform, prepared to dish out all the old platitudes. But, because I remember how much I suffered from long-winded lectures in the past, I shall try not to take advantage of my captive audience, but be brief and to the point. Be brief—that was the advice that the old preacher gave to the younger one, when he said: "Remember, no soul is saved after the first fifteen minutes." And so, my sermon—for there must always be a sermon on such occasions as this—my sermon will be brief.

My theme will be: the marks of a true artist. Have you ever asked yourself why you want to be an artist? Probably not: the true artist does not have to ask: he knows. There is nothing else in the world that he would rather be than an artist. To parody a Gilbert and Sullivan jingle:

301

> *In spite of all temptations*
> *To practise occupations*
> *He remains a painting man.*

No obstacle or handicap could discourage him from his chosen profession. In the old days it was harder to become an artist, and there were fewer of them. There were no academies or art schools. You were bound as an apprentice to some practising artist for seven years or so. During that time, you were his drudge and slave, but you learned something of your craft. You ground your master's colors, you roughed out his stone, you printed his woodcuts, you learned his secrets of drawing and painting and carving. Thereafter, you wandered around for a while as a journeyman, and finally, if you made good, you were admitted to the guild of artists as a master. I am not suggesting that this was an ideal arrangement. There is much to be said for the academy system. For one thing, you do not put your eggs all in one basket: you have contact with more than one artist and more than one man's ideas, and you do not run the risk of being apprenticed to a poor master. William Blake, for example, suffered for most of his life from the poor technique he acquired from the engraver Basire, to whom he had been bound as an apprentice. But, one thing the *bottega* or *atelier* system does do is to test the devotion of the pupil to his ultimate career.

The true artist, therefore, is dedicated to his profession. He has no other choice. Vollard tells a story about Degas. They happened to meet Vibert, the fashionable painter of Cardinals and other genre pictures. Vibert called to Degas and said: "You must come to see our new show of watercolors." Then, noticing Degas's shabby mackintosh, he went on patronizingly: "You may find our frames, our backgrounds, and our carpets a trifle too rich for your taste, but then, painting after all is a luxury, isn't it?" Degas retorted: "Painting may be a luxury for you, but for me it is an absolute necessity."

Necessity implies intensity, urgency. What was it that kept

old Cézanne working doggedly till the day he died? Or Michelangelo? Why is their work memorable? Let me put it this way. You are looking at an art exhibition. There are lots of nice pictures there. This one is fine, you say to yourself, and that and that. But there are a few that are more than just nice; they really get under your skin. You lie awake that night thinking about them. Now, in what mood do you think the artist painted those memorable pictures? Did he get up one morning, yawn, and stretch himself, and say "Well, I guess I will paint a masterpiece today." No, he wrestled and wrestled with an all-consuming problem. He worked in desperation and often in despair. Always the sense of urgency.

But emotional intensity is not enough. If it were, then a grief-stricken mother would be the greatest artist in the world. The artist must have disciplined and aesthetic emotions—the techniques to move and affect people in a very special way. Art is a language. There are certain conventions of the language to be learned. There are technical methods and mediums to be mastered, and various expressive and affective devices to be tested by experiment. All these constitute the painter's craft and technique, and are the backbone of academic training, for they are the things that can be taught. The student learns about technique at school, but he does not become a real master until he has absorbed the the technique and made it the vehicle of his personal expression. There is a vast difference between learning about something and making it your very own. Mastery is something that can not be taught: the student must achieve it by his own effort and experience. The student grasps only the externals. He believes that there is a virtue in method *per se,* and that if he acquires the methods, he has everything. Because he does not operate from within, he sometimes is impressed by the tricks and mannerisms that are obvious in the work of this or that successful artist. He hopes that if he can learn the tricks, he can be as successful as they are. In his inexperience, he does not realize that often the artist may be successful, not because of, but in spite of, his mannerisms.

As an example, however, of how a true artist thinks and talks about technique, let John Marin give testimony:

Seems to me, the true artist must perforce go from time to time to the elemental big forms—Sky, Sea, Mountain, Plain—and those things pertaining thereto, to sort of re-true himself, to recharge the battery. For these big forms have everything. But to express these, you have to love these, to be a part of these in sympathy. One doesn't get very far without this love, this love to enfold, too, the relatively little things that grow on the mountain's back. Which if you don't recognize, you don't recognize the mountain.

The glorious thing is that we cannot do, elementally do, other than our ancestors did. That is: that a round conveys to all who see it a similar definite, a triangle a similar definite, solids of certain forms similar definites, that a line—what I am driving at is that a round remains, a triangle remains, a line remains, and always was. So that the worker of today, as of old, picks up each of these things with recognition. . . .

And, that this, my picture, must not make one feel that it bursts its boundaries. The framing can not remedy. That would be a delusion; and I would have it, that nothing must cut my picture off from its finalities. And, too, I am not to be destructive within. I can have things that clash. I have a jolly good fight going on. There is always a fight going on when there are living things. But I must be able to control at will with a Blessed Equilibrium.

That was John Marin talking about the painter's craft.

Another point. The artist should be sincere and genuine. When we call an artist true or sincere, it is not to commend him for telling the truth in personal relations. We mean that he is true to his own expression, to the creative spark that is in him. I could perhaps have said that the real artist should be original, but I prefer to use the word genuine as a criterion. Originality, in the sense of something new or different, is apt to be based upon obvious and external features, and is measured by whatever is in vogue. Even a slight deviation from fashionable usage can furnish a quick and easy recipe for originality—perhaps even for a new commercial line of goods. The true artist, following his own star, pursues a course that may be either popular or unpopular, either successful or unsuccessful; he creates work that either may be traditional or may be original—so-called, but in every case, he is and must be genuine. The true artist worth his salt is apt to be a maverick, a lone wolf—one who does not follow the herd. It is well to keep in mind that the rest of the herd, or to change the metaphor, those who climbed aboard the bandwagon in the past, are more apt to be forgotten or known only to specialists, than the artists who were once the mavericks.

Such, then, are some of the distinguishing features of the real, the true artist: he must be passionately dedicated to his profession, intense in his application, possessed of a technique that he has shaped to his own ends, and guided by a purpose arising from his own inner drive. Young men and women, artists and artists to be, you are invited to strive for the arduous but blessed state of being a real artist!

Enough of this preaching! This should be a happy and joyous occasion. Awards are about to be made, and scholarship opportunities are about to be offered. The fortunate among you are about to embark on a great new adventure. For some of you there may have been heartbreak, but perhaps there will be better luck next time. Those of you who are about to become world travelers are in for an exciting experience. What a wonderful prospect: France, Italy, England, Germany, Spain, or wherever you go. I know what this can mean to a young student, because your elders——many of your teachers here—have told me what it meant to them, when they were young: the excitement, the stimulus, the chance to see and actually to study the world's great masterpieces, the revelation of other ways of life, the amenities of cafés and pubs and bistros. So, make the most of it. Don't insulate yourself, yield to all the blandishments of Europe. You are young only once!

You are doing what the journeyman in olden days did after they had served their apprenticeshop. They traveled around for a while to see the world and gain experience. You are lucky in that you are being staked; they had to work their way.

Art is a wonderful profession. Artists do get around. They may not make a lot of money, but they enjoy more of the good things of life than people with ten times their income. I like to be with artists. I find their talk stimulating and their friendship rewarding. I guess I just like artists. I had jolly well better like them, for, as a museum man, where would I be if there were no artists and none had ever existed? No artists, no museums. It is as simple as that. And so I say to you: "Travel and perfect yourself in your craft; strive to become great artists. Don't let a poor museum man down!"

Index of Names